W9-CYU-911

BAKER'S GUIDE TO CHRISTIAN DISTANCE EDUCATION

Other books by Jason D. Baker

Christian Cyberspace Companion
Parents' Computer Companion

Baker's Guide to

CHRISTIAN DISTANCE EDUCATION

ONLINE LEARNING FOR ALL AGES

Jason D. Baker

Baker Books

A Division of Baker Book House Co
Grand Rapids, Michigan 49516

© 2000 by Jason D. Baker

Published by Baker Books
a division of Baker Book House Company
P.O. Box 6287, Grand Rapids, MI 49516-6287

Printed in the United States of America

All rights reserved. No part of this publication may be reproduced, stored in a retrieval system, or transmitted in any form or by any means—for example, electronic, photocopy, recording—without the prior written permission of the publisher. The only exception is brief quotations in printed reviews.

Library of Congress Cataloging-in-Publication Data

Baker, Jason D.
    Baker's guide to Christian distance education : online learning for all ages / Jason D. Baker.
      p.   cm.
    ISBN 0-8010-6341-8 (paper)
    1. Distance education—United States—Directories. 2. University extension—United States—Directories. 3. Computer-assisted instruction—United States—Directories. 4. Church colleges—United States—Directories. I. Title: Guide to Christian distance education. II. Title.
LC5805.B35   2000
371.3'5'025—dc21   00-040382

Institutions listed in *Baker's Guide* have not paid for their listing and I do not take fees from institutions or prospective students. But I have been a distance learner at George Washington University, Jones International University, the University of Nebraska-Lincoln, and Regent University. And I have been an online instructor or consultant with Christian University GlobalNet, George Washington University, Jones International University, Reformed Theological Seminary, and Regent University.

Trademarked names appear throughout this book. Rather than list the names and entities that own the trademarks or insert a trademark symbol with each mention of the trademarked name, the author states that he is using the names only for editorial purposes and to the benefit of the trademark owner with no intention of infringing upon that trademark.

The information contained in this book does not constitute legal advice. The author and publisher have taken care in preparation of this book but make no expressed or implied warranty of any kind and assume no responsibility for errors or omissions. No liability is assumed for incidental or consequential damages in connection with or arising out of the use of the information contained herein. Please contact the author with any corrections or additions for future publications.

For current information about all releases from Baker Book House, visit our web site:
http://www.bakerbooks.com

For Julianne

He who finds a wife finds what is good
and receives favor from the LORD.

Proverbs 18:22

CONTENTS

ACKNOWLEDGMENTS

A few words of thanks are in order for:

Jennifer Leep—my editor at Baker Book House. Thanks for guiding *Baker's Guide* to publication.

Paul Engle—my former editor at Baker Book House. Thanks for being an advocate for this book.

John McFadden and Paul Smith—my former directors at Loyola College in Maryland. Thanks for your support of my writing and academic endeavors.

Online helpers—far too numerous to list. Thanks to all those who e-mailed me with information and updates about distance education programs.

Julianne—a wife worth far more than rubies. Thanks for your wisdom, advocacy, and presence throughout our journey together.

To God alone be the glory!

1

FROM CIRCULAR LETTERS TO ONLINE CLASSROOMS

One of the most significant educators in the early Christian church was the apostle Paul. Using circular letters, which were passed from church to church and read aloud to gatherings of believers, he was able to engage in fruitful education while traveling on his missionary journeys and even while locked away in prison. In many respects, this made Paul an early pioneer in the field of Christian distance education. Many years later, in 1901, Moody Bible Institute set a pattern for formal theological education at a distance by offering independent study correspondence courses. Since then, Moody's independent studies program has had more than a million enrollments.

Today distance education is a growing phenomenon with over two million students currently taking distance courses. From supplemental elementary school courses to full graduate-level degree programs, institutions are quickly developing off-campus and online versions of their most popular programs. Some schools are even developing distance-only programs to meet a growing student demand that is projected to increase dramatically over the coming years. Within the next few years, more than 80 percent of all colleges and universities are expected to offer distance education courses, with online classes representing the fastest-growing method of distance learning. And Christian institutions continue to lead the way in offering high-quality programs to students who aren't able to attend classes on campus. A recent collaborative venture by more than fifty Christian colleges and universities—Christian University GlobalNet—aims to reach over a million students per year through biblically based online courses.

WHY DISTANCE EDUCATION?

So why would you consider taking specific courses, or even pursuing an entire degree, through distance education? Availability and flexibility of such classes represent two of the major benefits of such a plan. It used to be that if you wanted to take classes for credit, you were limited to colleges and universities within driving distance. But even if you found the perfect program, you still had to make sure the class you wanted to take was offered at a convenient time. For people with significant job or family commitments, finding the right program offered at just the right time was often nearly impossible. Thanks to distance education, you can now take classes from literally anywhere in the world. And most distance courses lack fixed class meeting times, so you can plan your education according to your own schedule.

Distance education can benefit people from all walks of life:

- a home schooling couple looking for an online Christian high school for their children
- a sixteen-year-old student desiring to supplement her high school curriculum with some college-level courses
- a military officer seeking to take counseling courses while still on his tour in Germany
- a mother of three who is interested in finishing her degree without neglecting her full-time homemaking responsibilities
- a pastor who wants to earn his Master of Divinity degree without leaving his current congregation
- a corporate executive who wants to study organizational leadership within a biblical context

- a teacher who wants to earn her master's degree and explore a better-fitting job
- a father who is simply looking for courses to improve his Bible knowledge
- a small group leader looking for education courses to improve her teaching skills
- a missionary desiring to pursue a doctoral degree and start a local seminary without leaving the field for prolonged lengths of time

Real individuals in each of these circumstances have contacted me throughout the years via the *Baker's Guide* Web site (http:// www.bakersguide.com) looking for advice about finding a suitable distance program. I've been able to point every one of them (and countless others) to quality accredited programs that require little or no on-campus residency. The number of such distance education opportunities continues to grow, so there's a good chance you'll be able to find a program that meets your specific academic needs. And if you're not able to find exactly what you're looking for, there are a number of institutions that permit you to custom-design a degree program.

WHY THIS BOOK?

As you can see, distance education opens up a whole world of new learning opportunities for you to consider. Whether you're looking for K–12 home schooling classes or you want to earn an undergraduate or graduate college degree, distance learning is an option worth looking at. The number of schools, programs, and delivery methods can be quite overwhelming, though, and there are issues such as accreditation that you must consider when selecting a program. That's where *Baker's Guide to Christian Distance Education* comes in. This book will help you discover the many options available for Christian distance learning and will provide information and consultation about pursuing a suitable program.

Since *Baker's Guide* is a reference work, to best use the information found inside, you must understand how it's organized. The book is divided into two major sections: part 1 is a distance education primer featuring discussions of various aspects of distance education while part 2 is a distance education directory containing more than one hundred K–12, certificate, and degree programs. Specifically, the chapters break down as follows:

- Chapter 2 offers answers to commonly asked questions about distance education. In a sense, the whole first part of *Baker's Guide* is summarized in this chapter.
- Chapter 3 presents the most common types or models of distance course delivery. From audiotapes and workbooks to e-mail and Web pages, you'll learn how different programs are delivered.
- Chapter 4 walks you through a typical online learning experience. What does it feel like to take an online distance education course? How does it all work? How does a student attend class or submit homework? This chapter addresses these questions.
- Chapter 5 answers the question "How can I succeed as a distance learner?" by offering some specific tips for succeeding as a student.
- Chapter 6 contains an introduction to the accreditation issue. Since accreditation is so important, particularly within higher education, it's vital that you understand what accreditation is and how to ensure that the school you're interested in is truly accredited.
- Chapter 7 provides some practical suggestions for how to select a suitable distance program and what to do if you cannot find exactly what you're looking for.
- Chapter 8 features profiles of select Christian and secular distance education programs covering kindergarten through high school.
- Chapters 9 through 12 contain profiles of accredited Christian certificate and degree programs (ranging from bache-

lor's through doctoral degrees) that are delivered via a variety of distance education methods.

- Chapter 13 profiles a number of accredited degree programs that can be earned via prior learning or customized to fit your specific academic needs.

The book closes with further instructions about how to obtain more information about Christian distance education via the *Baker's Guide* Web site or electronic mail.

WHY MY PERSONAL INTEREST?

You may be wondering why I would want to write a book helping believers locate Christian distance learning opportunities. For many years I have been interested in nontraditional education—from home schooling to online learning—because of my passion to equip people with a biblical worldview. Distance education not only makes it possible for many people to receive a quality education that otherwise wouldn't be available to them, but it also, if done well, can actually deliver a better educational experience than the traditional lecture model. I have designed and taught a number of online courses and have seen the benefits and effectiveness of distance education for my students.

Finally, and perhaps most importantly, I've been a distance student myself. After earning my B.S. in electrical engineering through traditional means, I earned an M.A. in educational technology leadership from The George Washington University via online studies. Currently I'm enrolled in a Ph.D. program at Regent University that focuses on online communication and distance education and combines summer on-campus residency sessions with online courses in the fall and spring. Distance education has enabled me to pursue my vocational calling without sacrificing my family in the process. For this, I am grateful to God and those institutions that have developed such pioneering distance programs. I hope this book helps you to benefit from such opportunities as well.

PART 1

DISTANCE EDUCATION PRIMER

2

ANSWERS TO COMMON QUESTIONS

Despite its growing popularity, distance education still remains shrouded in mystery for many people. Numerous questions arise: Don't people learn better in a traditional classroom? Are distance courses easier than campus courses? How do I choose the best program? Will an online degree be recognized in the marketplace? This chapter answers these and many other common questions about distance education and online learning. When appropriate, answers include references to other chapters in *Baker's Guide* where you'll find more detailed information.

WHAT IS DISTANCE EDUCATION?

Distance education is learning that occurs in an environment where students are separated from the instructor and/or each other. It can incorporate a variety of media—including audiotapes, videotapes, telephone conferences, cable or satellite television, fax, electronic mail, or the World Wide Web—to deliver instruction or facilitate student interaction. Although distance education is not a new phenomenon—distance courses have been

available in the United States for more than a hundred years—
the educational possibilities created by the Internet and World
Wide Web have dramatically increased the availability of distance
programs.

ISN'T DISTANCE EDUCATION JUST INDEPENDENT STUDY?

At one time the only type of distance education was independent study correspondence courses. Although this remains
one approach to distance education, most programs have a much
higher level of interaction not only between the student and
instructor but also among fellow students within a class. Such
distance learning courses consist of a group of students who
interact over the Internet using e-mail, discussion forums, chat
rooms, and Web pages (chapter 4 offers a description of a typical online learning experience), or by means of a conference call
or videoconference. Sometimes programs also feature residency
sessions where you spend a few weeks on campus with your
classmates.

WHAT ARE THE BENEFITS OF DISTANCE LEARNING?

A significant benefit for many students is flexibility. Distance
education programs enable students to take classes or work on a
degree without sacrificing job or family commitments. They can
also benefit those who need timely training or who would learn
better without the rigid structure of a traditional program. Some
schools have a more flexible calendar for their distance programs,
so you may not be limited to fixed semester starting dates. Distance education can also be a valuable resource to parents (particularly those who home school their kids) who seek to increase
the educational opportunities for their children. In addition to the
convenience distance education affords students, it can also
enable them to learn directly from instructors who would normally be inaccessible. For example, a student living in Florida can
take a class taught by a favorite instructor who happens to live
in California.

IS DISTANCE EDUCATION RIGHT FOR ME?

If the aforementioned advantages sound attractive, then there's a good chance that distance education may be a good fit for you. Ask yourself these questions: Are you self-disciplined? Are you comfortable receiving instruction in ways other than traditional lectures? Are you able to interact well with others over e-mail, online discussions, telephone, and other non-face-to-face methods? and Are you competent with your personal computer? If you answered yes to these questions, then distance education is probably an option you should consider. For information about succeeding as a distance learner read chapter 5.

HOW DO ONLINE CLASSES WORK?

Most online courses have much in common with their traditional counterparts. Class "lectures" are generally delivered through a combination of Web pages, audio- or videotapes, and printed books and articles. Class discussions form the heart of the online distance experience—students congregate at a central course Web site and participate in a bulletin-board-style conversation about weekly discussion questions. Although there may be an occasional online or offline quiz, most assignments are written—research papers, case studies, and discussion question responses—and submitted to the instructor via electronic mail. The instructor then provides general class feedback by posting to the class discussion board and individual feedback via one-on-one e-mail communication.

DON'T PEOPLE LEARN BETTER IN A TRADITIONAL CLASSROOM?

Though it may be hard to believe (especially for those of us who teach for a living), the answer to this question appears to be no. Most research indicates that students learn and retain information delivered at a distance as well as, if not better than, that received in a traditional classroom. And the use of the Internet for online class discussion makes many distance courses more interactive than face-to-face courses. Home schoolers and others involved in nontraditional educational endeavors have already learned that the one-size-fits-all traditional classroom is not always the best solution. It's important to know how you learn best and then to select an educational approach that works for you. There are many choices out there (check out the directory listings in chapters 8 through 13!), so you should find something that works for you and go with it.

WHAT IS RESIDENCY?

Residency is generally defined as time spent on campus during a distance program. Residency sessions offer students the opportunity to develop relationships with their instructors and classmates in a supportive personal environment. Such residency sessions are usually either introductory workshops offered early in the program or weeklong intensive courses scattered throughout the program. Many distance programs don't require any on-campus residency sessions, but they still encourage students to come to campus for a seminar or graduation.

ARE DISTANCE EDUCATION COURSES EASIER THAN TRADITIONAL ONES?

Not at all. Sometimes distance sections are identical to on-campus courses right down to the taped lectures. Other distance courses involve increased reading, group projects, and class participation, which may actually make them harder than their on-campus counterparts. And if you are used to a professor constantly reminding you of upcoming deadlines, you may initially have a difficult time adjusting to the increased level of discipline and personal responsibility required by education outside the traditional classroom. Still, although the work won't be easier, the flexibility and potential better fit with your learning style may make your learning experience more enjoyable.

WHAT DEGREES CAN I EARN THROUGH DISTANCE EDUCATION?

Quality distance education programs are available at all educational levels. From the kindergarten curriculum offered by the

Calvert School of Baltimore to Regent University's multiple Ph.D. programs, there's sure to be a distance program that fits your interest.

WHAT IF I CANNOT FIND A PROGRAM THAT MATCHES MY NEEDS?

Many secular universities offer distance degree programs, from associate to doctoral level, that you can custom design to your specifications. For example, you might earn a B.A. in religion, an M.A. in biblical history, and a Ph.D. in theology and education through such personalized programs. Chapter 13 contains more information about accredited individualized degree options.

WHAT IS THE BEST DISTANCE SCHOOL?

There really is no "best" distance school or program. The real issue is finding the best distance program *for you*. Once you know that you're dealing with accredited institutions, the best way to select a program is to determine whether it fits your needs and learning style. It's important to consider whether the courses match your area of interest, how long the program will take, how much it costs, the possibility of transfer credits, and whether or not it requires you to participate in any on-campus residency sessions. Chapter 7 discusses the issues involved in selecting an appropriate distance program.

WHAT IS ACCREDITATION?

Accreditation is a measure of the accepted standard of academic quality within the United States. Institutions achieve accreditation by voluntarily submitting to a comprehensive review by an outside agency that ensures educational quality and institutional integrity. The most respected type of accreditation in the United States is "regional" accreditation in which an institution is accredited by one of six geographically dispersed associations approved by both the United States Department of Education and the Council for Higher Education Accreditation. More information on accreditation, including names of approved agencies, can be found in chapter 6.

IS ACCREDITATION REALLY IMPORTANT?

If you are pursuing a college degree through distance education, accreditation is a must. In other words, you should select a school that is accredited by one of the six regional agencies or by an approved specialized agency. An accredited degree is a prerequisite for many graduate programs and employers who simply discount unaccredited programs. Also, federal financial aid programs and tax credit benefits are available only for accredited programs. The primary exception to this rule applies if you are using distance education courses to supplement your home schooling curriculum. Most states and colleges already recognize the unique nature of home schooling and have additional quality-control checks in place for them.

Because accreditation is the accepted standard of academic quality, only accredited colleges, universities, and seminaries are listed in part 2 of this book.

ARE SCHOLARSHIPS OR FINANCIAL AID AVAILABLE FOR DISTANCE EDUCATION?

Yes. Many of the same student loan programs (e.g., the Federal Stafford Loan Program and VA benefits) are available for both on-campus and distance programs. Some schools permit distance students to compete for existing scholarship programs or even have special scholarships and financial aid programs available for them. And don't forget that the Hope Scholarship Credit and Lifetime Learning Credit can also be used to offset tuition costs as appropriate.

WILL A DISTANCE DEGREE BE LOOKED DOWN UPON?

As long as you stick with an accredited school (preferably a regionally accredited one), you should have no problem with the acceptability of your degree. Most schools don't distinguish between degrees earned on campus and those earned via distance education. Therefore, for any on-campus degree that is accepted, a corresponding distance program degree from the same school will likely be accepted as well. With the growing number of distance education programs offered, even by traditional schools such as Duke and Harvard, it's unlikely you will encounter any difficulties with a distance degree. Some employers may even commend you for having the foresight and self-discipline to seek out a distance program. I've actually spoken with individuals who received job offers specifically *because* they earned their degrees online.

3

MODELS OF DISTANCE COURSE DELIVERY

When someone says they're earning a degree through distance education, they could be referring to any number of different nontraditional learning experiences:

- viewing course material online and then interacting with classmates on a Web-based discussion forum,
- reading a required collection of articles and then participating in an online chat session with the instructor,
- listening to lectures on audiotape and corresponding with the instructor via e-mail,
- watching lectures on videotape and chatting with classmates via a telephone conference call, or
- visiting a special conference room and participating in a full-motion videoconference class.

The umbrella of distance education is broad enough to cover a variety of experiences ranging from independent study courses delivered with audiocassettes and workbooks to Internet-based classes where students receive their materials and interact with their instructor entirely online. Although online learning is responsible for most of the recent growth in distance education, many courses are still delivered through a mixture of online and offline media. This hybrid approach combines multiple media—for example, audiocassettes with Web-based discussion or videotapes and books with e-mail correspondence—and has proven to be quite effective and popular in the distance education community.

Rather than examining every possible hybrid combination, in this chapter we'll consider the fundamental issues of class size, instructional delivery, and interaction. By looking at the various building blocks for distance courses, you'll begin to recognize the major models of course delivery used in distance education programs. Each approach has its own particular strengths and weaknesses, and some approaches may be better suited to your learning style and life circumstances than others. This chapter will help clarify the variety of distance course options currently available.

CLASS SIZE

At one time independent study was the only type of distance education available. Distance leaders such as the Moody Bible Institute and The Open University (UK) continue to make extensive use of independent study courses to deliver high-quality instruction. However, because of the educational advantages of personal interaction, many distance education programs have adopted a tutorial or group approach.

INDEPENDENT STUDIES

Independent studies are fairly self-explanatory. You, the student, work through a course with little or no contact with other students or the instructor. Typically you receive a packet of information (lectures, books, and assignments) at the beginning of a course, then work through the material at your own pace. After completing all assignments and possibly a proctored final exam, you submit all materials and receive a grade for the course. The advantage of this approach is that you can usually work at your own pace (within general limits such as six months to a year per course) and study whenever it is convenient. The disadvantages, however, are that you lose the feedback of fellow classmates and lack regular interaction with your instructor.

TUTORIALS

The tutorial model attempts to address the second of those disadvantages by facilitating more frequent interaction between the instructor and the student. Like an independent study, you can often work through the tutorial at your own pace and in your own time, but you have regular interaction with the instructor. Some programs require weekly or monthly telephone conversations during which you discuss your learning activities. Other programs facilitate student-instructor interaction by requiring you to submit each assignment as you complete it, allowing time for the instructor to grade and return it before you continue. With the tutorial method you have an instructor to guide and mentor you, but if you have to sequentially submit each assignment, you may not be able to progress as quickly as you might with an independent study.

GROUP STUDIES

The group approach to distance education simulates a traditional classroom experience except, of course, for the fact that students are geographically scattered. Using various communication technologies (which we'll discuss further in the interaction section of this chapter), students interact with each other as well as the instructor throughout the duration of the class. This not only improves the learning experience, but it also greatly decreases the feeling of isolation often associated with distance learning. Sometimes a cohort is formed—in which the same group of students works through a series of courses together in pursuit of a degree—which makes it possible for distance students to develop substantive relationships over time. The drawback to group courses, though, is that they hamstring the student who wants to move through a program at a faster or slower rate than the academic calendar permits.

Class Size	Description	Advantages	Disadvantages
Independent Study	work through the course alone	learn at your own pace	isolation
Tutorial	work one-on-one with an instructor	benefit from instructor interaction while still largely learning at your own pace	not as time-flexible as independent study
Group	many students work through the course together	learn from other students throughout the course	tied to traditional academic calendar

INSTRUCTIONAL DELIVERY METHOD

In the distance arena there are a variety of ways to deliver the actual instruction, the lectures if you will, to the students. The five most common delivery modes are texts, audiocassettes, videotapes or television, videoconferences, and online communication. Let's briefly look at each of these methods.

TEXTS

Most distance education courses, like their traditional counterparts, incorporate a lot of reading. Textbooks, novels, magazines, articles, and individual handouts are commonplace. While traditional classes often contain lectures in addition to the books, some distance education courses deliver all instruction via texts. Typically students receive a book list at the beginning of the class, and the syllabus or study guide leads them through the required readings. Since reading has historically been part of education, text-based "lectures" are not that far removed from traditional learning. However, if you are a slow reader or don't learn well through books, you should probably avoid this method.

Audiocassettes

Audiocassette lectures have a number of advantages over other delivery methods. First, cassette tapes are inexpensive, thereby benefiting both the institution and the student. Second, they're very portable, which enables distance students to listen at home, in the car, while jogging, or wherever they have access to a cassette player. Third, audio lectures permit instructors to supplement reading with personal comments, suggestions, and other information normally shared in the classroom. Sometimes instructors simply tape their regular lectures; others create special talks specifically for distance students. Auditory learners will find this approach more beneficial than the text-only method, but visual learners will probably do better with videotapes or other media.

Videocassettes and Television

Videotaped or televised lectures add the sense of sight to the learning experience. As with audiocassettes, video lectures are sometimes created specifically for the distance program while at other times institutions simply stick a video camera into a classroom and record a regular lecture. Video lectures enable an instructor to use more charts, graphs, television clips, and other visual information that is precluded by audio lectures. They can also feel a bit more personal to students since they give a face to the instructor who is teaching. Furthermore, like audiocassettes, video lectures can be stopped, rewound, and watched again until a student grasps their content. However, since video production is more costly and labor-intensive than audio recording, many institutions lack the resources to produce professional-quality videotapes.

Videoconferencing

Videoconferencing, or full-motion teleconferencing, involves instructor and students located in specially-equipped rooms (with cameras, microphones, and television screens) that permit two-way conference calls. Everyone participates in a traditional class experience with the distinction that students are physically located in remote rooms. Still, students watch the instructor live, they can ask questions and mingle with fellow classmates, and often the instructor can view the various remote sites as well. This distance model offers the closest reconstruction of a traditional classroom, but it is also the most costly and inconvenient. To make this work the lead institution *and* the various students must have access to a compatible videoconferencing facility. Therefore, this is most commonly done between sites in a corporate training program or in a multicampus university system.

ONLINE

Online distance learning is the most recent trend—one that is growing phenomenally. Online classes really shine in the interactivity arena, but in the instructional delivery category they generally adopt one of the four previous models. Some programs place lecture material on the Internet for reading and printing, others deliver it using streaming audio or video technology, and a few even dabble with computer conferencing as a way to replicate the videoconferencing model. Sometimes course material is developed as an interactive multimedia presentation that is available online.

The advantage of online instructional delivery is that it offers the benefits of the other methods without any time delays. New materials can be distributed to students almost instantly. Of course, students must be at their computer in order to access the course content. The major limitation for the online approach is the connection speed of the students—those with slow modems cannot handle large multimedia files or streaming audio and video. But as connection speeds increase and the second-generation Internet is developed, these limitations will be eliminated and online learning may be the best way to go.

Delivery Method	Description	Advantages	Disadvantages
Text	book learning	low-cost; highly portable	auditory and visual learners at a disadvantage

(continued)

(continued)

Delivery Method	Description	Advantages	Disadvantages
Audio-cassette	audio lectures on tape	more custom-izable and per-sonal than text model; portable	lacks visual presentation options
Video-cassette or television	video lectures on tape	many presenta-tion options available; semi-portable	more expensive; longer lead time needed to produce
Video-conferencing	live video delivery just like a tradi-tional class-room lecture	very expensive; must have access to a compatible facility	
Online	computer-based mixture of other models	instant delivery and the ability to mix any of the other models	limited by modem connection speed

INTERACTION

Interaction with an instructor and with fellow students is an important part of one's learning experience. Distance learning programs offer four basic approaches to interaction: no interaction, audio- or videoconferencing, synchronous online chat sessions, and asynchronous online discussion. As you may guess, the class size and instructional delivery methods chosen often influence the selection of an interaction model.

No Interaction

Little to no interaction, with either instructor or student, is the hallmark of most independent study programs. Obviously a person must be a good independent learner to benefit from this approach. These are the students for whom class discussions and other forms of interaction actually detract from the learning experience. The zero interaction approach best suits students who prefer to simply interact with material and then take tests, write papers, and demonstrate their mastery of course content.

Audio- or Videoconferencing

Videoconferencing permits live interaction between instructor and students and shares the benefits of traditional classroom discussions. Some distance programs offer similar interaction using a telephone conference call. This audioconferencing approach offers the benefits of live discussion without the high costs associated with full-motion videoconferences.

Synchronous Online Chat

Online interaction falls into two categories—synchronous and asynchronous. Synchronous online interaction is the computer equivalent of a conference call—participants communicate with one another in real time—except that you use an online chat room rather than a telephone. Everyone in the class gets online at the same time and then logs on to a chat room for discussion. Instead of speaking to each other with voices, students type their interaction. This works best if you are a fast typist! With such online chats there are no long-distance fees or other high costs to absorb. However, slow typing speeds prevent you from accomplishing as much as you might with an audio or video conversation.

Asynchronous Online Discussion

Asynchronous discussions are time-delayed, and they don't require that everyone be online at the same time. Rather, you post your message at a time convenient to you, and others read it and post their response when they are online. Sometimes such "discussion" takes place using electronic mail, while others use electronic discussion forums. A discussion forum is the electronic equivalent of a bulletin board where each participant posts messages for others to read. Over time, students can read each posting and compose a response.

In addition to time benefits, the asynchronous approach provides an archive of all discussions throughout the course. You can reference or resume any previous conversation. This adds a new twist to the learning experience. Such discussion also enables participation from students who would normally be excluded from live discussions, either because they are quiet or because they don't think as fast as others. Asynchronous discussions do, however, lack the spontaneity associated with live interaction. Still, asynchronous discussion is the most common form of interaction in online courses.

Interaction	Description	Advantages	Disadvantages
None	no interaction	benefits independent learners	missing the insights of fellow students
Conference Call	live audio or video discussion	dynamic group discussions; real-time interaction	can be costly
Synchronous Online Chat	computer chat room	low cost; real-time interaction	slower than verbal chats
Asynchronous Online Discussion	e-mail or discussion forums	students don't all have to be connected simultaneously; archive of discussions	less spontaneous than live chats

Online models of instructional delivery and interaction, particularly Web-based courses using asynchronous discussion forums, have the most momentum right now and will probably become the de facto standard in the coming years. However, there is no single "best" model, and you may not always find your desired degree program offered with the exact combination of class size, instructional delivery, and interaction that you prefer. Therefore, consider which approaches work best for your circumstances and learning styles, then select a program that offers the closest fit to your ideal.

4

THE ONLINE
LEARNING EXPERIENCE

Once you adjust to the idea of learning in a virtual classroom rather than a physical one, you'll find that most distance courses are quite dynamic and interactive. And even the most cutting-edge online courses have much in common with on-campus classes—regular class schedules, student discussions, and plenty of deadlines. Some distance courses even include group projects, online presentations, and live chat sessions to help develop a sense of academic community among participating students. In this chapter we'll examine a typical online course design and the probable experiences of a new distance learner.

ONLINE COURSE DESIGN

Despite the variety of distance approaches available, most online courses have adopted a fairly similar style. Lecture material is usually delivered through printed online materials (e.g., PowerPoint presentations or text-laden Web pages) or through audio- or videotapes. Some courses substitute online audio or video streaming for mailing out tapes. This permits the instructors to record or revise lectures just before their delivery rather than relying on the stock lectures necessary for mass-produced tapes. Most online courses, like their on-campus counterparts, make use of numerous reading assignments from books and articles. Sometimes students are given a study guide to serve as an outline of, and running commentary on, weekly reading assignments. They may also incorporate online research especially for time-sensitive topics that may change faster than printed material can document. Figures 1 and 2 illustrate two sections of a typical course Web site delivered via Blackboard Course Info. The first picture shows a portion of an online syllabus and the second presents a number of options for student interaction.

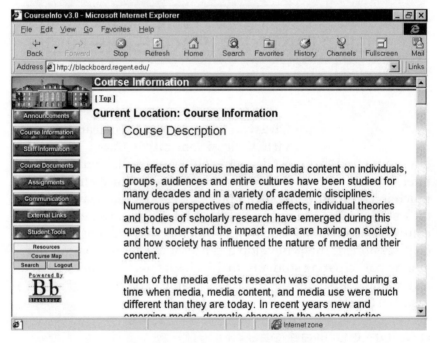

Figure 1: Section of Course Syllabus

Asynchronous Web-based discussion forms the heart of the online distance experience—students congregate at a course Web site and participate in a bulletin-board-style conversation about weekly discussion questions. Typically an instructor posts discussion questions addressing key points from the weekly reading at the beginning of each week. Students are expected to answer

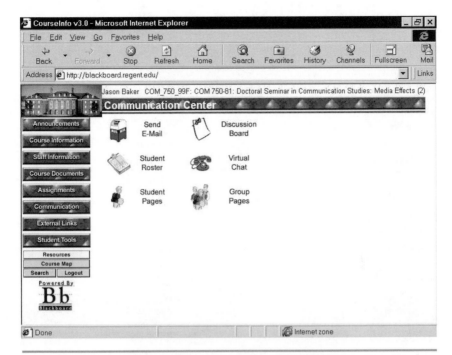

Figure 2: Interaction Options

the questions and respond to their classmates' postings. Instructors often monitor the online discussion and will interject comments throughout the week. But the core interaction occurs among the students themselves. Figure 3 shows an online discussion forum.

Course assignments are generally written (e.g., research papers, case studies, and discussion question responses) and are submitted to the instructor via electronic mail or posted onto a discussion board. The instructor provides personal feedback through e-mail and, as appropriate, posts general comments to the class using the discussion forum. Online quizzes are also becoming increasingly popular, sometimes as graded assignments and sometimes as evaluative tools to help both students and instructors gauge how well material is being learned. Some courses use proctored tests, often as midterm or final exams. In such cases students find a local librarian, pastor, or certified proctor to supervise them as they write an exam that then gets faxed or mailed to the instruc-

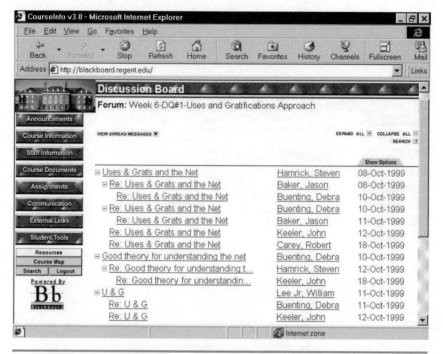

Figure 3: Discussion Forum

tor for grading. Many online courses also incorporate individual or group projects that challenge students to apply knowledge to real-world situations. This also not only helps to make learning practical, it can also encourage interaction among students in a class.

WALKING THROUGH AN ONLINE COURSE

From the very beginning, you'll notice that the online experience is much different from your recollection of campus life. First of all, when preparing to register for courses, you'll discover that many distance programs don't follow a traditional semester schedule. That means you're able to start courses at times other than September, January, or June. Once you've examined a series of programs and settled on a course that looks interesting, you may find that it happens to begin in two weeks. Upon further examination of the course schedule, you might also notice that it doesn't have a set class meeting time (e.g., Tuesday, 7–9 P.M.) but rather that it simply lists a starting and ending date. Feeling adventurous, you may click on the course registration link, type your credit card information into a secure Web form, and *voilà!* you've just registered for your first online course.

After your online registration has been accepted, you'll be directed to a virtual bookstore where you order your textbooks, reading packet, study guide, and videotapes. When the materials arrive a few days later you'll notice that the enclosed syllabus outlines the entire course (which is divided into weeks, rather than class sessions), including weekly readings, discussion questions, group projects, and major papers. The weekend before class begins, you receive a phone call from your instructor introducing herself to you and offering to answer any questions that you have about the course. After hearing that this is your first online course, she assures you that half of your classmates are in the same position and that she expects you to be a fluent online student in no time. Shortly after your phone conversation you receive e-mail with instructions on how to log into the course Web site using your newly issued username and password.

On the first day of class, you log into the Web site and read various messages posted by the instructor. She provides an overview of the class, commentary on the reading and videotape for the first week, instructions for how to use the Web-based discussion forum, and your first week's assignments. Your first task is to post a brief biographical sketch to the discussion forum as a way to introduce yourself to the nine other members of your class. Throughout the week you "meet" your classmates and begin discussions based on the interactive questions your instructor has posted. It may feel odd at first to have a discussion electronically, but soon you'll settle in and enjoy being able to compose (and revise) your responses before submitting them to the rest of the class. Figure 4 offers an example of a message composition form.

Rather than listening to a lecture for your class sessions, you are expected to watch a videotape featuring interviews with key leaders in your field, read a collection of journal articles, and review the notes and commentary provided by the instructor.

Subsequent weeks follow the same pattern, and throughout that time you begin to draft your first major paper relating this course

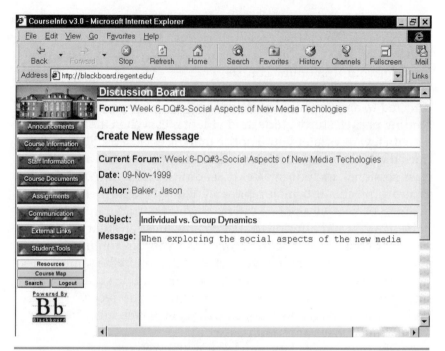

Figure 4: Composing a Message

to your current vocational efforts. As instructed, you e-mail your paper to a classmate (who e-mails you a draft of his in response) for peer review. Based on his comments and some further guidance from your instructor, you complete your paper and submit it via e-mail. Later that week you open a message from your instructor with a copy of your paper that has been electronically "marked-up" with various comments, questions, and suggestions. You're pleased to discover that you earned an A for your effort and are now feeling more comfortable with the whole online learning experience.

By this point, you've adjusted to the rhythm of an online class and you continue to excel throughout the rest of the semester. As the course draws to a close, you chat with some of your classmates and see whether any of them are interested in taking a follow-up course with you. It turns out that three of them are interested, so you return to the registration Web page and take the first step toward enrolling in your second online class. As your instructor promised during her initial phone call a few weeks earlier, you've become a veteran online learner.

Because the virtual classroom is such a new experience, it's easy to get caught up in the technical aspects of online learning and focus on e-mail, the Web, and other Internet tools. However, the online learning experience is ultimately about learning and not online computer technology. I hope this chapter has demonstrated that although there is a learning curve associated with distance education, you don't have to earn a computer science degree to prepare for an online course. Once you've made the adjustment to the online classroom, you'll find yourself spending your time in your academic studies. And you may even find that you learn better online than in a traditional classroom!

5

SUCCEEDING
AS A DISTANCE LEARNER

Once you've decided that you want to try distance education, it's important to make every effort to ensure a profitable learning experience. Studies conducted to determine what makes a successful distance learner have indicated that a student's intention to complete a course has a direct bearing on his or her level of success. In other words, a student who begins a course with a conscious intention to finish it is more likely to do so than someone who decides more tentatively to try a distance course.

Once you've made up your mind to complete a course, there are also other steps you can take to foster quality learning. The following tips, culled from my personal experience as both a distance instructor and a distance learner, will help you succeed as a distance learner.

Review the Course Syllabus Early—Spend some time reviewing the course syllabus before the semester begins, preferably before you enroll. This will prevent any surprises along the way.

Match Your Learning Style—Understand your preferred learning style(s) and select courses and programs that match those well.

45

Interact with Course Graduates—Talk to people who have already taken the course, and get their tips for course success.

Start Swiftly—Begin working on your coursework as soon as you receive your materials. Getting an early jump on readings and assignments will put you in a good position to do well.

Resolve Technical Problems Quickly—If you encounter any computer or technical problems, contact your institution and resolve them at once. A few days of lost e-mail or inability to access the Web can severely interrupt your progress.

Plan Your Time Well—Set interim deadlines to help you avoid waiting until the last minute on major assignments. Establish a regular study schedule and stick to it. Falling behind in your reading or assignments is the quickest way to lose control of a class.

Get Organized—If you don't already have a good filing system, start one. You will read and write many papers throughout your program and will save yourself a lot of time if you organize them well. The folder feature in most e-mail packages will help you organize your online interaction.

Take Good Notes—You will probably read a lot of material for your distance course, perhaps more than in traditional classes because you don't have lectures online. Take time to highlight and mark up your book, write up summary notes, and do whatever it takes to learn the material.

Ask Questions—Since the professor cannot tell by your expression how well you are grasping the material, ask questions of your instructor and classmates when you don't understand something.

Give Each Other the Benefit of the Doubt—Sometimes it's tough to discern someone's tone of voice in an e-mail message, so don't assume the worst. A little understanding goes a long way.

Don't Miss Deadlines—If you have an unusual situation that hinders your work during the week, let your instructor know about it immediately.

Save Everything You Write—You never know when you will want to refer to a paper that you wrote during your first class.

Perform Regular Self-Assessments—At select points throughout the course, honestly assess your progress. Don't hesitate to share your thoughts with your instructor and seek feedback. Make any necessary corrections to ensure that you finish strong.

Interact with Your Classmates Outside of Class—In addition to in-class online or voice/video interaction, drop notes or pick up the phone and call your classmates outside of class. Recount a recent life experience, inquire about someone's well-being, pray for each other, tell jokes, or share your struggles. If you're taking courses with others, remember that you're not alone. Encourage each other throughout the journey.

Don't Neglect Your Spiritual or Family Life—Distance studies are time-consuming and difficult, but don't neglect the relationships that are most important in your life. After all, what will it profit a distance learner to get an A but lose his or her soul?

Integrate Learning with Practice—Seek out opportunities to integrate your studies with your vocation, ministry, relationships, and other areas of interest. This will not only make your assignments more fruitful, but it will likely help you learn better also.

Take a Sabbath Rest—Preserving one day a week for worship and rest is a gift from God, so take advantage of it. You will be a better student during the other six days if you rest on one.

As you can see, many of the skills required to be a successful distance learner are the same skills necessary to succeed in the traditional classroom. And yet, because distance learning is such a new experience, there is often a much higher drop-out rate than with traditional courses. However, if you choose a suitable program and follow the suggestions in this chapter, you should find your learning experience to be fruitful, enjoyable, and successful.

6

UNDERSTANDING
ACCREDITATION

I've spoken with numerous people who have spent a great deal of time and money working on a degree via distance education, only to have it rejected by a prospective employer or graduate school. Their problem wasn't that their degree was earned via distance education (in fact, that was often considered a plus), but rather that it was earned from an unaccredited school. Accreditation is considered the benchmark for measuring the quality of an institution within the academic and business communities in the United States. Unfortunately, it can be a confusing topic. In this chapter I'll briefly define accreditation and explain how institutions acquire it, list the recognized accrediting agencies, and offer some comments on the importance of recognized accreditation.

WHAT IS ACCREDITATION?

Accreditation is a voluntary process by which primary and secondary schools, colleges, universities, and professional schools submit themselves to a review process by an approved agency that ensures compliance with a set of educational standards. While many countries require a governmental charter for operation of a

49

college or university, the United States lacks any such federal requirement. Some states do mandate a review and approval process, but many religious schools can simply seek an exemption from this requirement. Therefore, the accreditation process provides the only standard for validating academic quality and institutional integrity and promoting academic excellence.

The accreditation process relies heavily on self-study and institutional peer review. An institution first performs a self-study to ensure that the school meets general criteria for accreditation. During the self-study, objectives are outlined for institutional improvement. Then a team of outside reviewers, consisting of representatives from similar accredited schools, visits and reviews the institution in light of general accreditation criteria and specific goals outlined in the self-study.

This institutional peer-review approach encourages accredited institutions to carefully scrutinize new and renewal applications so that accreditation continues to reflect academic quality. At its best, this approach guarantees that institutions must achieve a certain level of quality to be accredited. If a subpar school were granted accreditation, the value of such accreditation would diminish, as well as the reputation of all accredited schools. At its worst, however, the peer-review approach has allowed issues that are academically controversial to be used against an institution. This happened in the 1980s when Westminster Theological Seminary's reaccreditation effort was hindered because of the school's policy of having only men on its governing board. Although the seminary did ultimately receive reaccreditation with the policy intact, the incident raised many concerns about potential anti-Christian biases inherent within the process. Still, while the accreditation process is imperfect, it remains the accepted standard of academic quality within the United States.

KEY ACCREDITING AGENCIES

The most credible type of accreditation in the United States is called "regional" accreditation, which means that an institution is accredited by one of the six geographically dispersed associations approved by both the United States Department of Education and the Council for Higher Education Accreditation (CHEA). Basically, the country is divided into six geographic regions, each with a corresponding regional accrediting agency.

The six approved regional agencies are the Middle States Association of Colleges and Schools, the New England Association of Schools and Colleges, the North Central Association of Colleges and Schools, the Northwest Association of Schools and Colleges, the Southern Association of Colleges and Schools, and the Western Association of Schools and Colleges.

There are also a number of specialized accrediting agencies, approved by both the Department of Education and CHEA, that focus on schools not by their geographic location but based on the type of school or program offerings. Three specialized agencies that are particularly relevant to Christian distance education include the Accrediting Association of Bible Colleges (AABC), the Association of Theological Schools in the United States and Canada (ATS), and the Distance Education and Training Council (DETC).

Some schools receive both regional and specialized accreditation. For example, a Bible college in Pennsylvania might seek both regional accreditation through the Middle States Association of Colleges and Schools (the regional agency covering Pennsylvania) as well as through the Accrediting Association of Bible Colleges. If you select a school that has only specialized accreditation, be aware that your efforts may not be as accepted if you apply to another institution for further study. For better or worse, there are various levels of respect associated with the different accrediting agencies, and the regional agencies are considered the standard. Specialized accreditation is, however, definitely preferable to no accreditation at all.

K–12 ACCREDITATION

Accreditation is a different animal on the K–12 level than on the higher education plane. Because of varied state regulations concerning home schooling (or any form of nontraditional learning) regional accreditation isn't as critical for K–12 programs as it is for colleges and universities. Furthermore, most of the regional accreditation agencies aren't equipped to handle the unique nature of primary and secondary distance schools. To address this issue, the regional accrediting agencies have created a new accrediting agency called the Commission on International and Transregional Accreditation (CITA). Distance institutions and programs for K–12 are encouraged to pursue CITA accreditation in addition to, or instead of, regional accreditation. Although CITA is fairly new, such accreditation is a recognized K–12 alternative to regional accreditation. The Distance Education and Training Council (DETC) mentioned earlier serves distance high schools as well as colleges and universities.

Accreditation by CITA or DETC is a good indication of the quality of a school. But lack of CITA accreditation shouldn't necessarily disqualify a school from your consideration. Both accredited and unaccredited K–12 schools are included in chapter 8 of this book. Regardless of what school you choose, be sure to check your state educational regulations about any steps that you must take to certify your child's K–12 learning experience. The Home School Legal Defense Association (HSLDA) can provide such information and also point you to organizations in your area for more information. You can reach HSLDA at 540-338-5600 or online at http://www.hslda.org.

THE IMPORTANCE OF ACCREDITATION

If you are pursuing a college degree through distance education, accreditation is a must. The school you choose must be accredited by one of the six regional agencies, or at least by AABC, ATS, or DETC. Many graduate programs and employers require an accredited degree and simply discount unaccredited programs. Furthermore, federal financial aid programs and tax credit benefits are only available for accredited programs.

Some nontraditional institutions, particularly within the Christian community, attempt to bypass the standard accreditation process by claiming accreditation from a different agency. Christian magazines are full of ads from schools claiming accreditation from organizations other than those mentioned above. Such claims lack meaning, though, within the current accreditation structure. To seek a degree from an institution that lacks recognized accreditation is to risk spending a lot of time and money for a degree that simply won't be recognized by other schools or employers. Furthermore, it is deceptive for an institution to claim that their unaccredited (or accredited through a nonrecognized agency) degrees stand on equal footing with accredited degree programs.

Not all unaccredited schools are bad—every new institution begins as an unaccredited school. Even newcomers such as Capella University and Jones International University were unaccredited just a few years ago. Some institutions, such as Bob Jones University (which has excellent distance programs available for home schooling through graduate school) or Pensacola Christian College, have sufficient academic quality to receive accreditation, but they decline to seek it for theological reasons. (These schools are quite forthright about their accreditation status and don't claim or seek accreditation from an unrecognized agency either.) But most unaccredited schools are unaccredited because, without substantial academic improvements, they would never pass an accreditation review.

My advice for those looking for distance degree programs is this: Be a good steward of your time and money and stick with an accredited institution. To get you started this book lists only accredited colleges and universities in chapters 9 through 13.

7

SELECTING A PROGRAM

Once you've ensured that an institution is accredited, you must select a distance education program that best fits your needs. It's important to consider whether courses match your area of interest, how long a program will take, how much it will cost, the possibility of transferring credits, and whether you need to participate in any on-campus residency sessions. It's also important to match the program to your learning style. One of the major benefits of distance learning is that you can not only fit courses into your life schedule, but you can select classes that will maximize your learning.

You may have several questions as you compare different programs. I've tried to answer them in the following pages.

CAN I EARN A HIGH SCHOOL DIPLOMA ONLINE?

Yes. Many of the programs listed in chapter 8 (e.g., the University of Nebraska-Lincoln Independent Study High School) offer recognized and accredited high school diploma programs. And depending on the regulations in your state, you may be able to pursue a high school education under the umbrella of home schooling and mix and match your studies from any number of Christian and secular institutions.

WHAT TYPE OF PROGRAM IS BEST?

Different programs work best with different people. Readings, audiotapes, videotapes, or online delivery of material will each appeal most to different individuals. If you know, for instance, that you're a strong visual learner, then find a program that uses videotapes rather than audiocassettes for lectures. One of the major benefits of distance learning is that you select courses that maximize your learning. Some learners may gravitate to an individually constructed degree program (e.g., the individualized Master of Arts program offered by the McGregor School of Antioch University that is listed in chapter 13) while others would do better in a more structured curriculum (e.g., Reformed Theological Seminary's Master of Arts [Religion] listed in chapter 11). Rather than assuming that one particular delivery method or curriculum structure is the best, select a program that fits your needs and learning style.

WHAT ARE THE DIFFERENCES BETWEEN DEGREES?

Academe is a veritable alphabet soup of degree titles—from A.A. to Ph.D. Following are some common degree titles with brief descriptions. (Note that required credit hours are approximate and will vary from program to program. For most programs, except those at the doctoral level, thirty credits is approximately equal to one year of full-time coursework.)

- A.A. (Associate of Arts)—undergraduate liberal arts degree; approximately sixty credits; typically spread over a number of disciplines (e.g., liberal arts, social sciences, general education, etc.)
- B.A. (Bachelor of Arts)—undergraduate liberal arts degree; approximately 120 credits; typically spread over a number of disciplines (e.g., liberal arts, social sciences, natural science, general education, etc.) as well as courses related to your major
- B.S. (Bachelor of Science)—undergraduate degree similar to the Bachelor of Arts; also has a distribution of credits, but typically a greater percentage of the 120 credits are concentrated in a major area of study

- M.A. (Master of Arts)—graduate research degree; approximately thirty-six to forty-five credits with either a thesis or a comprehensive exam
- M.S. (Master of Science)—graduate research or professional degree found within the natural science, social science, business, and technology fields; approximately thirty-six to forty-five credits
- M.B.A. (Master of Business Administration)—professional graduate degree in the area of business and management; approximately forty-five to sixty credits
- M.A.R. (Master of Arts in Religion)—graduate degree focused on the study of religion and theology; approximately forty-five to sixty credits
- M.Div. (Master of Divinity)—professional/practitioner graduate degree designed to prepare individuals for the pastoral ministry; approximately ninety credits
- Th.M. (Master of Theology)—research-oriented graduate degree designed for those who already hold an M.Div.; approximately thirty credits
- D.B.A. (Doctor of Business Administration)—doctoral level professional/practitioner degree designed primarily for those in the business/management community; approximately forty-five to sixty credits with an applied research dissertation
- Ed.D. (Doctor of Education)—doctoral level professional/practitioner degree designed primarily for those in the education community; approximately forty-five to sixty credits with an applied research dissertation
- D.Min. (Doctor of Ministry)—doctoral level professional/practitioner degree designed primarily for those in full-time ministry; approximately thirty to forty-five credits with an applied project/dissertation
- Ph.D. (Doctor of Philosophy)—doctoral level research degree; considered the *crème de la crème* of academic degrees; approximately sixty credits with comprehensive exams and an original research dissertation
- Th.D. (Doctor of Theology)—doctoral level research degree; historically designed as the theological counterpart to the

Ph.D. for those who already hold an M.Div., however, many seminaries have converted their Th.D. programs to Ph.D. programs in recent years; approximately sixty credits with comprehensive exams and an original research dissertation

If you're interested in teaching at a college or university, then you would be advised to stick with research-oriented degrees (e.g., M.A., Ph.D., etc.). On the other hand, professional/practitioner degrees (e.g., M.B.A., D.Min., etc.) may be more useful if you're looking for a more practical application of your studies.

CAN I EARN A DEGREE BASED ON PRIOR LEARNING?

Yes and no. On the undergraduate level, you can earn an entire associate's or bachelor's degree based on prior learning. Transfer credits, credit by examination, portfolio development and evaluation, and even other forms of prior learning can be applied toward an undergraduate degree. Many of the programs listed in chapter 10 offer such options toward advanced standing, and some of the custom programs listed in chapter 13 enable you to earn a degree based entirely on prior learning experiences.

This doesn't, however, apply to graduate programs. All accredited master's and doctoral degrees are based on new learning. If you closely examine the schools that advertise graduate degrees based on life experience, you'll notice that they aren't accredited by a Department of Education and CHEA-approved agency. Therefore, as I explained in the last chapter, you would be wise to avoid such programs.

HOW MUCH TIME DO I NEED TO SPEND ON CAMPUS?

On-campus residency requirements vary by program and degree level. With the exception of doctoral degrees, programs from kindergarten classes through master's degrees are not required to have any on-campus residency sessions. However, some institutions will require brief residency sessions periodically throughout their programs simply to assist students with their learning experience. Doctoral programs are generally required to have some on-campus residency in order to qualify for accreditation, but this can consist of as little as three to four weeks spread over the course of study.

CAN I EARN A DISTANCE DEGREE IF MY FIELD REQUIRES LICENSURE?

Yes. There are some programs that qualify you to sit for licensure examinations. For example, Liberty University's distance program for a Master of Arts in Counseling (see chapter 11) meets the licensure requirements of the National Board for Certified Counselors, the Council for Accreditation of Counseling and Related Educational Programs, and most state boards. It will, therefore, enable you to enter the field of professional counseling. When considering such a program, though, it's not only important to ensure that the program is accredited but also that it meets licensure criteria. Be sure to check with the appropriate licensure agency before enrolling in such a program.

CAN I DESIGN A CURRICULUM FOR MY UNIQUE NEEDS?

If you cannot find a program that meets your needs, there are a number of programs listed in chapter 13 that offer you the opportunity to design an individualized degree plan. Usually, you work with an academic advisor to outline a curriculum plan that meets program standards and is customized to your subject matter. On the undergraduate level you will be required to have a broad distribution of credits across a number of liberal arts fields, but on the graduate level you can be very targeted in your curriculum design.

I hope these first seven chapters have answered most of your questions and provided an introduction to the growing field of distance education. It's exciting to see an increasing number of schools, colleges, and companies offering online learning programs. I expect we'll see significantly more growth in the coming decade, which means you'll have even more learning opportunities at your fingertips. One Internet executive even declared that online learning will dwarf e-mail in terms of popularity and usage. While we haven't reached that point yet, there are clearly an abundance of learning opportunities available.

Part 2 of *Baker's Guide* serves as a directory of such opportunities. The chapters that follow feature a directory sorted by degree level with profiles for each program included. Each profile summarizes the specific grade, certificate, or degree program, offers credit and cost details, introduces the institution, and provides online and offline contact information. These profiles will enable you to find a suitable program that meets your learning needs.

PART 2

DISTANCE EDUCATION DIRECTORY

8

K-12 PROGRAMS

Distance programs for grades K–12 afford parents the opportunity to supplement a child's education with specialized courses or to deliver a complete, structured curriculum as an alternative to traditional public or private schools. The programs listed in this chapter represent leading Christian and secular institutions that offer kindergarten and elementary school courses as well as those that provide a complete high school diploma. Some are individualized and self-paced while others are modeled on traditional classrooms (except for students being scattered throughout the world!). Whether you're looking for a single advanced math course or a complete curriculum, you have many options from which to choose.

Alpha Omega Academy Online

300 N. McKemy Ave.
Chandler, AZ 85226-2618
877-688-2652
online@aopub.com

3rd through 12th Grade

Program Description

The Bridgestone OnLine Academy (BOLA) offers a home school, private school, and computer-based education all in one. Students complete their studies at home on the computer using the Switched-On Schoolhouse multimedia curriculum. Daily they link up to the BOLA Internet site and transfer their work to their teachers. Simultaneously, any grading and/or comments made by the teachers is transferred back to the students. An e-mail messaging system is built into the curriculum so that students and teachers can easily communicate. Using electronic "sticky notes" students can attach questions or comments directly to specific problems. Similarly, teachers also leave notes for students. BOLA teachers work with students to monitor their progress, address student concerns and questions, and make comments on student work.

Placement testing helps to customize the program for your student's educational needs. Lesson plans built around your own personalized school calendar set the due dates. BOLA provides the administrative and academic functions of a school. Progress reports and report cards are issued to inform parents of their student's achievements. Permanent records are kept and official transcripts provided. High school students earn graduation credits and their high school diplomas.

Institutional Description

Bridgestone OnLine Academy is a Christ-centered private school affiliated with Bridgestone Multimedia and Alpha Omega Publications, publishers of home schooling curriculum materials.

Tuition

4 Core Subjects: $750 (grades 3–6)
$875 (grades 7–12)

Electives: $225 per course (full-time)
$275 per course (part-time)

Denomination

None

Accreditation

None

Web Address

http://www.switchedonschoolhouse.com/aoao/

Bob Jones University HomeSat

1700 Wade Hampton Blvd.
Greenville, SC 29614
800-739-8199
hsatinfo@bju.edu

Elementary and High School Courses

Program Description

HomeSat is a service of Bob Jones University. The service has been available for over five years and offers elementary and secondary distance learning materials with a Christian emphasis. HomeSat assists home educators with a wide variety of courseware—kindergarten through high school—designed to interest and instruct distance learning students. Courses are prepared in a full-motion video format and delivered via satellite or on VHS tape.

The majority of the programs are developed at BJU's Center for Educational Technology. Courseware is based on BJU Press materials that have been used by Christian schools and home schools for almost twenty-five years. HomeSat's most popular courses are in the areas of math, science, and foreign languages.

Institutional Description

HomeSat is a service of Bob Jones University. Within the cultural and academic soil of liberal arts education, Bob Jones University exists to grow Christlike character that is scripturally disciplined, others-serving, God-loving, Christ-proclaiming, and focused above. BJU exists to teach men and women not only how to make a living but, more importantly, how to live.

Tuition

$39.95 per month
(10 months per year)

Denomination

None

Accreditation

None

Web Address

http://www.homesat.com

The Calvert School Home Instruction Department

105 Tuscany Rd.
Baltimore, MD 21210-3098
888-487-4652
inquiry@calvertschool.org

Kindergarten through 8th Grades

Program Description

The Calvert School program offers a complete home instruction curriculum for children ages kindergarten through eighth grade. Courses are drawn from the Calvert Day School curriculum. Teachers from the day school prepare the lessons and are in touch with students on a daily basis, so they are able to guide parents in practically every matter pertaining to a child's education. Materials for each grade include a step-by-step instruction manual to help the parent and tips to guide and encourage both parent and child.

Kindergarten through eighth grade courses are correlated study programs covering fundamental subjects as well as additional cultural studies. With the exception of the eighth grade material, each course is issued only as a full unit. To keep tuition costs at a minimum and because of the integrated subject approach, Calvert cannot individualize courses. Calvert also offers a wide variety of enrichment courses ranging from foreign language studies to reading guides. These courses are available independently and do not require a student to be enrolled in any other Calvert course.

Institutional Description

Calvert School, a nondenominational elementary school located just north of the Johns Hopkins University campus in Baltimore, Maryland, provides an excellent day school education to area boys and girls. The school also offers an educational opportunity to English-speaking children around the world through its home instruction department. Calvert School is incorporated as a nonprofit institution and is internationally recognized as an independent school. Both the day school and the home instruction department are fully approved by the Maryland State Department of Education.

Tuition

Varies by course

Denomination

None (secular institution)

Accreditation

Commission on International and Transregional Accreditation

Web Address

http://www.calvertschool.org

Christa McAuliffe Academy

3601 W. Washington Ave.
Yakima, WA 98903
509-575-4989
cma@cmacademy.org

7th through 12th Grades

Program Description

The Christa McAuliffe Academy system of education emphasizes individualized instruction using computer courseware delivered via the Internet. Student success is measured by mastery tests and a combination of written assessments and lab or practical learning activities in the various disciplines.

Each student chooses a CMA mentor (all of whom are certified teachers in their local jurisdictions) and determines his or her own pace and style of learning. Most CMA students accelerate their learning and graduate early. Those who need extra time to fully understand their courses will discover that CMA removes the pressure of time deadlines normally associated with group instruction. Group discussion and interaction with peers is accomplished through virtual learning sessions conducted weekly by each mentor.

An optional, extra-cost program of quarterly field excursions to important historic sites and exotic locations around the world is also available. This program is designed to develop student awareness of cultural diversity and to introduce real-life experiences into the curriculum.

Institutional Description

The Christa McAuliffe Academy is a private school offering individualized instruction for grades 7 through 12 using computer courseware delivered via the Internet. Our ultimate goal is to produce generations of excellent leaders, well-founded in traditional skills, knowledge, and values, but also highly capable in the use of advanced technology to help set the pace in an ever-changing society.

Tuition

$199 per month

Denomination

None (secular institution)

Accreditation

Commission on International and Transregional Accreditation

Web Address

http://www.cmacademy.org

Chrysalis School
14241 N.E. Woodinville-Duvall Rd., PMB 243
Woodinville, WA 98072
425-481-2228
info@chrysalis-school.com

High School

Program Description

Chrysalis School offers individualized courses online. A teacher will be available via e-mail, fax, and phone to give personal assistance and feedback on a frequent basis. The courses have been designed to appeal to a variety of learning styles and can be modified to be compatible with each student's ability, interests, and goals. Chrysalis is an independent study program whose goal is for students to become independent learners.

Enrollment in the distance program can be done two ways. You may choose to enroll in individual courses, paying for each course and taking up to a year to complete the work. If you are currently enrolled in a school in your area and need makeup credits, this would be the best option. The sooner you do the work, the sooner you earn the credit. You may also enroll month-to-month for the full-time program. In this program you pay on a monthly basis and work on five or six courses. These may include self-guided courses such as physical education, music lessons, volunteering, or part-time work experience. If you are not enrolled in another school and you work well independently, this would be a good option for you.

Institutional Description

Chrysalis is an independent private school accredited by the Northwest Association of Schools and Colleges. We have been in operation since 1983 and have had over a thousand families enrolled in our school. We have operated an Internet School Program since 1996.

Tuition

Single Course: $395

Full-time: $595 per month

Denomination

None (secular institution)

Accreditation

Northwest Association of Schools and Colleges

Web Address

http://www.chrysalis-school.com

Eagle Christian School
2526 Sunset Ln.
Missoula, MT 59804
888-324-5348
principal@eaglechristian.org
Junior High and High School

Program Description

Eagle Christian offers a complete online high school and junior high school program from a biblical perspective. Six classes in one semester constitutes a "full load" for both the junior high and high school curriculums. The high school program includes a number of elective possibilities. Assignments for a class are posted on the Internet on a weekly basis. Teachers have regular office hours and are available to be contacted "live" through chat software. Teachers seek to have regular contact with their students through e-mail, chat, and voice e-mail. Occasionally, a teacher will schedule an activity where all students "meet together" for a discussion or activity, but teachers are sensitive to the different time zones of their students.

Institutional Description

Eagle Christian School is the distance learning ministry of Valley Christian School. Eagle Christian School is an independent, interdenominational school committed to the Word of God as absolute truth, applicable to every area of life.

Tuition

Full-time: $750 per semester

Part-time: $150 per course

Denomination

None

Accreditation

None

Web Address

http://www.eaglechristian.org

Home Study International
P.O. Box 4437
Silver Spring, MD 20914-4437
301-680-6570
contact@hsi.edu

Kindergarten through 12th Grades

Program Description

Educational offerings include preschool, elementary, secondary, and higher education programs. These programs and courses, which respond to learner needs in the context of a lifetime learning experience, are available to all who can benefit from them. Parent study guides included with your course materials can help direct your learning. Such guides list learning objectives, include daily lesson plans, instruction, and supplemental information, and assign textbook reading and exercises for you to complete. Course supplies, such as textbooks, cassettes, lab equipment, or reading supplements can be used to assist you.

Institutional Description

As a global Seventh-day Adventist educational institution, the mission of Home Study International is to provide educationally sound, values-based, guided independent study and distance education programs that build a foundation for service to God, church, and society.

Tuition

Varies by grade level

Denomination

Seventh-day Adventist

Accreditation

Distance Education and Training Council

Web Address

http://www.hsi.edu

North Dakota Division of Independent Study
1510 12th Ave. N.
State University Station, P.O. Box 5036
Fargo, ND 58105-5036
701-231-6000
ensrud@sendit.NoDak.edu

5th through 12th Grades

Program Description

Independent study allows students to work at their own pace. Some students will work regularly and may finish quickly; others may take longer to complete coursework. Students have one year from the date of enrollment to complete a semester course. Tuition covers the teaching services provided by Division instructors and students use either a print-based or online study guide for each course.

Although the Division is a public distance education high school, our staff works closely with many students who are home educated. The independent study model of instruction lends itself well to home education since it is self-paced and individualized.

Institutional Description

The Division of Independent Study, a division of the North Dakota Department of Public Instruction, was established in 1935 by the North Dakota legislature to provide distance education courses for students in grades 5 to 12.

Tuition

$61 per half-credit course for North Dakota residents

$73 per half-credit course for non-residents

Denomination

None (secular institution)

Accreditation

North Central Association of Colleges and Schools

Web Address

http://www.dis.dpi.state.nd.us

NorthStar Academy

22571 Wye Rd.
Sherwood Park, AB, Canada T8C 1H9
888-464-6280
info@northstar-academy.org

7th through 12th Grades

Program Description

NorthStar Academy is a community of learners in an online school. It uses the Internet to link students with other students and with certified teachers. Teachers use conferencing software called FirstClass to send their lessons and assignments over the Internet. They also lead group discussions, evaluate students' assignments, and engage in most of the same teacher-student interactions that occur in traditional classrooms. Students complete assigned work using printed material and software provided by the school. Completed assignments and exams are sent back to teachers for marking and then returned to the students, all by e-mail.

NorthStar emulates nearly every learning interaction that happens in a traditional school: lectures, discussion (including the sorts of chatter that occur in the hallways), peer learning, group work, and student presentations.

Institutional Description

Northstar Academy is a private Christian online school offering grades 7 through 12. We are not an e-mail tutor nor a correspondence school; we are a fully staffed school offering full-time or part-time students the opportunity to be a part of our online community of learners.

Tuition

Full-time Students
• $2,650 for six full-time courses
• $2,450 with Saber Scholarship*

Part-time Students
• $450 per year-long course
• $250 per semester course
• $425 per year-long course with Saber Scholarship*
• $225 per semester course with Saber Scholarship*

*NorthStar Academy offers the Saber Scholarship to each full-time student who has a parent(s) working for a not-for-profit organization. NorthStar Academy also offers the Harris and Neva Poole (HNP) Scholarship—a partial (50 percent) scholarship awarded on the basis of both financial need and academic performance. Recipients must be full-time students.

Denomination

None

Accreditation

None

Web Address

http://www.northstar-academy.org

University of Nebraska-Lincoln Independent Study High School

Clifford Hardin Nebraska Center for Continuing Education
33rd and Holdrege, Room 255
Lincoln, NE 68583-9100
402-472-4321
unldde@unl.edu

High School

Program Description

The University of Nebraska-Lincoln Independent Study High School offers a complete four-year high school curriculum of more than 130 core and elective courses in sixteen subject areas. Students can earn a high school diploma by taking only distance education courses. However, more than 65 percent of the students enrolled in UNL distance education courses use the courses as a supplement to their high school curriculum.

CLASS (Communication, Learning, Assessment in a Student-centered System) is a dynamically interactive, student-centered course environment delivered electronically via the World Wide Web. An entire high school diploma sequence of fifty courses, including electives, is scheduled for completion in 2001.

Institutional Description

As part of the Department of Distance Education, the University of Nebraska-Lincoln Independent Study High School (ISHS), founded in 1929 to help small rural schools, currently serves nearly 14,000 enrollments annually from students in all fifty states and more than 135 other countries. The Independent Study High School is fully accredited by the North Central Association of Colleges and Schools and the Nebraska Department of Education and as such is authorized to grant a fully accredited high school diploma.

Tuition

Varies by course

Denomination

None (secular institution)

Accreditation

North Central Association of Colleges and Schools

Web Address

http://www.unl.edu
http://dcs.unl.edu/disted

The Sycamore Tree Online School

2179 Meyer Pl.
Costa Mesa, CA 92627
949-650-4466
sycamoretree@compuserve.com
4th through 12th Grades

Program Description

The Sycamore Tree Online School offers grades four through twelve. Students do their work on the computer each day and submit it via e-mail. All grading and tracking will be done by Sycamore Tree teachers. Enrollments are accepted at any time during the school year—even for high school students. Sycamore Tree students use the Switched-On Schoolhouse CD-ROM-based curriculum. Five subjects are available: Bible, English, math, science, and social studies. Teachers grade your student's work and respond with personalized academic assistance. Sycamore Tree offers official transcripts and a high school diploma through the online school. You may also use a combination of traditional curriculum and the online school.

Institutional Description

The Sycamore Tree, Inc. has been incorporated in California since 1982, and provides home school educational services to students in grades K–12 all over the world. Supporting the school or anyone needing Christian-based educational materials is a catalog purchasing service that provides a wide range of more than three thousand educational items.

Tuition

$200 each for Bible, math, social studies, and science courses
$250 for English courses

Denomination

None

Accreditation

None

Web Address

http://www.sycamoretree.com

9

CERTIFICATE PROGRAMS

Certificate programs, also called diploma programs, offer students the opportunity to pursue a "mini-degree" in a particular field of interest. Certificate programs typically require fewer credits than full degree programs and aren't usually tied to a traditional semester calendar. Many certificate programs have less stringent admission requirements and course prerequisites, and they may also have a lower tuition cost. Some certificates can be used to gain advanced standing in an undergraduate or graduate degree program if you decide to continue your education. So if you're looking for further study on a particular topic but aren't interested in earning a degree, a certificate program might be a perfect fit for you.

Baptist Bible College
628 E. Kearney
Springfield, MO 65803
800-228-5754
de-admin@bbcnet.edu

Certificate of Bible Knowledge

Program Description

The Certificate of Bible Knowledge is designed to help the layperson better prepare for church ministry. This program requires nineteen hours of study, including courses in Bible history, doctrine, evangelism, and teaching. Courses are offered in both self-paced correspondence and structured online formats.

Any course offered may be taken for personal growth without the intended purpose of working for a certificate, degree, or other college credit. Courses can also be taken to be transferred to another institution or for fulfillment of Baptist Bible College requirements.

Institutional Description

Baptist Bible College is an institution of higher learning with a distinctively biblical and historic Baptist curriculum, serving Christ and the Baptist Bible Fellowship International by training students to serve as pastors, missionaries, and other Christian workers for ministries in local churches.

Tuition

Varies by course

Denomination

Baptist Bible Fellowship International

Accreditation

Accrediting Association of Bible Colleges

Web Address

http://www.bbcnet.edu
http://www.bbcnet.edu/deinfo.html

Baptist Bible College
628 E. Kearney
Springfield, MO 65803
800-228-5754
de-admin@bbcnet.edu

Certificate of Church Ministries

Program Description

This program is designed to help the layperson better prepare for church ministry leadership. This program requires thirty-eight hours of study, including courses in Bible history, doctrine, evangelism, hermeneutics, and church ministries. Courses are offered in both self-paced correspondence and structured online formats.

Any course offered may be taken for personal growth without the intended purpose of working for a certificate, degree, or other college credit. Courses can also be taken to be transferred to another institution or for fulfillment of Baptist Bible College requirements.

Institutional Description

Baptist Bible College is an institution of higher learning with a distinctively biblical and historic Baptist curriculum, serving Christ and the Baptist Bible Fellowship International by training students to serve as pastors, missionaries, and other Christian workers for ministries in local churches.

Tuition

Varies by course

Denomination

Baptist Bible Fellowship International

Accreditation

Accrediting Association of Bible Colleges

Web Address

http://www.bbcnet.edu
http://www.bbcnet.edu/deinfo.html

Briercrest Bible College

510 College Dr.
Carenport, SK S0H 0S0, CANADA
800-667-5199
distance.learning@briercrest.ca

Certificate in Bible

Program Description

This thirty-two-credit certificate provides an overview of biblical and theological perspectives geared to students seeking growth in life and ministry, including courses in Old and New Testament, Christian ministry, and field education. This program makes up the entire first year of many three- and four-year B.A. programs offered at Briercrest Bible College. In addition to print correspondence courses, modes of delivery include extension classes, CD-ROM, and the Internet.

Institutional Description

The Bible College is operated on a postsecondary level to prepare men and women for the service of Christ through his church. The college offers one-year certificates, two-year A.A. degrees, a three-year general B.A. degree, and four-year professional B.A. degrees. Professional B.A. degrees include Bible teaching, business administration, theology, counseling, intercultural studies, leadership, pastoral leadership, and ministry degrees with specializations in children, sports, women, worship, and youth. The emphasis of all programs is on Bible and theology; over one-third of the credits in all B.A. programs are in these areas.

Tuition

$295 (USD) for a 3-credit-hour course

$390 (CAD) for a 3-credit-hour course

Denomination

None

Accreditation

Accrediting Association of Bible Colleges

Web Address

http://www.briercrest.ca/bdl/
http://www.briercrest.ca/bdl/programs/college.shtml

Briercrest Biblical Seminary

510 College Dr.
Carenport, SK S0H 0S0, CANADA
800-667-5199
distance.learning@briercrest.ca

Certificate of the Seminary

Program Description

This thirty-credit introductory program is of special interest to students already engaged in ministry and looking for personal and professional development. It includes courses in Bible, theology, history, research, and specialized courses of your choice. In addition to print correspondence courses, modes of delivery include extension classes, CD-ROM, and the Internet.

Institutional Description

The seminary is a theological institution for graduate education that influences students to extend, refocus, rethink, retool, and recommit themselves to strategic ministry in their generation. It is a graduate school where experienced people reflect and refine ministry skills for service to Christ and his church. Briercrest Biblical Seminary offers Master of Divinity degrees and Master of Arts degrees with majors in administration, adolescent ministries, biblical counseling, biblical studies, Christian ministries, communication, and historical theology.

Tuition

$375 (USD) for a 3-credit-hour course
$495 (CAD) for a 3-credit-hour course

Denomination

None

Accreditation

Association of Theological Schools

Web Address

http://www.briercrest.ca/bdl/
http://www.briercrest.ca/bdl/programs/seminary.shtml

Canadian Theological Seminary

4400 Fourth Ave.
Regina, SK S4T 0H8, CANADA
306-545-1515
admissions@cbccts.sk.ca

Diploma in Christian Studies

Program Description

The thirty-two-credit Diploma in Christian Studies provides preparation for lay ministry that has been enhanced by concentrated study in Bible and theology. This diploma can be applied fully to the Master of Arts in religion, and can be taken entirely through alternative course formats such as Connections. Connections courses are independent studies utilizing audiotaped lectures by recognized evangelical scholars. Each course is directed by regular CTS faculty and must be completed within six months of registration.

The thirty-two credits include courses in biblical studies, church history, Christian thought, pastoral studies, world missions, and Christian education.

Institutional Description

Canadian Theological Seminary exists to glorify the triune God by preparing pastors, missionaries, teachers, and others for ministering the Word and for leading the church in its worldwide mission. Though the primary purpose of the seminary is to serve the Christian and Missionary Alliance, we welcome the opportunity to prepare workers from other Christian communions and to develop lay Christians for their role in Christ's service. We seek to accomplish these purposes by a holistic preparation for ministry that relates to the individual's understanding, ministerial practice, and spiritual life, and which motivates and equips the student for a lifetime of learning.

Tuition

$157 per credit

Denomination

Christian and Missionary Alliance

Accreditation

Association of Theological Schools

Web Address

http://www.cbccts.sk.ca
http://www.cbccts.sk.ca/cts/dip_cs.html

Columbia International University
7435 Monticello Rd., P.O. Box 3122
Columbia, SC 29230-3122
800-777-2227
extoff@ciu.edu
Certificate in Biblical Studies

Program Description

Columbia Bible College and Columbia Biblical Seminary & Graduate School of Missions offer distance learning studies available worldwide at extension sites and through independent distance learning studies (audio/video) for graduate or college credit or personal enrichment. You can enroll in an independent distance learning (IDL) course at any time. Once enrolled you'll receive a package including a syllabus, study guide, audiotaped or videotaped lectures, and textbooks. Students studying for credit also have access to the holdings of the Columbia Library for research and collateral reading assignments.

The one-year curriculum (thirty-one semester hours) is designed to provide a practical bridge between secular education and vocational or lay ministry. Its flexibility lies in the fact that while it marks the completion of basic study for those who terminate after one year, it also may be applied toward a degree for those who continue, although no more than six IDL courses may be applied toward a degree. Non-resident students in the program must complete spiritual formation and ministry skills components designed to meet the objectives normally met through campus life experiences. All students in the program must be active members in an evangelical church.

Institutional Description

Columbia International University (CIU) is a multidenominational, biblically based, Christian institution with one of the leading missionary training programs in the world. Although CIU is denominationally unaffiliated, it serves students from many different denominations and independent churches.

Tuition

Undergraduate tuition: $125 per semester hour

Graduate tuition: $165 per semester hour

Denomination

None

Accreditation

Southern Association of Colleges and Schools

Accrediting Association of Bible Colleges

Association of Theological Schools

Web Address

http://www.ciu.edu
http://www.ciuextension.com

Covenant Theological Seminary
12330 Conway Rd.
Saint Louis, MO 63141-8914
800-264-8064
webmaster@covenantseminary.edu

Graduate Certificate

Program Description

The Graduate Certificate is designed for individuals who desire advanced biblical study but are not seeking a master's degree. The program is ideal for Sunday school teachers, small group leaders, or short-term missionaries. It is also helpful in making total Christian truth and activity meaningful and relevant for individuals in various professions. Teachers in schools and colleges and people engaged in politics, law, business, literature, or science will find their vocations enhanced and their Christian witness more effective because of this formal Bible education. Admission to the graduate certificate program requires a bachelor's degree from a recognized college or university. Graduation from the program requires thirty hours of study, all of which can be completed from an extension site. Courses taken toward the graduate certificate may be transferred to a master's degree with faculty approval.

Courses are under the direct supervision of Covenant faculty and are offered through a structured environment that includes interaction between the extension student and faculty assistants at our main campus via mail, phone, and e-mail. These audio and video courses are specially designed to supply personal and social interaction within the context of academic study.

Institutional Description

The purpose of Covenant Theological Seminary is to train servants of the triune God to walk with God, to interpret and communicate his Word, and to lead his people. We believe that a seminary education is successful only if—at its end—the student knows Jesus Christ more intimately than at its beginning.

Tuition

$135 per credit hour

Denomination

Presbyterian Church in America

Accreditation

North Central Association of Colleges and Schools

Association of Theological Schools

Web Address

http://www.covenantseminary.edu
http://www.covenantseminary.edu/externalstudy/degreeprograms.htm

Eastern Pentecostal Bible College

780 Argyle St.
Peterborough, ON K9H 5T2, CANADA
800-295-6368
ici@epbc.edu

Christian Ministry Certificate
in General Church Leadership

Program Description

This thirty-credit certificate provides an overview of biblical theology, New Testament, church leadership, and Pentecostal history and distinctives. Courses are offered in print correspondence or online formats.

Institutional Description

Eastern Pentecostal Bible College is Canada's largest denominational undergraduate theological institution. Founded in 1939, Eastern has a long history of excellence in education and innovation in the accomplishment of its mission. Courses and programs are available at our campus in Peterborough, Ontario, Canada, or through a variety of distance education options.

Tuition

Varies by course

Denomination

The Pentecostal Assemblies of Canada

Accreditation

Accrediting Association of Bible Colleges

Web Address

http://www.epbc.edu
http://www.epbc.edu/disted/

Eastern Pentecostal Bible College
780 Argyle St.
Peterborough, ON K9H 5T2, CANADA
800-295-6368
ici@epbc.edu

Ministerial Diploma

Program Description

This ninety-nine-credit diploma provides three years of coursework on a variety of topics including biblical theology, New Testament, church leadership, Pentecostal history and distinctives, and personal ministry development. Courses are offered in print correspondence or online formats.

Institutional Description

Eastern Pentecostal Bible College is Canada's largest denominational undergraduate theological institution. Founded in 1939, Eastern has a long history of excellence in education and innovation in the accomplishment of its mission. Courses and programs are available at our campus in Peterborough, Ontario, Canada, or through a variety of distance education options.

Tuition

Varies by course

Denomination

The Pentecostal Assemblies of Canada

Accreditation

Accrediting Association of Bible Colleges

Web Address

http://www.epbc.edu
http://www.epbc.edu/disted/

Fuller Theological Seminary

135 N. Oakland Ave.
Pasadena, CA 91182
626-584-5290 or 800-999-9578
idl@fuller.edu

Certificate of Christian Studies

Program Description

The Certificate of Christian Studies can be completed entirely through distance learning. It requires the successful completion of six graduate courses of the student's choice. The certificate offers students an opportunity to complete a focused course of study or a sampling of master's-level courses from the School of Theology or the School of World Missions. As it requires less coursework than degree programs, the certificate can be completed in a shorter period of time. Because each individual's course of study is personalized, students can achieve a wide range of goals, including training for a specific church or parachurch ministry, a specialized work in missions, or spiritual and personal enrichment.

Courses use audiocassette lectures and notebooks, supplemented by readings and some videos. Students and teachers interact via mail, telephone, e-mail, and fax. Online interactive distance courses are offered in ten-week quarters and require interaction over the Internet.

Institutional Description

Fuller Theological Seminary is an evangelical, multidenominational, international, and multiethnic graduate institution dedicated to the preparation of men and women for the manifold ministries of Christ and his church. Founded in 1947 by radio evangelist Charles Fuller and pastor-scholar Harold Ockenga, Fuller has grown to be one of the largest evangelical seminaries with over three thousand students from over sixty-three countries and one hundred denominations. Under the authority of Scripture, Fuller seeks to fulfill its commitment to ministry through graduate education, professional development, and spiritual formation while striving for excellence in the service of Jesus Christ, under the guidance and power of the Holy Spirit to the glory of the Father.

Tuition

$192 per quarter credit

Denomination

Multidenominational

Accreditation

Western Association of Schools and Colleges

Association of Theological Schools

Web Address

http://www.fuller.edu
http://www.fuller.edu/cll/html/idl.html
http://www.fulleronline.org

Gordon Conwell Theological Seminary

130 Essex St.
South Hamilton, MA 01982
978-468-7111
info@gcts.edu

Diploma

Program Description

Independent study courses for diploma students can be taken through the Ockenga Institute of Gordon-Conwell Seminary and are designed for you to do your work at home. These courses include lectures that have been put on cassette tapes and an accompanying notebook to supplement lecture material. This is a personalized learning method using audiocassette-taped lectures with a course syllabus and study guide supplemented by textbooks, reference materials, and, in some cases, video resources, Internet, and CD-ROM formats. A diploma student must complete fifteen units in biblical studies, Christian thought, ministry, and electives to complete the program.

Institutional Description

Our Lord has given Gordon-Conwell Theological Seminary a mission—to train men and women who have commitment, vision, and scholarly competence to reach the world for Jesus. Our vision is to provide an environment in which people who hear the call of God on their lives can prepare ... where they can be challenged, discipled, loved, taught, and mentored ... where they can become great preachers and teachers, evangelists and missionaries, counselors and scholars, theologians and pastors.

Tuition

$337.50 per course

Denomination

None

Accreditation

New England Association of Schools and Colleges

Association of Theological Schools

Web Address

http://www.gcts.edu
http://www.gcts.edu/ock/

Northwestern College
3003 Snelling Ave. N.
St. Paul, MN 55113-1598
651-631-5100
distance@nwc.edu

Certificate in Bible

Program Description

The Certificate in Bible is designed for those wishing concentrated training in the Word of God. It assists students to become established in the faith, rooted and grounded in the Word, and fortified with answers to man's primary questions regarding life's purpose and destiny. It provides tools for continuing Bible study and for effective Christian witness. It is of value to professional men and women going to the mission field and needing such a concentrated study of the Bible. The Certificate of Bible is granted upon completion of forty-five credits of selected Bible courses. Course materials are delivered using various technologies including video- or audiocassettes, textbooks, and computers.

Institutional Description

Northwestern College exists to provide Christ-centered higher education that equips believers (1) to grow intellectually and spiritually, (2) to serve effectively in their professions, and (3) to give God-honoring leadership in the home, church, community, and world. Northwestern upholds its heritage of biblical distinctives through the vital integration of human knowledge and divine revelation. The goal of the college is to help develop the whole person, characterized by personal development, spiritual maturity, ethical conviction, intellectual curiosity, cultural sensitivity, professional achievement, and faithful service to society and the world.

Tuition
$180 per credit

Denomination
Nondenominational

Accreditation
North Central Association of Colleges and Schools

Web Address
http://www.nwc.edu
http://www.nwc.edu/disted/

Oral Roberts University

7777 S. Lewis Ave.
Tulsa, OK 74171
888-900-4678
slle@oru.edu

Certificate of Theology

Program Description

The Certificate of Theology is designed for equipping laypeople for ministry through the local church. The certificate is awarded upon completion of a twelve-course, noncredit correspondence program that includes courses covering Old and New Testament studies, end-time events, the Holy Spirit at work today, Christian leaders who shaped America, how to witness, and more. These courses are noncredit courses with a more practical than academic design. Students will learn more about themselves, their ministries, the Bible, and the world.

Certificate study is done by correspondence. Students work from a packet that consists of textbooks and a study guide. They mail in completed assignments, which are, in turn, graded and returned to students by the Adult Learning Service Center. This program functions on the basis of a rolling enrollment. Students may enroll at any time. Once enrolled, students have one full year to complete a course.

Institutional Description

Oral Roberts University was founded as a result of the evangelist Oral Roberts's obedience to God's mandate to build a university on God's authority and the Holy Spirit. God's commission to Oral Roberts was: "Raise up your students to hear My voice, to go where My light is dim, where My voice is heard small, and My healing power is not known, even to the uttermost bounds of the earth. Their work will exceed yours, and in this I am well pleased."

Oral Roberts University is a charismatic university founded in the fires of evangelism and upon the unchanging precepts of the Bible. The board of regents and the president and chief executive officer are dedicated to upholding the university's founding purpose.

Tuition

$40 per course

Denomination

Nondenominational

Accreditation

North Central Association of Colleges and Schools

Web Address

http://www.oru.edu

Prairie Bible College

Box 4000, 330 6th Ave. N.
Three Hills, AB TOM 2N0, CANADA
800-661-2425
distance.ed@pbi.ab.ca

Certificate in Bible

Program Description

Whether you continue on to further education, enter the marketplace, or want to be more effective in local church ministry, the Certificate in Bible will give you a solid biblical perspective for successful living. The Certificate consists of three required Bible courses, two elective Bible courses, two theology courses, two ministry courses, and two elective courses. All credits earned can be transferred to degree programs.

Institutional Description

Prairie Bible Institute is an interdenominational, biblically based Christian educational institution offering K–12 through college instruction in Three Hills, Alberta, Canada, and a graduate school in Calgary, Alberta, as well as distance education courses and degrees worldwide.

Tuition

$119 per credit

Denomination

None

Accreditation

Accrediting Association of Bible Colleges

Web Address

http://www.pbi.ab.ca
http://www.pbi.ab.ca/distanceed/

Prairie Graduate School

Box 4000, 330 6th Ave. N.
Three Hills, AB TOM 2N0, CANADA
800-661-2425
distance.ed@pbi.ab.ca

Certificate in Christian Ministry

Program Description

Earn a sixteen-credit Prairie Graduate School Certificate through distance education. Designed to give you a basic understanding of the Bible and ministry, this program requires six months of active lay or vocational ministry. Credits are fully transferable to other Prairie Graduate School programs. Most courses incorporate tapes, workbooks, textbooks, and other reading materials while online courses are also under development.

Institutional Description

Prairie Bible Institute is an interdenominational, biblically based Christian educational institution offering K–12 through college instruction in Three Hills, Alberta, Canada, and a graduate school in Calgary, Alberta, as well as distance education courses and degrees worldwide.

Tuition

$139 per graduate credit

Denomination

None

Accreditation

Accrediting Association of Bible Colleges

Web Address

http://www.pbi.ab.ca
http://www.pbi.ab.ca/distanceed/

Reformed Theological Seminary

2101 Carmel Rd.
Charlotte, NC 28226
800-227-2013
distance.education@rts.edu

Certificate Programs

Biblical Studies	Historical Studies	Theological Studies
General Studies	Missions	

Program Description

Each of the five certificate programs available through distance education requires thirty credit hours of study. Since the certificate program is not a degree program, there is no admissions process and a baccalaureate degree is not required. Courses consist of audiotapes, workbooks, articles and books, and numerous assignments. A regular assessment of your progress will be provided through midterm and final exams. If admitted to a degree program at RTS, particular courses completed in the external education program may be applied toward the degree upon review by the academic dean.

Institutional Description

The purpose of Reformed Theological Seminary is to serve the church in all branches of evangelical Christianity, especially the Presbyterian and Reformed family, by training its leaders (with a priority on pastors and including missionaries, educators, counselors, and others) through a program of theological education on the graduate level, based upon the authority of the inerrant Word of God and committed to the Reformed faith as set forth in the Westminster Confession of Faith and the Larger and Shorter Catechisms as originally adopted by the Presbyterian Church in the United States. This program shall be characterized by biblical fidelity, confessional integrity, and academic excellence.

Tuition

$220 per semester hour

Denomination

None

Accreditation

Southern Association of Colleges and Schools
Association of Theological Schools

Web Address

http://www.rts.edu
http://www.rtsvirtual.org

Regent College

5800 University Blvd.
Vancouver, BC V6T 2E4, CANADA
604-224-3245
admissions@regent-college.edu

Certificate in Christian Studies

Program Description

The Certificate in Christian Studies is a twenty-four-credit program designed to give students from all walks of life a basic understanding of the Christian faith and to provide them with the tools for an ongoing life of Christian study, meditation, and practical service. Central to the concerns of the certificate is a vision for the integration of faith and life, that is, the need to bring the insights of faith to bear on personal, social, and cultural issues.

Students may elect to earn the certificate through on-campus offerings (summer school, winter school, fall or spring terms), in classes located at extension centers, or by audiocassette correspondence courses. Any combination of these formats may be selected. Students may also choose to audit courses. Most correspondence courses will be offered in two-credit-hour packages, whereas most courses held on the Vancouver campus will be offered in the three-credit-hour format.

Institutional Description

Regent College is a graduate school of Christian studies that seeks to educate, nurture, and equip men and women from around the world to live and work as mature leaders. Recognizing that God calls his people to claim the whole of human life for Jesus Christ as they spread the good news of his saving grace, the college shapes its corporate life to produce believers who can fulfill this calling with insight and skill in varied vocations worldwide. In support of this, the college seeks also to prepare those who will further this mission through the ministry of local congregations.

Tuition

$260 per credit hour

Denomination

None

Accreditation

Association of Theological Schools

Web Address

http://www.regent-college.edu

Regent University
1000 Regent University Dr.
Virginia Beach, VA 23464-9800
757-226-4000
govschool@regent.edu

Public Policy Certificate

Program Description

The certificate program allows individuals to attain a working knowledge of principles and public policies for influencing and participating in government at local, state, national, and international levels. Students select their own choice of twenty-four credit hours of core, electives, and skills courses to complete this degree. All courses are interactive and delivered via the Internet.

Institutional Description

Regent University is the nation's premier Christian graduate university offering master's and doctoral degrees from a Judeo-Christian perspective. With a commitment to academic excellence and innovation, Regent prepares men and women to make a positive impact upon American society and the world. Twenty-two degree programs are offered on the Virginia Beach campus, and several are offered in the northern Virginia/Washington, D.C., area. Students may also pursue degree programs via the Internet. The eight graduate fields of study offered at Regent University include business, communication, counseling and psychology, divinity, education, government, law, and organizational leadership.

Tuition

$340 per credit

Denomination

Nondenominational

Accreditation

Southern Association of Colleges and Schools

Web Address

http://www.regent.edu
http://www.regent.edu/acad/schgov/admissions/distance.html

Taylor University World Wide Campus
1025 W. Rudisill Blvd.
Fort Wayne, IN 46807-2197
800-845-3149
wwcampus@tayloru.edu

Justice and Ministry Certificate

Program Description

An eighteen-hour program aimed at equipping individuals working with at-risk populations and/or inmates, this certificate will offer an interdisciplinary approach to understanding ministry needs and the essentials in criminal justice. Individuals seeking to obtain this certificate will need to complete six of the eighteen hours on campus. Coursework may be completed by either correspondence or online learning.

Institutional Description

The World Wide Campus is the virtual campus of Taylor University emphasizing the integration of faith and learning through distance education. It offers three associate of arts degrees, two certificate programs, and more than seventy courses from most academic disciplines. Courses are offered for undergraduate credit and/or non-credit in a variety of delivery formats to meet individual learning needs.

Tuition

$169 per credit hour online

$119 per credit hour correspondence

Denomination

Interdenominational/ Nondenominational

Accreditation

North Central Associationof Colleges and Schools

Web Address

http://wwcampus.tayloru.edu
http://wwcampus.tayloru.edu/degrees_certificates/frm3.htm

Taylor University World Wide Campus
1025 W. Rudisill Blvd.
Fort Wayne, IN 46807-2197
800-845-3149
wwcampus@tayloru.edu

Christian Worker Certificate

Program Description

The Christian Worker Certificate is an eighteen-hour program of study designed for in-depth study of God's Word. This certificate is ideal for potential missionaries, pastors, and volunteer laypeople who desire greater knowledge of the Bible and a better understanding of the professional challenges of ministry. Coursework may be completed by either correspondence or online learning.

Institutional Description

The World Wide Campus is the virtual campus of Taylor University emphasizing the integration of faith and learning through distance education. It offers three associate of arts degrees, two certificate programs, and more than seventy courses from most academic disciplines. Courses are offered for undergraduate credit and/or noncredit in a variety of delivery formats to meet individual learning needs.

Tuition

$169 per credit hour online

$119 per credit hour correspondence

Denomination

Interdenominational/
Nondenominational

Accreditation

North Central Association of Colleges and Schools

Web Address

http://wwcampus.tayloru.edu
http://wwcampus.tayloru.edu/degrees_certificates/frm3.htm

Tennessee Temple University

1815 Union Ave.
Chattanooga, TN 37404
800-553-4050
ttuinfo@tntemple.edu

Diploma of Theology

Program Description

The Diploma of Theology is a three-year, ninety-four-credit, independent study correspondence course program offered through the School of External Studies. The program includes forty-six credits of core courses in Bible and theology, communication, computer skills, history, humanities, mathematics or science, physical education, psychology, social studies, and Christian service. In addition, the student can take a variety of concentration courses and electives. For any student taking more than 50 percent of coursework through correspondence, the diploma will be tagged from the School of External Studies.

Institutional Description

Tennessee Temple University is a distinctively Christian institution offering an education that is characterized by its goal of academic excellence in the classroom and its effort to build biblical character and ethical values in its students. Tennessee Temple University is multifaceted, with undergraduate programs at the associate's and bachelor's levels and a graduate master's program in education. The university's purpose is to prepare Christian men and women for life through emphasis on knowledge acquisition, biblical application, skill development, evangelism, and godly living. Tennessee Temple University balances a traditional liberal arts program with a historical Baptist position regarding doctrine and conduct. Its unique characteristic is its emphasis on local church ministries through affiliation with the Highland Park Baptist Church of Chattanooga, Tennessee. Tennessee Temple University is dedicated to providing a Christ-centered education to a diverse population of students from many geographical locations. All classes are taught by dedicated Christian professors who integrate the knowledge of their respective fields with biblical perspectives.

Tuition

$250 per 2-credit-hour course

$325 per 3-credit-hour course

$400 per 4-credit-hour course

Denomination

None

Accreditation

Accrediting Association of Bible Colleges

Web Address

http://www.tntemple.edu
http://www.tntemple.edu/external_studies/

Western Seminary

5511 S.E. Hawthorne Blvd.
Portland, OR 97215
800-547-4546
western@westernseminary.edu

Certificate in Theology or Church Ministries

Program Description

A certificate may be earned on the way to a diploma or degree, or it may be the final goal for a student. Certificate programs are offered in theology and church ministries and require twelve semester credits. Western's external courses are available to both credit and noncredit students, and may be taken on an independent basis or with a study group. As a result, you have a choice of how you take the courses. Courses are offered in both video-based format—taped from campus courses—and audio-based courses using tapes developed by the Institute of Theological Studies.

Institutional Description

Western Seminary is an educational institution nurturing godly leaders committed to and competent for Christ's redemptive purpose throughout the world.

Tuition

Varies by course

Denomination

Conservative Baptist Association

Accreditation

Northwest Association of Schools and Colleges

Web Address

http://www.westernseminary.edu
http://www.westernseminary.edu/external.html

Western Seminary

5511 S.E. Hawthorne Blvd.
Portland, OR 97215
800-547-4546
western@westernseminary.edu

Diploma in Theological Studies or Ministerial Studies

Program Description

There are currently two diplomas available through external studies: a diploma in theological studies and a diploma in ministerial studies. Each requires thirty semester credits of work. Western's external courses are available to both credit and noncredit students and may be taken on an independent basis or with a study group. As a result, you have a choice of how you take the courses. Courses are offered in both video-based format—taped from campus courses—and audio-based courses using tapes developed by the Institute of Theological Studies.

Institutional Description

Western Seminary is an educational institution nurturing godly leaders committed to and competent for Christ's redemptive purpose throughout the world.

Tuition

Varies by course

Denomination

Conservative Baptist Association

Accreditation

Northwest Association of Schools and Colleges

Web Address

http://www.westernseminary.edu
http://www.westernseminary.edu/external.html

Westminster Theological Seminary

P.O. Box 27009
Philadelphia, PA 19118
800-373-0119

Certificate in Christian Studies

Program Description

A Certificate in Christian Studies program is offered for men and women who desire graduate-level courses from Westminster but do not desire to enter a degree program. The certificate will be earned after the completion of twenty-five semester hours of graduate courses. All courses in the certificate program must be taken under the auspices of Westminster Theological Seminary. Courses are master's-level, audio-programmed, independent studies. Taped lectures are supplemented by a syllabus, study questions, and bibliography under the guidance of a Westminster faculty member. Admission to the certificate program requires the same qualifications as admission for graduate degree programs. Registration, tuition charges, and all academic procedures and prerequisites are also the same.

Institutional Description

Westminster Theological Seminary prepares leaders for ministry, developing graduates with a depth of understanding of God's Word and a heartfelt desire to use that knowledge in God's service. A Westminster education starts with the Bible. Grounded in the Reformed tradition, Westminster teaches that the Christian religion is true, and that in-depth study of the Bible and its historical contexts will reveal this truth, building a bedrock foundation for Christian ministry. Challenged and mentored by skilled faculty and supporting each other as members of a learning community, students grow intellectually and spiritually, confident in their faith, as the power and significance of the Word changes their lives and prepares them to offer God's message to others. Westminster is a world leader in seminary education, committed to the highest academic standards. What connects the students who learn here is profound knowledge of the Word, kindled by passion for the Christian faith, and delivered to a world that needs it.

Tuition

$320 per semester hour

Denomination

None

Accreditation

Middle States Association of Colleges and Schools

Association of Theological Schools

Web Address

http://www.wts.edu
http://www.wts.edu/disted/

Wheaton College
501 College Avenue
Wheaton, IL 60187-5593
800-888-0141
admissions@wheaton.edu

Certificate of Advanced Biblical Studies

Program Description

The twenty-six-credit Certificate of Advanced Biblical Studies—Distance Learning option is designed for students who desire advanced training in biblical and theological studies without working for a master's degree. It provides flexibility while offering an adequate introduction to the subject matter. Knowledge of a biblical language is not required because studies are based on the English text. The certificate program provides professional development opportunities for pastors, teachers in Christian schools, missionaries, and other Christian workers. It also provides a way for those working in other vocations and disciplines to attain a theological and biblical foundation necessary for the deep integration of faith, learning, and living. It is a suitable program for lay persons who desire biblical and theological training to better equip themselves for personal Christian living and service in the church. To receive the Certificate of Advanced Biblical Studies—Distance Learning Option, students must complete twenty-six hours in biblical and theological studies. Each student's program is worked out individually in consultation with a faculty adviser and all courses are delivered online.

Institutional Description

Wheaton College exists to help build the church and improve society worldwide by promoting the development of whole and effective Christians through excellence in programs of Christian higher education. Committed to the principle that truth is revealed by God through Christ "in Whom are hid all the treasures of wisdom and knowledge" Wheaton College seeks to relate Christian liberal arts education to the needs of contemporary society. The curricular approach is designed to combine faith and learning in order to produce a biblical perspective needed to relate Christian experience to the demands of those needs.

Tuition

$380 per credit hour

Denomination

None

Accreditation

North Central Association of Colleges and Schools

Web Address

http://www.wheaton.edu
http://www.wheatononline.org

10
BACHELOR'S DEGREE PROGRAMS

The bachelor's degree is the most common undergraduate degree. It consists of approximately four years of coursework covering a wide array of subjects. Some degrees (e.g., the Bachelor of Arts in General Studies) are broad-based programs with coursework in the humanities, social sciences, natural sciences, mathematics, and education. Others (e.g., the Bachelor of Science in Business Administration) have an interdisciplinary core of courses followed by numerous courses in your area of specialization.

In addition to the prescribed coursework, many distance bachelor's programs found in this chapter also have generous policies concerning transfer credit, credit by examination, and other opportunities to earn credits based on life experience. Such policies are worth examining. They may make it easier, faster, and cheaper for you to earn your undergraduate degree. Regardless of your area of interest, you'll find that Christian institutions offer a variety of bachelor's degree distance programs. You can pursue biblical studies, marketing, accounting, counseling, education, psychology, and many other majors through the distance degrees listed in this chapter.

Atlantic Union College
338 Main St.
South Lancaster, MA 01561
800-282-2030
adp@atlanticuc.edu

Bachelor of Arts

Art	History	Psychology
Behavioral Science	Interior Design	Religion
Business	Interdisciplinary Majors	Theology
Communications	Modern Languages	Philosophy
Computer Science	Personal Ministries	Women's Studies
Education	Physical Education	

Program Description

The adult degree program at Atlantic Union College provides adults with the opportunity to complete a degree through distance learning. Students attend two on-campus seminars per year, in January and July, where they individually design their study programs. They receive guidance from faculty mentors as they study independently at home. The program is open to adults twenty-five years of age or older who present evidence of being capable of self-directed work and having the necessary skills for research, writing, and organized study. A student can obtain a bachelor's degree through the adult degree program in four years by completing one unit of study (sixteen semester credits) every six months. The student can complete one unit in six months by studying an average of twenty hours per week.

Institutional Description

Atlantic Union College is a four-year accredited, coeducational, liberal arts institution with a number of professional and preprofessional programs, several alternative education programs, and a master's degree program in education. Although established by the Seventh-day Adventist Church, it welcomes applications from all students who desire a campus atmosphere consciously structured on Christian principles. The college also serves educational needs of adults who cannot study in conventional programs and offers programs designed for students ranging from preparatory students to retired adults. It is committed to the belief that each person has the capacity to learn and to change, no matter what the age or background of the individual.

Tuition

$136 per credit

Denomination

Seventh-day Adventist

Accreditation

New England Association of Schools and Colleges

Web Address

http://www.atlanticuc.edu/
http://www.atlanticuc.edu/academics/adp/degree.html

Berean University of the Assemblies of God

1475 Campbell
Springfield, MO 65802
800-443-1083
berean@ag.org

Bachelor of Arts

Bible/Christian Counseling
Bible/Christian Education
Bible/Missions Evangelism

Bible/Pastoral Ministries
Bible/Theology

Program Description

Berean University School of College Studies offers bachelor's and associate's degrees entirely by independent study. The bachelor's degree requires a total of 128 credits. Courses are delivered through a variety of methods including individual correspondence courses, one of Berean's five hundred National Study Centers, or online courses via Berean's Virtual Study Center.

Institutional Description

Berean University of the Assemblies of God has one purpose: to fulfill the mandate of our Master, Jesus Christ, to make disciples. The college, as an integral part of the Assemblies of God, embraces Bible-based objectives that include ministry to the Lord, ministry to his saints, and ministry to those who do not as yet know him as Lord. Students with the discipline for distance learning will find the programs they need to prepare for God's calling on their life.

Berean University and ICI University are combining efforts to form one entity known as Global University of the Assemblies of God. Global University will offer a variety of programs from evangelism courses to graduate-level degrees. Delivery systems will primarily be print but will also include the Internet, CD-ROM, and video-conferencing.

Tuition

$69 per credit

Denomination

Assemblies of God

Accreditation

Distance Education and Training Council

Web Address

http://www.berean.edu
http://www.berean.edu/catalog/collegedegree/html/b.a._degree.htm

Bethany College

800 Bethany Dr.
Scotts Valley, CA 95066
800-843-9410
edp@bethany.edu

Bachelor of Arts

Addiction Studies
Applied Professional Studies
Biblical and Theological Studies
Business
Church Leadership

Early Child Development
General Ministries
Liberal Studies
Psychology
Social Science

Program Description

All students in Bethany's external degree program first attend a four-day orientation workshop. Students then return to their homes and complete all assignments according to their personal schedules. Course syllabi received from instructors provide step-by-step assistance through assignments. Exams are administered by approved proctors. By calling the toll-free number during office hours or by using e-mail, students may contact professors for answers to questions. Weekly contact with professors via phone or e-mail is required. Each subsequent semester, students return to Bethany's campus for a two-day progress review. Experiential learning credit is also available.

Institutional Description

Bethany is a comprehensive Christian college affiliated with the Assemblies of God churches of Northern California and Nevada. While a majority of our students are from Assemblies of God churches, more than 40 percent are from other evangelical, charismatic, and pentecostal churches and denominations. Bethany's pentecostal heritage is evident in our doctrinal statement, our chapels and classes, and in our faculty and staff. The character of Bethany College is distinctly Christian, and the school seeks to teach students practical ways to live our lives in a manner that follows biblical principles. Daily required chapel services, residence hall devotions, spiritual emphasis weeks, missions emphasis weeks, and required student involvement in Christian service are all demonstrations of Bethany's commitment to biblical Christianity.

Tuition

Varies by course

Denomination

Assemblies of God

Accreditation

Western Association of Colleges and Schools
Accrediting Association of Bible Colleges

Web Address

http://www.bethany.edu
http://www.bethany.edu/edp/

Briercrest Bible College
510 College Dr.
Carenport, SK S0H 0S0, CANADA
800-667-5199
distance.learning@briercrest.ca

Bachelor of Arts in Christian Studies

Program Description

The B.A. in Christian Studies is a one-hundred-credit-hour degree program that consists of courses in Bible/theology, ministry preparation, general education, and field education. Briercrest Distance Learning provides a unique opportunity to complete a degree program in your own environment with church involvement and support as an integral part of the program. In addition to print correspondence courses, modes of delivery include extension classes, CD-ROM, and the Internet.

Institutional Description

The Bible College is operated on a postsecondary level to prepare men and women for the service of Christ through his church. The college offers one-year certificates, two-year A.A. degrees, a three-year general B.A. degree, and four-year professional B.A. degrees. Professional B.A. degrees include Bible teaching, business administration, theology, counseling, intercultural studies, leadership, pastoral leadership, and ministry degrees with specializations in children, sports, women, worship, and youth. The emphasis of all programs is on Bible and theology; over one-third of the credits in all B.A. programs are in these areas.

Tuition

$295 (USD) for a 3-credit-hour course
$390 (CAD) for a 3-credit-hour course

Denomination

None

Accreditation

Accrediting Association of Bible Colleges

Web Address

http://www.briercrest.ca/bbc/
http://www.briercrest.ca/bdl/programs/college.shtml

Concordia University
275 Syndicate St. N.
St. Paul, MN 55104
651-641-8897 or 800-211-3370
gradstudies@luther.csp.edu

Bachelor of Arts in Child Development

Program Description

The Bachelor of Arts in Child Development for early childhood educators is a B.A. degree completion program that requires students to have about two years of previous college coursework. The child development major is designed to educate learners to work with young children and families in early childhood settings. Students will understand the major developmental theories, as well as define the best characteristics and processes of developmentally appropriate practice. The distance education program requires a five-day residency at the Concordia University campus. Following the residency, coursework is completed by using media such as Internet chat rooms, bulletin boards, and e-mail.

Institutional Description

Concordia University is a four-year, liberal arts university owned and operated by the Lutheran Church—Missouri Synod. Concordia University offers a variety of traditional undergraduate programs on campus, as well as degree completion programs and graduate programs for adult learners. Several degree completion programs and graduate programs are offered through Web-based distance education, where learners may earn their degree without taking traditional classes on Concordia's campus. Concordia University was established in 1893 and admits students of any race, color, gender, national and ethnic origin to all rights, privileges, programs, and activities generally accorded or made available to students at the university.

Tuition

$11,550 for 22-month program

Denomination

Lutheran Church—Missouri Synod

Accreditation

North Central Association of Colleges and Schools

Web Address

http://www.csp.edu/
http://www.csp.edu/hspd

Concordia University

275 Syndicate St. N.
St. Paul, MN 55104
651-641-8897 or 800-211-3370
gradstudies@luther.csp.edu

Bachelor of Arts in School-Age Care

Program Description

The Bachelor of Arts in School-Age Care is a B.A. degree completion program that requires students to have about two years of previous college coursework. The school-age care major is designed for those people who are working with children in before- and after-school programs. This program emphasizes the development of social skills for children ages five to twelve, and the coursework allows students to immediately apply what they learn to their work. The distance education program requires a five-day residency at the Concordia University campus. Following the residency, coursework is completed by using media such as Internet chat rooms, bulletin boards, and e-mail.

Institutional Description

Concordia University is a four-year, liberal arts university owned and operated by the Lutheran Church—Missouri Synod. Concordia University offers a variety of traditional undergraduate programs on campus, as well as degree completion programs and graduate programs for adult learners. Several degree completion programs and graduate programs are offered through Web-based distance education, where learners may earn their degree without taking traditional classes on Concordia's campus. Concordia University was established in 1893 and admits students of any race, color, gender, national and ethnic origin to all rights, privileges, programs, and activities generally accorded or made available to students at the university.

Tuition

$11,550 for 22-month program

Denomination

Lutheran Church—Missouri Synod

Accreditation

North Central Association of Colleges and Schools

Web Address

http://www.csp.edu/
http://www.csp.edu/hspd

Concordia University
275 Syndicate St. N.
St. Paul, MN 55104
651-641-8897 or 800-211-3370
gradstudies@luther.csp.edu

Bachelor of Arts in Youth Development

Program Description

The Bachelor of Arts in Youth Development is a B.A. degree completion program that requires students to have about two years of previous college coursework. The focus of the youth development major is to facilitate positive development in youth. Students learn how to build needed life skills in youth by developing meaningful activities for them. The distance education program requires a five-day residency at the Concordia University campus. Following the residency, coursework is completed by using media such as Internet chat rooms, bulletin boards, and e-mail.

Institutional Description

Concordia University is a four-year, liberal arts university owned and operated by the Lutheran Church—Missouri Synod. Concordia University offers a variety of traditional undergraduate programs on campus, as well as degree completion programs and graduate programs for adult learners. Several degree completion programs and graduate programs are offered through Web-based distance education, where learners may earn their degree without taking traditional classes on Concordia's campus. Concordia University was established in 1893 and admits students of any race, color, gender, national and ethnic origin to all rights, privileges, programs, and activities generally accorded or made available to students at the university.

Tuition

$11,550 for 22-month program

Denomination

Lutheran Church—Missouri Synod

Accreditation

North Central Association of Colleges and Schools

Web Address

http://www.csp.edu/
http://www.csp.edu/hspd

Concordia University

275 Syndicate St. N.
St. Paul, MN 55104
651-641-8897 or 800-211-3370
gradstudies@luther.csp.edu

Bachelor of Arts in Criminal Justice

Program Description

The Bachelor of Arts in Criminal Justice is a B.A. degree completion program that requires students to have about two years of previous college coursework. The criminal justice major focuses on fostering ethical standards by increasing sensitivity and consideration of moral issues among those who enforce our system. Our programs encourage students to develop a continuing relationship with learning and service. The distance education program requires a five-day residency at the Concordia University campus. Following the residency, coursework is completed by using media such as Internet chat rooms, bulletin boards, and e-mail.

Institutional Description

Concordia University is a four-year, liberal arts university owned and operated by the Lutheran Church—Missouri Synod. Concordia University offers a variety of traditional undergraduate programs on campus, as well as degree completion programs and graduate programs for adult learners. Several degree completion programs and graduate programs are offered through Web-based distance education, where learners may earn their degree without taking traditional classes on Concordia's campus. Concordia University was established in 1893 and admits students of any race, color, gender, national and ethnic origin to all rights, privileges, programs, and activities generally accorded or made available to students at the university.

Tuition

$11,550 for 22-month program

Denomination

Lutheran Church—Missouri Synod

Accreditation

North Central Association of Colleges and Schools

Web Address

http://www.csp.edu/
http://www.csp.edu/hspd

Concordia University

275 Syndicate St. N.
St. Paul, MN 55104
651-641-8897 or 800-211-3370
gradstudies@luther.csp.edu

Bachelor of Arts in Management of Human Service Organizations

Program Description

The Bachelor of Arts in Management of Human Service Organizations is a B.A. degree completion program that requires students to have about two years of previous college coursework. The management of human service organizations major teaches skills for preventative and developmental care for people of all ages. Students will learn to solve problems with a community-based method and become agents of change in their organization. The distance education program requires a five-day residency at the Concordia University campus. Following the residency, coursework is completed by using media such as Internet chat rooms, bulletin boards, and e-mail.

Institutional Description

Concordia University is a four-year, liberal arts university owned and operated by the Lutheran Church—Missouri Synod. Concordia University offers a variety of traditional undergraduate programs on campus, as well as degree completion programs and graduate programs for adult learners. Several degree completion programs and graduate programs are offered through Web-based distance education, where learners may earn their degree without taking traditional classes on Concordia's campus. Concordia University was established in 1893 and admits students of any race, color, gender, national and ethnic origin to all rights, privileges, programs, and activities generally accorded or made available to students at the university.

Tuition

$11,550 for 22-month program

Denomination

Lutheran Church—Missouri Synod

Accreditation

North Central Association of Colleges and Schools

Web Address

http://www.csp.edu/
http://www.csp.edu/hspd

Dallas Baptist University

3000 Mountain Creek Pkwy.
Dallas, TX 75211-9299
214-333-6893
online@dbuonline.org

Bachelor of Arts and Sciences in Business Administration

Program Description

A student who graduates with a Bachelor of Arts and Sciences in Business Administration will have demonstrated competence in the foundational areas of business, as well as the technical skills and knowledge in a chosen major area. This level of competence in the business disciplines will enable the student to assume entry-level roles and assignments in his or her chosen career. Students may earn up to thirty hours of undergraduate credit for knowledge gained through life and work experience. The integration of faith and learning provides both knowledge and wisdom for successful living. Courses are delivered online.

Institutional Description

The purpose of Dallas Baptist University is to provide Christ-centered quality higher education in the arts, sciences, and professional studies at both the undergraduate and graduate levels to traditional age and adult students in order to produce servant leaders who have the ability to integrate faith and learning through their respective callings.

Tuition

$990 per undergraduate course

Denomination

Southern Baptist

Accreditation

Southern Association of Colleges and Schools

Web Address

http://www.dbu.edu
http://www.dbuonline.org

Eastern Pentecostal Bible College
780 Argyle St.
Peterborough, ON K9H 5T2, CANADA
800-295-6368
ici@epbc.edu

Bachelor of Theology (Pastoral Ministry Major)

Program Description

This 129-credit degree provides five years of coursework on a variety of topics including biblical theology, New Testament, church leadership, Pentecostal history and distinctives, teaching, preaching, Greek or Hebrew, pastoral counseling, and personal ministry development. Courses are offered in print correspondence or online formats.

Institutional Description

Eastern Pentecostal Bible College is Canada's largest denominational undergraduate theological institution. Founded in 1939, Eastern has a long history of excellence in education and innovation in the accomplishment of its mission. Courses and programs are available at our campus in Peterborough, Ontario, Canada, or through a variety of distance education options.

Tuition

Varies by course

Denomination

The Pentecostal Assemblies of Canada

Accreditation

Accrediting Association of Bible Colleges

Web Address

http://www.epbc.edu/disted/
http://www.epbc.edu/disted/programs3.html

Eastern Pentecostal Bible College

780 Argyle St.
Peterborough, ON K9H 5T2, CANADA
800-295-6368
ici@epbc.edu

Bachelor of Religious Education (Pastoral Ministry Major)

Program Description

This seventy-eight-credit program is a shortened degree for university and community college graduates. (University graduates can upgrade this degree to a Bachelor of Theology with the completion of either Greek I and II or Hebrew I and II.) Five years of coursework on a variety of topics includes biblical theology, Old Testament, church leadership, preaching, Greek or Hebrew, and personal ministry development. Courses are offered in print correspondence or online formats.

Institutional Description

Eastern Pentecostal Bible College is Canada's largest denominational undergraduate theological institution. Founded in 1939, Eastern has a long history of excellence in education and innovation in the accomplishment of its mission. Courses and programs are available at our campus in Peterborough, Ontario, Canada, or through a variety of distance education options.

Tuition

Varies by course

Denomination

The Pentecostal Assemblies of Canada

Accreditation

Accrediting Association of Bible Colleges

Web Address

http://www.epbc.edu/disted/
http://www.epbc.edu/disted/programs3.html

Florida Baptist Theological College

5400 College Dr.
Graceville, FL 32440
800-328-2660
mail@fbtc.edu

Bachelor of Science in Biblical Studies

Program Description

This degree is an external degree program that uses associate's degrees from regionally accredited institutions as a basis for admission. Students who do not have an associate's degree may be given advanced standing in this program through transcript evaluation. It is designed to meet the needs of adult learners who wish to acquire upper-level theological education through various distance learning systems. Sixty credits of this degree can be earned through online courses at FBTC. Coursework is available in the areas of Bible, Christian education, leadership, Christian history, Christian counseling, and evangelism.

Institutional Description

Florida Baptist Theological College is committed to providing preparation for lifetime Christian service. Specifically, the college's purpose is to educate and train God-called men and women. Owned and operated by the Florida Baptist Convention, the college offers four-year and two-year programs in the fields of theology, Christian education, and church music. Instruction centers around the Bible as the infallible Word of God. To fulfill its purpose, the college seeks to develop qualities in students that contribute to effective ministry. In the area of personal growth, we seek to: foster a desire for knowledge; develop cultural awareness by introducing students to a wide range of knowledge; nurture the ability to acquire, evaluate, assimilate, and use information; and promote personal and social maturity. For spiritual growth, we provide resources for gaining biblical and religious data and assist students in learning and living the Christian life. In terms of professional growth, students are enabled to gain the credentials that enhance opportunities for ministry, and they learn to master a specialized body of knowledge. At the same time, we encourage positive attitudes toward ministry and foster both an awareness of and a loyalty to the Southern Baptist heritage.

Tuition

$120 per semester hour

Denomination

Southern Baptist

Accreditation

Southern Association of Colleges and Schools

Web Address

http://www.fbtc.edu
http://www.fbtconline.org

Griggs University
P.O. Box 4437
Silver Spring, MD 20914-4437
301-680-6570

Bachelor of Arts in Religion or Theological Studies

Program Description

Griggs University is the collegiate division of Home Study International, a Christian distance learning provider of K–12 and college programs. Griggs and HSI are part of the Seventh-day Adventist school system. Griggs offers four-year B.A. degrees in religion and theological studies.

Institutional Description

The mission of Griggs University is to provide students with a well-balanced education that will enrich the quality of their lives and their ability to serve others, as well as give them the tools to serve their church as ministers, religious workers, business leaders, religion teachers, and lay church leaders. As a global Seventh-day Adventist educational institution, the mission of GU/HSI is to provide educationally sound, values-based, guided independent study and distance education programs that build a foundation for service to God, church, and society.

Tuition

$170 per semester hour

Denomination

Seventh-day Adventist

Accreditation

Distance Education and Training Council

Web Address

http://www.griggs.edu

Griggs University

P.O. Box 4437
Silver Spring, MD 20914-4437
301-680-6570

Bachelor of Science in Church Business Management or Religious Education

Program Description

Griggs University is the collegiate division of Home Study International, a Christian distance learning provider of K–12 and college programs. Griggs and HSI are part of the Seventh-day Adventist school system. Griggs offers four-year B.S. degrees in church business management and religious education.

Institutional Description

The mission of Griggs University is to provide students with a well-balanced education that will enrich the quality of their lives and their ability to serve others, as well as give them the tools to serve their church as ministers, religious workers, business leaders, religion teachers, and lay church leaders. As a global Seventh-day Adventist educational institution, the mission of GU/HSI is to provide educationally sound, values-based, guided independent study and distance education programs that build a foundation for service to God, church, and society.

Tuition

$170 per semester hour

Denomination

Seventh-day Adventist

Accreditation

Distance Education and Training Council

Web Address

http://www.griggs.edu

Hope International University

2500 E. Nutwood Ave.
Fullerton, CA 92831
714-879-3901 or 800-839-2351
excel.office@hopeonline.edu

Bachelor of Science in Organizational Management

Program Description

The organizational management major in the EXCEL degree completion program is designed for those seeking increased effectiveness in their communication, management, and leadership skills in business settings. Courses include the study of group and organizational communication; human resource management and supervision; business strategy, economics, marketing, and accounting; ethics and strategies for service; and servant leadership based on a Christian biblical foundation.

EXCEL is an accelerated degree completion program designed primarily for working adults who have earned some previous college credit. With the Hope online EXCEL degree completion program, you will be able to finish your bachelor's degree in organizational management in about eighteen months. EXCEL requires that students have the equivalent of two years (forty-five units) of college coursework completed prior to enrolling in the program.

Institutional Description

Hope International University was founded in 1928 and has grown to three schools, all educating students for the purpose of service to society through various careers. Over the years of growth, Hope has expanded its schools and developed new programs, always striving to meet the needs of students in search of a quality education. Hope International University continues the seventy-year tradition of preparing servant leaders throughout its academic programs. Each school adds strength to this tradition as we build leaders who have a foundation of ethics, principles, and outreach. Hope International University is a place that cares about the future and about those who will lead in their professions and their callings. The school wants to be known and recognized as a place where servant leaders prepare for a lifetime of service to the world in Christ's name. It all begins here at Hope . . . where learning leads to serving.

Tuition

$4,500 per semester

Denomination

Christian Church

Accreditation

Western Association of Schools and Colleges

Web Address

http://www.hiu.edu
http://hopeonline.edu

Hope International University

2500 E. Nutwood Ave.
Fullerton, CA 92831
714-879-3901 or 800-839-2351
excel.office@hopeonline.edu

Bachelor of Science in Human Development

Program Description

The human development major in the EXCEL degree completion program is for individuals interested in the social sciences, teaching, counseling, or other helping professions. Courses include the study of individuals and group interaction; developmental, learning, and counseling theories; abnormal psychology; cultural diversity; research methods; ethics and strategies for service; and servant leadership based on a Christian biblical foundation.

EXCEL is an accelerated degree completion program designed primarily for working adults who have earned some previous college credit. With the Hope online EXCEL degree completion program, you will be able to finish your bachelor's degree in human development in about eighteen months (three semesters). EXCEL requires that students have the equivalent of two years (forty-five units) of college coursework completed prior to enrolling in the program.

Institutional Description

Hope International University was founded in 1928 and has grown to three schools. Over the years, Hope has expanded its schools and developed new programs, always striving to meet the needs of students in search of a quality education. Hope International University continues the seventy-year tradition of preparing servant leaders throughout its academic programs. Each school adds strength to this tradition as we build leaders who have a foundation of ethics, principles, and outreach. Hope International University is a place that cares about the future and about those who will lead in their professions and their callings. The school wants to be known and recognized as a place where servant leaders prepare for a lifetime of service to the world in Christ's name. It all begins here at Hope . . . where learning leads to serving.

Tuition

$4,500 per semester plus books

Denomination

Christian Church

Accreditation

Western Association of Schools and Colleges

Web Address

http://www.hiu.edu
http://hopeonline.edu

ICI University
6300 N. Belt Line Rd.
Irving, TX 75063
972-751-1111
info@ici.edu

Bachelor of Arts
Bible and Theology, Religious Education, or Missions

Program Description

The Bachelor of Arts (B.A.) program is a 128-credit-hour program. The B.A. in Bible and Theology is designed to provide the educational background needed by those preparing for a pastoral or preaching ministry. Students can study independently or in groups—using print, audio, video, electronic mail, seminars, teleconferencing, and online—and in classes held in cooperation with resident institutions.

Institutional Description

The global mission of ICI University is fivefold: evangelism, discipleship, training lay workers, ministerial training, and training for other educational vocations. This mission is based on a Christian worldview and is accomplished by providing access to educational and training programs that meet the needs of students, cooperating institutions, churches, and the communities served by the churches. All levels of education and training are included. As this mission is pursued, the body of Christ (the church) is enlarged, edified, and equipped, and society as a whole benefits. Our two mottos succinctly describe the nature of ICI University. "Our Campus Is the World" expresses the global nature of our institution and its distance learning methods. "From All Nations to All Nations" places special emphasis on the fact that we have highly qualified faculty from other nations whose input is shared with the rest of the world.

ICI University and Berean University are combining efforts to form one entity known as Global University of the Assemblies of God. Global University will offer a variety of programs from evangelism courses to graduate-level degrees. Delivery systems will primarily be print, but will also include the Internet, CD-ROM, and videoconferencing.

Tuition

$75 per credit hour

Denomination

Assemblies of God

Accreditation

Distance Education and Training Council

Web Address

http://www.ici.edu
http://www.ici.edu/undergrad/
http://www.globaluniversity.edu

Judson College
302 Bibb St.
Marion, AL 36756
334-683-5100
Mtew@future.judson.edu

Bachelor of Arts

Business	History	Psychology
Criminal Justice	Ministry Studies	Religious Studies
English	Music	

Program Description

This 128-credit bachelor's degree includes basic core requirements in English, speech, history, Bible, social science, physical science, computer science, math, and fine arts. Students also take at least thirty-three hours (for the major) and eighteen hours (for the minor) of specified courses in any of the following disciplines: business, criminal justice, English, history, ministry studies, music (by permission), psychology, and religious studies. In addition to taking courses at Judson, students can earn credit via transfer courses from accredited institutions, seminary extension diploma courses, standardized credit-by-examination options, and credit by assessment of prior learning experiences.

Institutional Description

Since 1838, Judson has been and continues to be a remarkable place for women. While Judson seeks to embrace students from diverse backgrounds and religions, the college is unapologetically Christian in its worldview. This mission has continued unchanged while the college's educational programs have evolved through the years to meet the needs of each new generation. The Adult Studies Program of Judson College offers education opportunities for students who find it impossible to attend traditional classes on campus due to the responsibilities of maintaining a job or caring for a family, or both. Through ASP, women and men can work out flexible plans leading toward a bachelor's degree.

Tuition

$204 per semester hour

Denomination

None

Accreditation

Southern Association of Colleges and Schools

Web Address

http://www.judson.edu
http://www.judson.edu/academic/external/exthow.html

Judson College
302 Bibb St.
Marion, AL 36756
334-683-5100
Mtew@future.judson.edu
Bachelor of Ministry

Program Description

This 128-credit bachelor's degree includes basic core requirements in English, speech, history, Bible, social science, physical science, computer science, math, and fine arts. Students also take major and minor requirements in ministry studies and ministry skills studies. Approved diploma courses offered by seminary extension (a ministry education system of the six theological seminaries of the Southern Baptist Convention) and recommended for credit by the American Council on Education may be accepted in transfer and applied toward the B.A. in Ministry Studies or Bachelor of Ministry degree.

Institutional Description

Since 1838, Judson has been and continues to be a remarkable place for women. While Judson seeks to embrace students from diverse backgrounds and religions, the college is unapolo-getically Christian in its worldview. This mission has continued unchanged while the college's educational programs have evolved through the years to meet the needs of each new generation. The Adult Studies Program of Judson College offers education opportunities for students who find it impossible to attend traditional classes on campus due to the responsibilities of maintaining a job or caring for a family, or both. Through ASP, women and men can work out flexible plans leading toward a bachelor's degree.

Tuition
$204 per semester hour

Denomination
None

Accreditation
Southern Association of Colleges and Schools

Web Address

http://www.judson.edu
http://www.judson.edu/academic/external/exthow.html

Judson College
302 Bibb St.
Marion, AL 36756
334-683-5100
Mtew@future.judson.edu

Bachelor of Science in Business or Psychology

Program Description

This 128-credit bachelor's degree includes basic core requirements in English, speech, history, Bible, social science, physical science, computer science, math, and fine arts. Students also take at least thirty-three hours (for the major) and eighteen hours (for the minor) of specified courses in business or psychology. In addition to taking courses at Judson, students can earn credit via transfer courses from accredited institutions, seminary extension diploma courses, standardized credit-by-examination options, and credit by assessment of prior learning experiences.

Institutional Description

Since 1838, Judson has been and continues to be a remarkable place for women. While Judson seeks to embrace students from diverse backgrounds and religions, the college is unapolo-getically Christian in its worldview. This mission has continued unchanged while the college's educational programs have evolved through the years to meet the needs of each new generation. The Adult Studies Program of Judson College offers education opportunities for students who find it impossible to attend traditional classes on campus due to the responsibilities of maintaining a job or caring for a family, or both. Through ASP, women and men can work out flexible plans leading toward a bachelor's degree.

Tuition

$204 per semester hour

Denomination

None

Accreditation

Southern Association of Colleges and Schools

Web Address

http://www.judson.edu
http://www.judson.edu/academic/external/exthow.html

Lee University
P.O. Box 3450
Cleveland, TN 37320-3450
423-614-8370
inquiry@leeonline.org

Bachelor's Degree in Christian Ministry
(specializations in Bible, Christian Education, Pastoral Ministries, Theology, or Urban Ministries)

Program Description

The Lee University department of external studies offers a baccalaureate-level degree program in the area of Christian ministry. The degree program is a total of 130 credit hours, with specializations in Bible, Christian education, pastoral ministries, theology, and urban ministries. From urban ministry to the classroom, this program will prepare you for Christian ministry to the contemporary world.

The department offers courses in various formats, including independent study, the Ministerial Internship Program College Option, extension classes, LeeOnline, and resident non-traditional campus training.

Institutional Description

Lee University is a Christian institution that offers liberal arts and professional education on both the baccalaureate and master's levels. It seeks to provide education that integrates biblical truth as revealed in the Holy Scriptures with truth discovered through the study of the arts and sciences and in the practice of various professions. A personal commitment to Jesus Christ as Lord and Savior is the controlling perspective from which the educational enterprise is carried out. The foundational purpose of all educational programs is to develop within the students the knowledge, appreciation, understanding, ability, and skills that will prepare them for responsible Christian living in the modern world.

Tuition

$90 per credit

Denomination

Church of God

Accreditation

Southern Association of Colleges and Schools

Web Address

http://www.leeuniversity.edu
http://www.leeonline.org

Liberty University

1971 University Blvd.
Lynchburg, VA 24502
804-582-2000
wcpenn@liberty.edu

Bachelor of Science in Business

(specializations in Accounting, Management,
Finance, and Marketing)

Program Description

A forty-five-credit undergraduate curriculum of required basic general education courses underlies the total program of each student. The curricula offered by the external degree program have been adapted for adult learners from the university's on-campus programs. All courses offered through the external degree program are provided on standard VHS format T–120 videocassettes. The student will purchase a worktext and a textbook to accompany the lectures on videocassettes. Examinations for each course will be mailed to the faculty-approved proctor designated by the student. Each course has a specific examination schedule that is provided with the course materials.

Candidates for the bachelor's degree must complete twelve hours on campus. Students may satisfy this requirement either by attending modular courses or by attending other regularly scheduled classes at Liberty University. Modular courses are one-week intensive sessions scheduled during summer and other selected times during the year. The 120-credit B.S. business major has concentrations in accounting, management, finance, and marketing.

Institutional Description

Liberty University is a Christian academic community in the tradition of evangelical institutions of higher education. Liberty's mission is to produce Christ-centered men and women with the values, knowledge, and skills required to impact tomorrow's world. This mission is carried out for external students in a comparable academic program but without the structure of a resident community.

Tuition

$180 per semester hour

Denomination

None

Accreditation

Southern Association of Colleges and Schools

Web Address

http://www.liberty.edu
http://www.liberty.edu/admissions/

Liberty University

1971 University Blvd.
Lynchburg, VA 24502
804-582-2000
wcpenn@liberty.edu

Bachelor of Science in Multidisciplinary Studies

Program Description

A forty-five-credit undergraduate curriculum of required basic general education courses underlies the total program of each student. The curricula offered by the external degree program have been adapted for adult learners from the university's on-campus programs. All courses offered through the external degree program are provided on standard VHS format T–120 videocassettes. The student will purchase a worktext and a textbook to accompany the lectures on videocassettes. Examinations for each course will be mailed to the faculty-approved proctor designated by the student. Each course has a specific examination schedule that is provided with the course materials.

Candidates for the bachelor's degree must complete twelve hours on campus. Students may satisfy this requirement either by attending modular courses or by attending other regularly scheduled classes at Liberty University. Modular courses are one-week intensive sessions scheduled during summer and other selected times during the year. The 120-credit multidisciplinary studies degree offers concentrations in business, psychology, and religion.

Institutional Description

Liberty University is a Christian academic community in the tradition of evangelical institutions of higher education. Liberty's mission is to produce Christ-centered men and women with the values, knowledge, and skills required to impact tomorrow's world. This mission is carried out for external students in a comparable academic program but without the structure of a resident community.

Tuition

$180 per semester hour

Denomination

None

Accreditation

Southern Association of Colleges and Schools

Web Address

http://www.liberty.edu
http://www.liberty.edu/admissions/

Liberty University
1971 University Blvd.
Lynchburg, VA 24502
804-582-2000
wcpenn@liberty.edu
Bachelor of Science in Religion

Program Description

A forty-five-credit undergraduate curriculum of required basic general education courses underlies the total program of each student. The curricula offered by the external degree program have been adapted for adult learners from the university's on-campus programs. All courses offered through the external degree program are provided on standard VHS format T–120 videocassettes. The student will purchase a worktext and a textbook to accompany the lectures on videocassettes. Examinations for each course will be mailed to the faculty-approved proctor designated by the student. Each course has a specific examination schedule that is provided with the course materials.

Candidates for the bachelor's degree must complete twelve hours on campus. Students may satisfy this requirement either by attending modular courses or by attending other regularly scheduled classes at Liberty University. Modular courses are one-week intensive sessions scheduled during summer and other selected times during the year. The 120-credit B.S. in Religion is designed to provide a thorough, biblically-based, cognitive and spiritual foundation for effective ministry. Specializations are offered in order to prepare students for pastoral, youth, or cross-cultural ministries or for further graduate studies.

Institutional Description

Liberty University is a Christian academic community in the tradition of evangelical institutions of higher education. Liberty's mission is to produce Christ-centered men and women with the values, knowledge, and skills required to impact tomorrow's world. This mission is carried out for external students in a comparable academic program but without the structure of a resident community.

Tuition
$180 per semester hour

Denomination
None

Accreditation
Southern Association of Colleges and Schools

Web Address
http://www.liberty.edu
http://www.liberty.edu/admissions/

Liberty University

1971 University Blvd.
Lynchburg, VA 24502
804-582-2000
wcpenn@liberty.edu

Bachelor of Science in Psychology

Program Description

A forty-five-credit undergraduate curriculum of required basic general education courses underlies the total program of each student. The curricula offered by the external degree program have been adapted for adult learners from the university's on-campus programs. All courses offered through the external degree program are provided on standard VHS format T–120 videocassettes. The student will purchase a worktext and a textbook to accompany the lectures on videocassettes. Examinations for each course will be mailed to the faculty-approved proctor designated by the student. Each course has a specific examination schedule that is provided with the course materials.

Candidates for the bachelor's degree must complete twelve hours on campus. Students may satisfy this requirement either by attending modular courses or by attending other regularly scheduled classes at Liberty University. Modular courses are one-week intensive sessions scheduled during summer and other selected times during the year. The B.S. in Psychology consists of a total of 120 credit hours and is designed to develop a conceptual framework that embraces relevant facts and concepts of human behavior as well as an understanding of the history of the discipline that goes beyond knowledge of major figures and their contributions and includes the sociocultural context in which psychology emerged.

Institutional Description

Liberty University is a Christian academic community in the tradition of evangelical institutions of higher education. Liberty's mission is to produce Christ-centered men and women with the values, knowledge, and skills required to impact tomorrow's world. This mission is carried out for external students in a comparable academic program but without the structure of a resident community.

Tuition

$180 per semester hour

Denomination

None

Accreditation

Southern Association of Colleges and Schools

Web Address

http://www.liberty.edu
http:// www.liberty.edu/admissions/

Moody Bible Institute
820 N. LaSalle Blvd.
Chicago, IL 60610
312-329-4000
xstudies@moody.edu

Bachelor of Science in Biblical Studies

Program Description

The Center for External Studies designed the Bachelor of Science in Biblical Studies degree for the mature individual who desires to obtain a degree in Bible. The program prepares the student in the skillful use of the Bible and the application of its principles to life situations. It is geared toward individuals currently in or anticipating a lay ministry in their church, but also serves to supplement the knowledge of ministry professionals wishing to enhance their effectiveness or any qualified individual desiring a better understanding of the Scriptures.

Individuals pursuing the degree take their courses through MBI's independent studies program. This allows them to study by mail, at their own pace, in the comfort of their own homes, and to do it anywhere in the world. Students in the Chicago area can fulfill the requirements at Moody's main campus extension school.

Institutional Description

Under the authority of God and his Word and in commitment to Christ and his church, the Moody Bible Institute exists to equip and motivate people to advance the cause of Christ through ministries that educate, edify, and evangelize.

Tuition

$100 per semester hour

Denomination

None

Accreditation

North Central Association of Colleges and Schools

Accrediting Association of Bible Colleges

Web Address

http://www.moody.edu
http://www.moody.edu/ed/xs/independent/welcome.htm

Nazarene Bible College
1111 Academy Park Loop
Colorado Springs, CO 80910
800-873-3873
info@nbc.edu

Bachelor of Biblical Studies

Program Description

The Bachelor of Biblical Studies is a program built upon the Associate of Arts in Biblical Studies degree. After completing ninety-six quarter-credits in the A.A. program, students earn an additional ninety-six quarter-credits (for a total of 192 quarter-credits) in the B.B.S. program through online courses. Online computer-mediated education is an outgrowth of the technological transformation and a response to the increasing use of computers and modems for communication. The online campus currently enrolls degree-seeking adult students from all over the United States. It is a group-based learning environment offering the kind of interaction and support that take place in a traditional, face-to-face seminar-style classroom.

Institutional Description

The General Assembly of the Church of the Nazarene mandated the founding of Nazarene Bible College and continues to sponsor it for the specific purpose of providing undergraduate ministerial preparation. The Church of the Nazarene in the United States is the focus of Nazarene Bible College with a primary campus in Colorado Springs. Nazarene Bible College exists to glorify Jesus Christ as Lord by preparing adults to evangelize, disciple, and minister to the world. Nazarene Bible College is an undergraduate, professional school of ministry. As a learning community, it is committed to academic and practical programs designed to prepare the whole person for ministry in contemporary society. The college offers baccalaureate and associate degree programs in biblical studies, Christian education, church music, and lay ministries. Academic preparation is undergirded by a variety of student development strategies and programs.

Tuition

$110 per quarter-credit hour

Denomination

Church of the Nazarene

Accreditation

Accrediting Association of Bible Colleges

Web Address

http://www.nbc.edu
http://www.nbc.edu/online/online_main.htm

Nazarene Bible College
1111 Academy Park Loop
Colorado Springs, CO 80910
800-873-3873
info@nbc.edu

Bachelor of Christian Education

Program Description

The Bachelor of Christian Education is a program built upon the Associate of Arts Degree in Christian Education. After completing ninety-six quarter-credits in the A.A. program, students earn an additional ninety-six quarter-credits (for a total of 192 quarter-credits) in the B.C.E. program through online courses. Online computer-mediated education is an outgrowth of the technological transformation and a response to the increasing use of computers and modems for communication. The online campus currently enrolls degree-seeking adult students from all over the United States. It is a group-based learning environment offering the kind of interaction and support that take place in a traditional, face-to-face seminar-style classroom.

Institutional Description

The General Assembly of the Church of the Nazarene mandated the founding of Nazarene Bible College and continues to sponsor it for the specific purpose of providing undergraduate ministerial preparation. The Church of the Nazarene in the United States is the focus of Nazarene Bible College with a primary campus in Colorado Springs. Nazarene Bible College exists to glorify Jesus Christ as Lord by preparing adults to evangelize, disciple, and minister to the world. Nazarene Bible College is an undergraduate, professional school of ministry. As a learning community, it is committed to academic and practical programs designed to prepare the whole person for ministry in contemporary society. The college offers baccalaureate and associate degree programs in biblical studies, Christian education, church music, and lay ministries. Academic preparation is undergirded by a variety of student development strategies and programs.

Tuition

$110 per quarter-credit hour

Denomination

Church of the Nazarene

Accreditation

Accrediting Association of Bible Colleges

Web Address

http://www.nbc.edu
http://www.nbc.edu/online/online_main.htm

Northwestern College
3003 Snelling Ave. N.
St. Paul, MN 55113-1598
651-631-5100
distance@nwc.edu

Bachelor of Arts in Intercultural Ministries

Program Description

The Intercultural Ministries program is a degree completion program designed specifically for those preparing for or currently involved in serious missionary endeavors. To enroll in the program, prospective students must meet Northwestern College's admissions requirements and must have already accumulated the equivalent of two years of qualifying credits.

Each of the four modules comprising the Intercultural Ministries program is designed to be completed in seventeen weeks, with an investment in study time of approximately twenty-four hours per week. Following this schedule, a student could complete the bachelor's degree in two years or less.

As students complete the four modules of study, they will come to understand God's evangelistic purposes from the beginning of time through the present. It provides a solid foundation in the study of missions, Bible, anthropology, world religions, global history, and even some basics in science and languages.

Institutional Description

Northwestern College exists to provide Christ-centered higher education that equips believers (1) to grow intellectually and spiritually, (2) to serve effectively in their professions, and (3) to give God-honoring leadership in the home, church, community, and world. Northwestern upholds its heritage of biblical distinctives through the vital integration of human knowledge and divine revelation. The goal of the college is to help develop the whole person, characterized by personal development, spiritual maturity, ethical conviction, intellectual curiosity, cultural sensitivity, professional achievement, and faithful service to society and the world.

Tuition

$110 per credit

Denomination

Nondenominational

Accreditation

North Central Association of Colleges and Schools

Web Address

http://www.nwc.edu
http://www.nwc.edu/disted/

Oral Roberts University

7777 S. Lewis Ave.
Tulsa, OK 74171
888-900-4678
slle@oru.edu

Bachelor of Science

Business Administration
Christian Care and Counseling
Church Ministries

Elementary Christian School
Education
Liberal Studies

Program Description

The external degree program offers an accredited 129-credit Bachelor of Science degree. External study is done by correspondence. Students work from a packet that consists of textbooks and a study guide. They mail in completed assignments, which are, in turn, graded and returned to students by the Adult Learning Service Center. This program functions on the basis of a rolling enrollment. Students may enroll at any time. Once enrolled, students have four months to complete a course.

Institutional Description

Oral Roberts University was founded as a result of the evangelist Oral Roberts's obedience to God's mandate to build a university on God's authority and the Holy Spirit. God's commission to Oral Roberts was: "Raise up your students to hear My voice, to go where My light is dim, where My voice is heard small, and My healing power is not known, even to the uttermost bounds of the earth. Their work will exceed yours, and in this I am well pleased."

Oral Roberts University is a charismatic university, founded in the fires of evangelism and upon the unchanging precepts of the Bible. The board of regents and the president and chief executive officer are dedicated to upholding the university's founding purpose.

Tuition

$105 per credit

Denomination

Nondenominational

Accreditation

North Central Association of Colleges and Schools

Web Address

http://www.oru.edu

Prairie Bible College
Box 4000, 330 6th Ave. N.
Three Hills, AB TOM 2N0, CANADA
800-661-2425
distance.ed@pbi.ab.ca
Bachelor of Ministry

Program Description

This program is designed to give you a firsthand Bible knowledge with basic skills for interpreting and understanding the text, along with a comprehension of major Christian doctrines. You will expand your biblical worldview to include a Christian perspective of various humanities, integrate biblical studies with ministry and general studies, and develop a Christian understanding of how modern concepts and issues are rooted in history. You will grow spiritually as well as in personal and ministry skills. Your developing giftedness will enable you to effectively participate in accomplishing your part in the church's global mandate.

The Ministry Internship offers you eighteen credit hours of intensive ministry skills development. You will serve under the direction of a local supervisor and mentor and be evaluated regularly. The program includes a number of requirements relating to church involvement and other activities designed to help you grow. Most courses incorporate tapes, workbooks, textbooks, and other reading materials while online courses are also under development. To ensure maximum benefits, you are encouraged to be connected to the Internet. An increasing number of courses will be available online and you will be encouraged and motivated by dialoguing with other B.Min. students as well as your course instructors.

Institutional Description

Prairie Bible Institute is an interdenominational, biblically based Christian educational institution offering K–12 through college instruction in Three Hills, Alberta, Canada, and a graduate school in Calgary, Alberta, as well as distance education courses and degrees worldwide.

Tuition

$99 per undergraduate credit

Denomination

None

Accreditation

Accrediting Association of Bible Colleges

Web Address

http://www.pbi.ab.ca
http://www.pbi.ab.ca/distanceed/

Southern Christian University

P.O. Box 240240
Montgomery, AL 36124-0240
800-351-4040
onlinecourses@southernchristian.edu

Bachelor of Arts or Bachelor of Science in Biblical Studies

Program Description

A ninety-six-quarter-hour program designed for people with an A.A. or equivalent. Most on-campus courses on the bachelor's and master's levels, including all required courses, are offered through the videotape-based extended learning program. Campus classes are recorded on videotape and mailed to the students. In effect, distance learning students are in the same class and receive the same quality of instruction as on-campus students. They must complete the same assignments, meet the same deadlines, and take the same tests. They are graded on the same basis.

Faculty members establish telephone hours for off-campus students to call with any questions or problems. Students may also submit questions or comments by mail or e-mail when they return the tapes. Professors typically start each lecture by restating and answering questions received since the last class. Class content may be adjusted to meet the needs and interests of extended learning students, just as for on-campus students.

Institutional Description

Southern Christian University offers upper-level undergraduate programs, master's programs, and a doctoral program that are designed to train Christian ministers, missionaries, counselors, and other church workers. Admission is open to all persons of good character and good reputation whose backgrounds and abilities qualify them for undergraduate or graduate education. Southern Christian University does not discriminate on the basis of race, color, national or ethnic origin, religion, sex, or handicap in the administration of its educational policies, programs, and activities except where necessitated by the specific religious tenets held by the institution. Southern Christian University is a private religious school affiliated by common purpose and cooperative effort with the Churches of Christ, an undenominational fellowship of independent congregations that strive to reproduce New Testament Christianity today.

Tuition

$230 per semester hour

Denomination

Churches of Christ

Accreditation

Southern Association of Colleges and Schools

Web Address

http://www.southernchristian.edu
http://www.southernchristian.edu/extended.html

Southwestern Adventist University

100 Hillcrest Dr.
Keene, TX 76059
800-433-2240
webmaster@swau.edu

Bachelor of Arts

Program Description

Southwestern Adventist University's Adult Degree Program enables you to complete a degree wherever you are with only an initial six-day seminar on our campus to get started. Attendance at the seminar, combined with a post-seminar portfolio, carries three hours of college credit that is included in your first twelve-hour package. In the seminar, you'll cover things such as building your own portfolio to prove the skills and knowledge you've acquired outside the formal classroom, how to write a college research paper and how to best use the library, how to study for tests, financial aid for ADP students, setting up your degree plan, and choosing your major and minor. The rest of the program is offered at-a-distance. Some of the majors offered in the Adult Degree Program are broadcasting, business administration, computer information systems, English, history, international affairs, journalism, mathematics, religion, and theology.

Institutional Description

SWAU offers a master's degree in elementary education, bachelor's degrees in twenty-eight fields, preprofessional preparation, and associate degrees in five major fields. SWAU is part of the international Seventh-day Adventist educational system, the second largest denominational system in the world. A majority of students are Seventh-day Adventist Christians, but students from many other denominations choose SWAU because of its comfortable Christian atmosphere. Since 1990, the university has seen a consistent increase in enrollment. With innovative off-campus programs for adult education and a continued emphasis on small classes and work opportunities, projections show enrollment will continue to increase steadily. SWAU now serves students from across the United States and thirty-one countries.

Tuition

$299 per credit hour

Denomination

Seventh-day Adventist

Accreditation

Southern Association of Colleges and Schools

Web Address

http://www.swau.edu
http://www.swau.edu/adp/

Southwestern Assemblies of God University
1200 Sycamore
Waxahachie, TX 75165
888-937-7248
info@sagu.edu

Bachelor of Arts of Bachelor of Science

Program Description

During the initial semester of enrollment, students attend a two-day orientation course at the campus which is located in the Greater Dallas/Fort Worth Metroplex. Three hours of credit are earned upon completion. After the two-day orientation, students register for the courses they will be taking that semester. Courses are then opened in fifty-minute segments over the following two days. After the initial semester, students will only need to return to the campus for the registration and course opening seminars.

Students then return home to begin their coursework. Contact with professors and staff is maintained through an electronic mail system and a toll-free telephone line. Study sessions are also enhanced by videotaped lectures of the professor. Courses follow a traditional semester format. Semesters begin in January, May, and August of each year. The completed degree is a Bachelor of Arts or Sciences in the chosen field of study.

Institutional Description

Southwestern Assemblies of God University understands that every person has a divine destiny that can be realized if God-given endowments are trained for optimum performance. This premise is held to be the primary justification for institutional education by the Assemblies of God, the parent body of Southwestern Assemblies of God University.

Southwestern is committed to the task of contributing to the training of Christian individuals to carry the gospel to the ends of the earth while fulfilling their divinely approved place in the kingdom of God.

Tuition
Varies by course

Denomination
Assemblies of God

Accreditation
Southern Association of Colleges and Schools

Web Address
http://www.sagu.edu
http://www.sagu.edu/sde/

Tennessee Temple University

1815 Union Ave.
Chattanooga, TN 37404
800-553-4050
ttuinfo@tntemple.edu

Bachelor of Science in Biblical Studies

Program Description

The Bachelor of Science in Biblical Studies is a four-year, 128-credit, independent study correspondence course program offered through the School of External Studies. The program includes forty-six credits of core courses in Bible and theology, communication, computer skills, history, humanities, mathematics and science, physical education, psychology, social studies, and Christian service. In addition, students select a minor and choose a variety of concentration courses and electives. For any student taking more than 50 percent of coursework through correspondence, the diploma will be tagged from the School of External Studies. The Bachelor of Science in Biblical Studies degree must be completed within twelve years from the time of enrollment.

Institutional Description

Tennessee Temple University is a distinctively Christian institution offering an education that is characterized by its goal of academic excellence in the classroom and its effort to build biblical character and ethical values in its students. Tennessee Temple University is multifaceted, with undergraduate programs at the associate's and bachelor's levels and a graduate master's program in education. The University's purpose is to prepare Christian men and women for life through emphasis on knowledge acquisition, biblical application, skill development, evangelism, and godly living. Tennessee Temple University balances a traditional liberal arts program with a historical Baptist position regarding doctrine and conduct. Its unique characteristic is its emphasis on local church ministries through affiliation with the Highland Park Baptist Church of Chattanooga, Tennessee. Tennessee Temple University is dedicated to providing a Christ-centered education to a diverse population of students from many geographical locations.

Tuition

$250 per 2-credit-hour course
$325 per 3-credit-hour course
$400 per 4-credit-hour course

Denomination

None

Accreditation

Accrediting Association of Bible Colleges

Web Address

http://www.tntemple.edu
http://www.tntemple.edu/external_studies/

Western Baptist College
5000 Deer Park Dr. S.E.
Salem, OR 97301
800-764-1383
asd@wbc.edu

Bachelor of Science in Family Studies or Management and Communication

Program Description

These degree completion programs are offered in a complete distance format. Students participate in a distance cohort and complete a degree in approximately sixteen months. To enter the program students must complete at least sixty semester credit hours of previous college credit. Distinctives of the program include a Christian learning environment; faculty who are Christian social service, education, and ministry professionals; a curriculum that integrates biblical principles; and learning that integrates life experience. Throughout the program, readings will be completed and discussion questions posted through a software program that allows students to make comments on their reading. Students will be able to read comments of fellow students as well as add personal comments and reflections. One of the greatest benefits of this format is the scheduling flexibility for participating in "classroom" discussions.

Institutional Description

Western Baptist College has been in Salem, Oregon, since 1969 as a Christian college offering majors in the areas of ministry, liberal arts, and professional studies. Western's purpose is to educate Christians who will make a difference in the world for Jesus Christ. Western endeavors to equip growing Christians who are competent thinkers, informed citizens, and effective communicators; to provide Bible-centered baccalaureate programs built on the foundations of our Judeo-Christian and Baptist heritage; to provide opportunities for students to apply their academic knowledge and exercise their ministry gifts and abilities; and to develop healthy, balanced lives through a variety of programs and activities designed to meet the needs of a diversified student body.

Tuition
$11,800 for the total program

Denomination
None

Accreditation
Northwest Association of Schools and Colleges

Web Address
http://www.wbc.edu
http://www.wbc.edu/prospect/degree/fso.html
http://www.wbc.edu/prospect/degree/mo.html

11
MASTER'S DEGREE PROGRAMS

Master's degree programs come in a wide variety of styles. Most Master of Arts (M.A.) and Master of Science (M.S.) programs require approximately thirty-six to forty-five credits and involve coursework and thesis, a major project, and/or comprehensive examination. However, there are also master's degrees such as the Master of Education (M.Ed.) and Master of Divinity (M.Div.) that are geared more toward practitioners—the former for teachers and the latter for pastors. Such programs have a more integrated approach that attempts to weave coursework and practice together. The distance programs in this chapter include a variety of subjects, learning approaches, and delivery methods. The growing number of master's degree distance programs (many with little or no on-campus residency requirements) make it more convenient than ever to earn that graduate degree you've always wanted.

Amber University

1700 Eastgate Dr.
Garland, TX 75041
972-279-6511
websysop@ambernet.amberu.edu

Master of Arts in Professional Development

Program Description

The M.A. in Professional Development is a special graduate program designed to allow the college-trained person to expand his or her knowledge beyond the boundaries of traditional education. The program is intended for the student who has earned the bachelor's degree and seeks a terminal graduate degree that offers the broader educational experience not normally available through traditional programs. The degree is designed for individuals who desire a learning experience that can be a helpful resource in decision making, leadership, and personal growth. The curriculum is both broad and diversified, with major emphasis on the study of ideas. Courses include those that focus on the psychological, social, political, and business aspects of contemporary society. Essentially interdisciplinary and nonvocational, the Master of Arts in Professional Development does not emphasize specialization.

Amber University offers conference courses as an alternative learning method designed for the working adult who has responsibilities that prevent predictable scheduling of time. Conference courses are identical to classroom courses in terms of learning outcomes but require that the student exhibit independent organizational skills, self-discipline, and a talent for unsupervised research. The learning competencies for conference courses are the same as those for classroom courses. Conference classes are taught by the same instructors who teach campus-based lecture classes. However, in a conference class setting, there is a one-on-one relationship best described as a tutorial learning process.

Institutional Description

Amber University is a private, non-traditional, specialized upper-division and graduate institution catering exclusively to mature working adults who seek a relevant educational opportunity in a Christian atmosphere.

Tuition

$165 per credit hour

Denomination

None

Accreditation

Southern Association of Colleges and Schools

Web Address

http://www.amberu.edu
http://www.amberu.edu/DL.HTM

Amber University

1700 Eastgate Dr.
Garland, TX 75041
972-279-6511
websysop@ambernet.amberu.edu

Master of Business Administration
(General Business, Management, Stragetic Leadership)

Program Description

The M.B.A in General Business is intended for individuals who desire a broad-based business curriculum. The M.B.A. in Management concentrates on developing graduates capable of pursuing positions of responsibility in organizations faced with the challenges of a rapidly changing environment. The program is intended to meet the present and future educational needs of men and women striving for excellence in the world of business. The M.B.A. in Strategic Leadership is intended to prepare management personnel with the necessary skills to empower organizations to face challenges, create opportunities, and establish themselves as viable centers for productive work. The degree is multidisciplinary and integrates course work that focuses on leadership development rather than the typical broad-based business curricula.

Amber University offers conference courses as an alternative learning method designed for the working adult who has responsibilities that prevent predictable scheduling of time. Conference courses are identical to classroom courses in terms of learning outcomes but require that the student exhibit independent organizational skills, self-discipline, and a talent for unsupervised research. The learning competencies for conference courses are the same as those for classroom courses. Conference classes are taught by the same instructors who teach campus-based lecture classes. However, in a conference class setting, there is a one-on-one relationship best described as a tutorial learning process.

Institutional Description

Amber University is a private, non-traditional, specialized upper-division and graduate institution catering exclusively to mature working adults who seek a relevant educational opportunity in a Christian atmosphere.

Tuition

$165 per credit hour

Denomination

None

Accreditation

Southern Association of Colleges and Schools

Web Address

http://www.amberu.edu
http://www.amberu.edu/DL.HTM

Amber University
1700 Eastgate Dr.
Garland, TX 75041
972-279-6511
websysop@ambernet.amberu.edu

Master of Science in Human Relations and Business

Program Description

The M.S. degree in Human Relations and Business is a multidisciplinary program designed to meet the needs of administrators, managers, and leaders. The program recognizes the interrelationships between people, communications, and organizational goals. Specifically, the program is designed for individuals who, because of their technical success, have been promoted or seek to be promoted to managerial and leadership positions.

Amber University offers conference courses as an alternative learning method designed for the working adult who has responsibilities that prevent predictable scheduling of time. Conference courses are identical to classroom courses in terms of learning outcomes but require that the student exhibit independent organizational skills, self-discipline, and a talent for unsupervised research. The learning competencies for conference courses are the same as those for classroom courses. Conference classes are taught by the same instructors who teach campus-based lecture classes. However, in a conference class setting, there is a one-on-one relationship best described as a tutorial learning process.

Institutional Description

Amber University is a private, non-traditional, specialized upper-division and graduate institution catering exclusively to mature working adults who seek a relevant educational opportunity in a Christian atmosphere.

Tuition

$165 per credit hour

Denomination

None

Accreditation

Southern Association of Colleges and Schools

Web Address

http://www.amberu.edu
http://www.amberu.edu/DL.HTM

Berean University of the Assemblies of God

1475 Campbell
Springfield, MO 65802
800-443-1083
berean@ag.org

Master of Arts in Biblical Studies

Program Description

The M.A. in Biblical Studies degree is a thirty-six-credit program designed for mature adults who desire to improve their knowledge and ministry skills. The degree includes twelve credits of core courses, eighteen credits of New Testament concentration courses, and six credits of thesis work. At least twenty-four semester hours of undergraduate coursework in Bible and theology must have been completed prior to enrollment in the M.A. program, and a student should also have a background of Greek or Hebrew language studies. As part of nontraditional programs, individual courses may include audio- and video-tapes, lecture outlines, reading and study guides, online interaction, and suggestions for independent learning. A close relationship between a mentor/instructor and the student is a key component of this program.

Institutional Description

Berean University of the Assemblies of God has one purpose: to fulfill the mandate of our Master, Jesus Christ, to make disciples. The college, as an integral part of the Assemblies of God, embraces Bible-based objectives, which include ministry to the Lord, ministry to his saints, and ministry to those who do not as yet know him as Lord. Students with the discipline for distance learning will find the programs they need to prepare for God's calling on their life.

ICI University and Berean University are combining efforts to form one entity known as Global University of the Assemblies of God. Global University will offer a variety of programs from evangelism courses to graduate-level degrees. Delivery systems will primarily be print, but will also include the Internet, CD-ROM, and videoconferencing.

Tuition

$129 per credit

Denomination

Assemblies of God

Accreditation

Distance Education and Training Council

Web Address

http://www.berean.edu
http://www.berean.edu/catalog/graduatestudies/
http://www.globaluniversity.edu

Berean University of the Assemblies of God
1475 Campbell
Springfield, MO 65802
800-443-1083
berean@ag.org

Master of Arts in Christian Counseling

Program Description

The M.A. in Christian Counseling degree is designed for those who want to serve in pastoral counseling and for those who seek ministry opportunities in counseling. Since licensure laws for counseling vary from state to state, individuals interested in becoming a Licensed Professional Counselor (LPC) are encouraged to contact their state governmental agency regarding licensure requirements.

Students participate in programs that combine academic and clinical studies. The clinical component takes place under the direction of qualified supervisors at EMERGE Ministries, Inc. and approved agencies in the student's locality. Three (separate) one-week intensive sessions scheduled at EMERGE in Akron, Ohio, are needed for the practicum requirement. All three practicum experiences are usually available within any fifteen-month period. These sessions will include both pre- and post-session assignments.

Institutional Description

Berean University of the Assemblies of God has one purpose: to fulfill the mandate of our Master, Jesus Christ, to make disciples. The college, as an integral part of the Assemblies of God, embraces Bible-based objectives, which include ministry to the Lord, ministry to his saints, and ministry to those who do not as yet know him as Lord. Students with the discipline for distance learning will find the programs they need to prepare for God's calling on their life.

ICI University and Berean University are combining efforts to form one entity known as Global University of the Assemblies of God. Global University will offer a variety of programs from evangelism courses to graduate-level degrees. Delivery systems will primarily be print but will also include the Internet, CD-ROM, and videoconferencing.

Tuition

$129 per credit

Denomination

Assemblies of God

Accreditation

Distance Education and Training Council

Web Address

http://www.berean.edu
http://www.berean.edu/catalog/graduatestudies/
http://www.globaluniversity.edu

Berean University of the Assemblies of God

1475 Campbell
Springfield, MO 65802
800-443-1083
berean@ag.org

Master of Arts in Ministerial Studies

Program Description

The M.A. in Ministerial Studies degree is a thirty-six-credit program designed for mature adults who desire to improve their knowledge and ministry skills. The degree includes twelve credits of core courses, eighteen credits of concentration courses in leadership, education, or missions, and six credits of thesis work. At least twenty-four semester hours of undergraduate coursework in Bible and theology must have been completed prior to enrollment in the M.A. program. As part of nontraditional programs, individual courses may include audio- and videotapes, lecture outlines, reading and study guides, online interaction, and suggestions for independent learning. A close relationship between a mentor/instructor and the student is a key component of this program.

Institutional Description

Berean University of the Assemblies of God has one purpose: to fulfill the mandate of our Master, Jesus Christ, to make disciples. The college, as an integral part of the Assemblies of God, embraces Bible-based objectives, which include ministry to the Lord, ministry to his saints, and ministry to those who do not as yet know him as Lord. Students with the discipline for distance learning will find the programs they need to prepare for God's calling on their life.

ICI University and Berean University are combining efforts to form one entity known as Global University of the Assemblies of God. Global University will offer a variety of programs from evangelism courses to graduate-level degrees. Delivery systems will primarily be print but will also include the Internet, CD-ROM, and videoconferencing.

Tuition

$129 per credit

Denomination

Assemblies of God

Accreditation

Distance Education and Training Council

Web Address

http://www.berean.edu
http://www.berean.edu/catalog/graduatestudies/
http://www.globaluniversity.edu

Bethel Theological Seminary
3949 Bethel Dr.
St. Paul, MN 55112
800-255-8706
bsem-admit@bethel.edu

Master of Arts in Children's and Family Ministry

Program Description

This degree will prepare you for ministry with children and families in church and parachurch settings. All courses are taught using a combination of on-campus, two-week sessions that meet twice a year and distance education courses facilitated through electronic media. By coming to the campus twice a year for an intensive learning experience and completing additional courses at home, up to seven courses per year can be completed in this program. The entire degree can be accomplished in approximately forty months.

The distance education courses are highly interactive. Significant communication between faculty and students and among students themselves occurs through Internet and e-mail services. In total, twelve courses are offered on campus and twelve courses are conducted through electronically mediated, at-a-distance instruction.

Institutional Description

The passion of Bethel Seminary is to advance the gospel of Jesus Christ among all people in culturally sensitive ways. As a Spirit-empowered, biblically grounded community of learning, Bethel strives to develop and equip whole and holy persons to serve and lead so that churches and ministry agencies can become all they are called to be and do all they are called to do in the world for the glory of God.

Tuition

$177 per credit hour

Denomination

Baptist General Conference

Accreditation

North Central Association of Colleges and Schools

Association of Theological Schools

Web Address

http://www.bethel.edu/seminary/btshome.htm
http://www.bethel.edu/seminary/acad/mastarts/bscfm.htm
http://www.globaluniversity.edu

Bethel Theological Seminary
3949 Bethel Dr.
St. Paul, MN 55112
800-255-8706
bsem-admit@bethel.edu
Master of Divinity

Program Description

The in-ministry Master of Divinity program makes the M.Div. degree available to nonresident students currently serving in ministry positions. The ministry setting provides the laboratory for application of course material as well as the questions posed in the courses.

Students attend courses on campus twice a year, taking two one-week courses during each session. Advance assignments are mailed to students several weeks prior to their arrival on campus. Students have four weeks after the campus experience to complete the in-ministry application assignments. This allows students to complete four on-campus courses a year. Students also take two distance courses a year in their ministry setting. These courses will be mediated through a telephone bridge with the instructor and a variety of other appropriate technologies, such as computer bulletin boards and audio- and videotapes. One ministry practicum is completed each year. The on-campus and distance courses combine to allow students to take seven courses a year and to complete the Master of Divinity in approximately five years.

Institutional Description

The passion of Bethel Seminary is to advance the gospel of Jesus Christ among all people in culturally sensitive ways. As a Spirit-empowered, biblically grounded community of learning, Bethel strives to develop and equip whole and holy persons to serve and lead so that churches and ministry agencies can become all they are called to be and do all they are called to do in the world for the glory of God.

Tuition

$177 per credit hour

Denomination

Baptist General Conference

Accreditation

North Central Association of Colleges and Schools

Association of Theological Schools

Web Address

http://www.bethel.edu/seminary/btshome.htm
http://www.bethel.edu/seminary/catalog/programs/bsinmin.htm

Concordia University

275 Syndicate St. N.
St. Paul, MN 55104
800-211-3370
gradstudies@luther.csp.edu

Master of Arts in Education

(Early Childhood, School-Age Care, Youth Development,
Parish Education and Administration)

Program Description

Concordia offers a thirty-six-credit Master of Arts in Education program with concentrations in Early Childhood, School-Age Care, Youth Development, or Parish Education and Administration. The Early Childhood track focuses on leadership, advocacy, and professionalism in the field of early childhood. It's a broad look at educational issues with a focus on the skills and theories that practitioners need to be more effective in their work. The School-Age Care emphasis is designed to improve the learner's leadership and advocacy skills. The learner will explore the skills needed to be a more effective practitioner and a leader in the field. The Youth Development degree is for those who already are, or would like to be, a leader in the field of youth development. This program surveys both educational issues and the youth development field. The degree emphasis in Parish Education and Administration is designed for those who work in the congregational setting, particu- larly those who are in educational ministries. Learners will explore a variety of educational and theological topics.

Institutional Description

Concordia University is a four-year, liberal arts university owned and operated by the Lutheran Church—Missouri Synod. Concordia University offers a variety of traditional undergraduate programs on campus, as well as degree completion programs and graduate programs for adult learners. Several degree completion programs and graduate programs are offered through Web-based distance education, where learners may earn their degree without taking traditional classes on Concordia's campus.

Tuition

$240 per credit

Denomination

Lutheran Church—Missouri Synod

Accreditation

North Central Association of Colleges and Schools

Web Address

http://www.csp.edu/
http://www.cshs.csp.edu

Concordia University
275 Syndicate St. N.
St. Paul, MN 55104
800-211-3370
gradstudies@luther.csp.edu

Master of Arts in Human Services
(Family Studies, Leadership)

Program Description

Concordia offers a forty-credit Master of Arts in Human Services program with concentrations in Family Studies or Leadership. The Family Studies program will help family life education professionals get a deeper understanding of the family, family diversity and needs, and the family's role in society. The Master of Arts in Human Services with an emphasis in Leadership degree is for those working in a leadership or management capacity in a human service setting. There is a heavy emphasis on organizational diagnosis, problem-solving, and strategy from a systems perspective.

The distance education program begins with a five-day residency at the Concordia University campus in St. Paul, Minnesota. At the residency, students learn the technology they will be using, and begin their first class. They will meet the instructors, and will have a chance to ask questions about specific courses. Students will also meet the department staff and learn the support services that are available. Finally, the residency is a time to meet the other members of the cohort, a group of ten to fifteen people who will travel through the program together. Throughout the program, cohort members will interact with each other and the university in online discussion groups, e-mail, and phone conferences

Institutional Description

Concordia University is a four-year, liberal arts university owned and operated by the Lutheran Church—Missouri Synod. Concordia University offers a variety of traditional undergraduate programs on campus, as well as degree completion programs and graduate programs for adult learners. Several degree completion programs and graduate programs are offered through Web-based distance education, where learners may earn their degree without taking traditional classes on Concordia's campus.

Tuition
$250 per credit

Denomination
Lutheran Church—Missouri Synod

Accreditation
North Central Association of Colleges and Schools

Web Address
http://www.csp.edu/
http://www.cshs.csp.edu

Concordia University Wisconsin
12800 N. Lake Shore Dr.
Mequon, WI 53097
262-243-5700
sarah.weaver@cuw.edu

Master of Business Administration

Program Description

The Master of Business Administration offers eleven concentrations in the following areas: church administration, finance, health-care administration, human resources, global business, management, marketing, management information systems, managerial communication, public administration, and risk management. The program is designed to provide the opportunity of a professional education for the working student. The curriculum provides the broad base of knowledge needed by middle- and upper-level managers. While the M.B.A. program is designed for those in business professions, it is readily adapted to meet the needs of students from engineering, health, nonprofit, religious, and other fields.

Institutional Description

Concordia University Wisconsin is a coeducational, liberal arts school in the Concordia University System that is owned and operated by The Lutheran Church—Missouri Synod. Concordia provides a variety of educational opportunities for students who are preparing for vocations in the ministry of the church and for various professional and business careers in the community. The program of studies emphasizes a liberal arts curriculum and course offerings provide educational experiences that cultivate personal and vocational skills. The total program is centered in the Christian philosophy with a confessional Lutheran emphasis. It is governed by sound educational standards and is focused on the spiritual, academic, social, and physical development of students.

Tuition

$300 per credit

Denomination

Lutheran Church—Missouri Synod

Accreditation

North Central Association of Colleges and Schools

Web Address

http://www.cuw.edu
http://www.cuw.edu/graduate/distance_learning.htm

Concordia University Wisconsin

12800 N. Lake Shore Dr.
Mequon, WI 53097
262-243-5700
sarah.weaver@cuw.edu

Master of Science in Education

Program Description

The graduate program at Concordia University is designed to prepare graduate students for leadership roles in professional education careers. The purpose of the graduate academic program is to provide qualified students with a challenging course of study that will enhance their intellectual development, personal growth, and career satisfaction. The master's degree requires thirty semester hours of credit including a thesis or project. A non-thesis thirty-six-credit-hour master's degree is also available. The program includes a sequence of required courses with electives selected to meet the requirements of a master's degree in school administration, curriculum studies, early childhood, family studies, and student personnel administration. A separate counseling track is also available.

Institutional Description

Concordia University Wisconsin is a coeducational, liberal arts school in the Concordia University System that is owned and operated by The Lutheran Church—Missouri Synod. Concordia provides a variety of educational opportunities for students who are preparing for vocations in the ministry of the church and for various professional and business careers in the community. The program of studies emphasizes a liberal arts curriculum, and course offerings provide educational experiences that cultivate personal and vocational skills. The total program is centered in the Christian philosophy with a confessional Lutheran emphasis. It is governed by sound educational standards and is focused on the spiritual, academic, social, and physical development of students.

Tuition

$300 per credit

Denomination

Lutheran Church—Missouri Synod

Accreditation

North Central Association of Colleges and Schools

Web Address

http://www.cuw.edu
http://www.cuw.edu/graduate/distance_learning.htm

Concordia University Wisconsin

12800 N. Lake Shore Dr.
Mequon, WI 53097
262-243-5700
sarah.weaver@cuw.edu

Master of Science in Nursing

Program Description

The purpose of the Master of Science in Nursing program is to prepare professional nurse leaders competent to fulfill advanced practice nursing roles as family nurse practitioners, geriatric nurse practitioners, and nurse educators. The family nurse practitioners and geriatric nurse practitioners programs consist of forty-three credits while the nurse educator program requires fifty credits. The distance learning model is available to students living fifty or more miles from CUW. Degree requirements are met by completing reading and writing assignments specified for each course. Exams, if a class requirement, are proctored at a testing center near the student. All courses have modules explaining course requirements, and many courses have complementing classroom videotapes. Students are encouraged to interact and correspond with their instructor via e-mail, telephone, fax, or mail. Residency sessions are also expected of all students during their tenure.

Institutional Description

Concordia University Wisconsin is a coeducational, liberal arts school in the Concordia University System that is owned and operated by The Lutheran Church—Missouri Synod. Concordia provides a variety of educational opportunities for students who are preparing for vocations in the ministry of the church and for various professional and business careers in the community. The program of studies emphasizes a liberal arts curriculum, and course offerings provide educational experiences that cultivate personal and vocational skills. The total program is centered in the Christian philosophy with a confessional Lutheran emphasis. It is governed by sound educational standards and is focused on the spiritual, academic, social, and physical development of students.

Tuition

$300 per credit

Denomination

Lutheran Church—Missouri Synod

Accreditation

North Central Association of Colleges and Schools

Web Address

http://www.cuw.edu
http://www.cuw.edu/graduate/distance_learning.htm
http://www.cuw.edu/graduate_nursing/

Dallas Baptist University

3000 Mountain Creek Pkwy.
Dallas, TX 75211-9299
214-333-6893
online@dbuonline.org

Master of Business Administration

Program Description

The Master of Business Administration (M.B.A.) program exists to serve the educational needs of professionals who desire to enhance their management skills and acquire new ones for more effective service in their organizations. DBU's management concentration covers concepts and theories for understanding and resolving human problems in organizational settings. Courses are delivered online.

Institutional Description

The purpose of Dallas Baptist University is to provide Christ-centered, quality higher education in the arts, sciences, and professional studies at both the undergraduate and graduate levels to traditional age and adult students in order to produce servant leaders who have the ability to integrate faith and learning through their respective callings.

Tuition

$1,014 per graduate course

Denomination

Southern Baptist

Accreditation

Southern Association of Colleges and Schools

Web Address

http://www.dbu.edu
http://www.dbuonline.org

George Fox University
414 N. Meridian St.
Newberg, OR 97132-2697
503-538-8383
sheadly@georgefox.edu

Master of Education

Program Description

The Master of Education program allows you flexibility in designing and developing your own M.Ed. degree plan. You will work with a faculty advisor to evaluate your options, incorporate possible transfer credits, and achieve your personal and career goals. The M.Ed. program offers online as well as on-site courses, evening courses during the school year, a flexible summer schedule, and up to ten hours that may be accepted in transfer. The program incorporates innovative classroom techniques, computer technologies, and a broad spectrum of educational, psychological, and sociological issues.

Upon completing the M.Ed. degree, you will be eligible for the Oregon Continuing License. (In some cases, additional professional tests may be required.) The flexibility of the program often allows students to meet the licensure or recertification requirements of other states as well. If you're not an Oregon resident, you'll need to check your own state's licensing criteria before designing your M.Ed. program.

Institutional Description

George Fox University is Christ-centered. Our heritage as a Quaker-founded institution gives us distinctives common to the Friends Church, such as a concern for social justice, a commitment to peace and nonviolence, and a belief in the equality of all people. While approximately 9 percent of our undergraduate students are Friends, more than fifty denominations are represented on campus, the largest being Baptist. Students of all faiths are welcome. While we don't require a signed statement of faith, we are a Christian community, and as such, ask and expect our students and employees to abide by the university's community responsibilities and expectations. In keeping with our mission of Christian higher education, all employees—faculty, administration, and staff—are committed evangelical Christians.

Tuition

$355 per credit hour

Denomination

Evangelical Friends

Accreditation

Northwest Association of Schools and Colleges

Web Address

http://www.georgefox.edu
http://voyager.georgefox.edu/med/

Golden Gate Baptist Theological Seminary

201 Seminary Dr.
Mill Valley, CA 94941
888-442-8701
admissions@ggbts.edu

Master of Theology

Program Description

This online Th.M. degree is essentially a distance equivalent of GGBTS's on-campus Th.M. program. Like the campus program, the online Th.M. requires incoming students to hold an M.Div. degree and then take twenty-eight credits of coursework including a research methods seminar (two credits), six seminars related to the primary area of study (eighteen credits), and an eight-credit-hour thesis.

The on-line intensive Th.M. program requires the formation of a learning community (referred to as a "cohort") with a minimum of eight and a maximum of fifteen participants who covenant to move through a predetermined sequence of intensive and online seminars together on the following schedule. The program begins with an intensive two-week on-campus summer seminar during which participants are introduced to each another, to GGBTS, and to the Th.M. faculty. They select their faculty advisors, complete the research methods seminar, and receive an introduction to the three online seminars scheduled during the following academic year (September–May). Subsequent years will follow a similar pattern of on-campus seminars and online courses.

Institutional Description

Under the lordship of Christ, Golden Gate Baptist Theological Seminary provides educational and ministry experiences to shape Christian leaders through programs that emphasize spiritual growth, biblically based scholarship, and ministry skills development—all within a multicultural setting.

Within this strategic setting, the seminary equips men and women to walk more closely with God, understand more clearly the heart of the Christian faith, develop a passion for fulfilling Christ's Great Commission, strengthen God-given gifts to serve and equip others, and minister effectively to people of all cultures.

Tuition

$1,500 per year for Southern Baptist students

$3,000 per year for non–Southern Baptist students

Denomination

Southern Baptist Convention

Accreditation

Western Association of Schools and Colleges

Association of Theological Schools

Web Address

http://www.ggbts.edu
http://www.ggbts.edu/courses/onlinethm.html

Grand Rapids Baptist Seminary

1001 East Beltline N.E.
Grand Rapids, MI 49525
800-697-1133
grbs@cornerstone.edu

Master of Religious Education

Program Description

The in-ministry Master of Religious Education degree program is a professional continuing education degree program. This thirty-two-semester-hour degree program is designed for persons who have had a minimum of three years of full-time ministry experience. The in-ministry M.R.E. consists of a twelve-hour core in Bible and theology and a twenty-hour ministry concentration. Students choose one of the four ministry concentrations: pastoral studies, Christian education, missions, or Christian school administration. This particular degree program is achieved through a combination of extension study and summer in-residence study.

Institutional Description

Grand Rapids Baptist Seminary is in the business of educating and mentoring men and women for service to Christ through ministry leadership. We firmly believe that the continued global advancement of the church of Jesus Christ in the world requires the continued development of leaders who engage in authentic Christian ministry. The mission statement of Grand Rapids Baptist Seminary declares that the seminary is primarily engaged in "preparing leaders who are authentically Christian and culturally sensitive."

Tuition

$257 per credit

Denomination

General Association of Regular Baptist Churches

Accreditation

North Central Association of Colleges and Schools

Web Address

http://www.cornerstone.edu/grbs.nsf
http://www.cornerstone.edu/grbs.nsf/degree+programs?openpage

Hope International University

2500 E. Nutwood Ave.
Fullerton, CA 92831
714-879-3901
palexander@hiu.edu

Master of Arts in Ministry: Intercultural Studies

Program Description

This Internet-based program is designed to meet the needs of those who wish to enhance their skills in crossing boundaries for witness and ministry while using a combination of distance learning and a qualified mentor. In this program course readings are both introduced and reviewed by audio-taped mini-lectures and/or videotapes by highly qualified professors. To provide the crucial student-teacher interaction, we provide a carefully designed study guide that requires thinking and writing, together with weekly meetings and a face-to-face mentor approved by Hope International University.

Mentors are similar to field supervisors of student interns, or, in some cases, like teaching assistants. In weekly discussions, mentors may help these less-experienced students apply their studies to the real world of ministry wherever they are.

Institutional Description

Hope International University was founded in 1928 and has grown to three schools, all educating students for the purpose of service to society through various careers. Over the years of growth, Hope has expanded its schools and developed new programs, always striving to meet the needs of students in search of a quality education. Hope International University continues the seventy-year tradition of preparing servant leaders throughout its academic programs. Each school adds strength to this tradition as we build leaders who have a foundation of ethics, principles, and outreach. Hope International University is a place that cares about the future and about those who will lead in their professions and their callings. The school wants to be known and recognized as a place where servant leaders prepare for a lifetime of service to the world in Christ's name. It all begins here at Hope . . . where learning leads to serving.

Tuition

Varies by course

Denomination

Christian Church

Accreditation

Western Association of Schools and Colleges

Web Address

http://www.hiu.edu
http://www.hiu.edu/grad/mam.html

Hope International University
2500 E. Nutwood Ave.
Fullerton, CA 92831
714-879-3901
palexander@hiu.edu

Master of Business Administration in International Development

Program Description

The forty-eight-credit M.B.A. in International Development emphasizes strong management skills along with sound technical and cross-cultural competence. You are prepared to serve in international, national, or local community development agencies where management skills and application are featured. The program emphasizes enterprise development and income generation, particularly microenterprise in international urban and rural settings. Community-based business, cooperatives, and grassroots economic development organizations are studied in parallel with the more conventional or traditional business environments in the student's setting.

The M.B.A. is delivered via distance learning, including e-mail, and made possible through collaboration with international agencies that have an existing, extensive international network of field offices and projects.

Institutional Description

Hope International University was founded in 1928 and has grown to three schools, all educating students for the purpose of service to society through various careers. Over the years of growth, Hope has expanded its schools and developed new programs, always striving to meet the needs of students in search of a quality education. Hope International University continues the seventy-year tradition of preparing servant leaders throughout its academic programs. Each school adds strength to this tradition as we build leaders who have a foundation of ethics, principles, and outreach. Hope International University is a place that cares about the future and about those who will lead in their professions and their callings. The school wants to be known and recognized as a place where servant leaders prepare for a lifetime of service to the world in Christ's name. It all begins here at Hope . . . where learning leads to serving.

Tuition

Varies by course

Denomination

Christian Church

Accreditation

Western Association of Schools and Colleges

Web Address

http://www.hiu.edu
http://www.hiu.edu/grad/mid.html

Hope International University
2500 E. Nutwood Ave.
Fullerton, CA 92831
714-879-3901

Master of Science in International Development and Crisis Management

Program Description

The thirty-six-credit M.S. in International Development emphasizes skills in developing partnerships with communities and local resources while responding to community needs and empowering community members to meet those needs. You are prepared to serve in international, national, or local agencies where relief or community development is the major emphasis.

The program is delivered via distance learning, including e-mail, and made possible through collaboration with international agencies that have an existing, extensive international network of field offices and projects.

Institutional Description

Hope International University was founded in 1928 and has grown to three schools, all educating students for the purpose of service to society through various careers. Over the years of growth, Hope has expanded its schools and developed new programs, always striving to meet the needs of students in search of a quality education. Hope International University continues the seventy-year tradition of preparing servant leaders throughout its academic programs. Each school adds strength to this tradition as we build leaders who have a foundation of ethics, principles, and outreach. Hope International University is a place that cares about the future and about those who will lead in their professions and their callings. The school wants to be known and recognized as a place where servant leaders prepare for a lifetime of service to the world in Christ's name. It all begins here at Hope . . . where learning leads to serving.

Tuition

Varies by course

Denomination

Christian Church

Accreditation

Western Association of Schools and Colleges

Web Address

http://www.hiu.edu
http://www.hiu.edu/grad/mid.html

ICI University
6300 N. Belt Line Rd.
Irving, TX 75063
972-751-1111
sgs@ici.edu

Master of Arts in Biblical Studies

Program Description

The ICI M.A. programs allow students to earn a Master of Arts degree through an individually structured distance-education format that utilizes mentors and printed materials. The ICI enrollment policy allows year-round open enrollment and is not based on a semester system. The M.A. in Biblical Studies program has concentrations in New Testament and Old Testament. Through various types of research and writing activities, the program is designed to prepare qualified students for a high level of service and proficiency in present and future ministry activities.

The M.A. degree awarded by ICI University requires students to complete thirty-six credit hours beyond the B.A. degree. This includes a six-credit thesis for students who choose the thesis route. Students who choose a non-thesis degree will be required to take and pass a written, proctored comprehensive examination.

Institutional Description

The global mission of ICI University is fivefold: evangelism, discipleship, training lay workers, ministerial training, and training for other educational vocations. This mission is based on a Christian worldview and is accomplished by providing access to educational and training programs that meet the needs of students, cooperating institutions, churches, and the communities served by the churches. All levels of education and training are included. As this mission is pursued, the body of Christ (the church) is enlarged, edified, and equipped, and society as a whole benefits. Our two mottos succinctly describe the nature of ICI University. "Our Campus Is the World" expresses the global nature of our institution and its distance learning methods. "From All Nations to All Nations" places special emphasis on the fact that we have highly qualified faculty from other nations whose input is shared with the rest of the world.

Tuition

$126 per credit

Denomination

Assemblies of God

Accreditation

Distance Education and Training Council

Web Address

http://www.ici.edu
http://www.ici.edu/grad/

ICI University

6300 N. Belt Line Rd.
Irving, TX 75063
972-751-1111
sgs@ici.edu

Master of Arts in Ministerial Studies

Program Description

The ICI M.A. degree programs allow students to earn a Master of Arts degree through an individually structured distance-education format by utilizing mentors and printed materials to guide students in their chosen courses of study and research. The ICI enrollment policy allows year-round open enrollment and is not based on a semester system. The M.A. in Ministerial Studies program has concentrations in missions, education, leadership. Through various types of research and writing activities, the program is designed to prepare qualified students for a high level of service and proficiency in present and future ministry activities.

The M.A. degree awarded by ICI University requires students to complete thirty-six credit hours beyond the B.A. degree. This includes a six-credit thesis for students who choose the thesis route. Students who choose a non-thesis degree will be required to take and pass a written, proctored comprehensive examination.

Institutional Description

The global mission of ICI University is fivefold: evangelism, discipleship, training lay workers, ministerial training, and training for other educational vocations. This mission is based on a Christian worldview and is accomplished by providing access to educational and training programs that meet the needs of students, cooperating institutions, churches, and the communities served by the churches. All levels of education and training are included. As this mission is pursued, the body of Christ (the church) is enlarged, edified, and equipped, and society as a whole benefits. Our two mottos succinctly describe the nature of ICI University. "Our Campus Is the World" expresses the global nature of our institution and its distance learning methods. "From All Nations to All Nations" places special emphasis on the fact that we have highly qualified faculty from other nations whose input is shared with the rest of the world.

Tuition

$126 per credit

Denomination

Assemblies of God

Accreditation

Distance Education and Training Council

Web Address

http://www.ici.edu
http://www.ici.edu/grad/

Indiana Wesleyan University

4301 S. Washington St.
Marion, IN 46953-5279
800-621-8667
fbrown@indwes.edu

Master of Business Administration

Program Description

The M.B.A. online program spans a twofold structure of integration and application of knowledge. The foundational core provides managers with context and background as they face complex, global managerial decisions. The functional core focuses on how a firm actually develops a product or service, efficiently produces or delivers it, effectively markets it, and finances overall operations. At the heart of the functional core is the manager, engaging in strategic decision-making that has short- and long-term impact.

Students will receive proactive and personalized technical assistance before beginning their program, including startup documents, e-mail addresses, and usernames. Ongoing technical assistance continues throughout the students' educational experience. All courses will be delivered via the Internet, with the exception of one that is delivered in a three-day (Thursday through Saturday), on-site, intensive learning experience with opportunities for significant interaction with university experts and corporate executives. Indiana Wesleyan offers students a virtual classroom as a forum to interact with faculty and fellow professionals on a broad range of management issues. The technology allows for both asynchronous and synchronous interaction among class members and faculty.

Institutional Description

Indiana Wesleyan University is a community of scholars whose mission is to create a Christ-centered educational climate where students are equipped for lifelong learning and service. A distinctly Christian approach and dynamic growth characterize Indiana Wesleyan University. The university is a community of scholars who integrate biblical principles, values, and faith in and out of the classroom. Students, faculty members, and administrators are expected to attend chapel three days a week. Each semester begins with Spiritual Emphasis Week, a weeklong series of chapel services featuring some of the nation's top evangelical thinkers.

Tuition

$345 per credit hour

Denomination

Wesleyan Church

Accreditation

North Central Association of Colleges and Schools

Web Address

http://www.indwes.edu
http://www.indwes.edu/mbaonline

Johnson Bible College

7900 Johnson Dr.
Knoxville, TN 37998
800-669-7889
mketchen@jbc.edu

Master of Arts in Marriage and Family Therapy

Program Description

The objective of this degree is to provide professional therapy education for individuals intending to minister in churches, community mental health agencies, children and family service agencies, institutional settings, or private practice. This program combines the theoretical, experiential, and spiritual aspects of marriage and family therapy. The curriculum is intended to prepare graduates for state licensure in marriage and family therapy. Marriage and family therapy training is by nature interdisciplinary and, therefore, includes relevant courses in ethics, health, law, family, theology, sociology, psychology, and marriage and family therapy. The program leads to a Master of Arts degree with a concentration in marriage and family therapy.

Nontraditional learning students travel to the campus and stay for two-week sessions. They identify supervisors and complete internships near their homes. Three classes of three credits each are offered each semester. One additional course is offered by video correspondence. In a typical class, the student must complete 1,500 to 3,000 pages of reading and present critiques of the material before taking the class. The student must do a project after the class to show that he or she has integrated all of the material. The student must complete 12 two-week sessions, 1 three-credit-hour video correspondence course, and 300 hours of direct clinical experience to earn the degree (51 credit hours). The degree may be completed in a minimum of two years and a maximum of six years.

Institutional Description

Johnson Bible College is a private, coeducational institution of higher learning offering associate's, bachelor's, and master's degrees. Johnson Bible College educates students for specialized Christian ministries with emphasis on the preaching ministry. Because Christian ministry requires that students have a Christian worldview, understanding themselves as well as the Word of God and the world of people, the college stresses holistic education including spiritual, intellectual, professional, social, and physical development.

Tuition

$150 per credit hour

Denomination

None

Accreditation

Southern Association of Colleges and Schools

Web Address

http://www.jbc.edu
http://www2.jbc.edu/johnsonbiblecollege/MAFTProgram.htm

Johnson Bible College

7900 Johnson Dr.
Knoxville, TN 37998
800-669-7889
mketchen@jbc.edu

Master of Arts in New Testament

Program Description

Johnson Bible College's New Testament master's program encourages renewal in the church by increasing the depth and quality of New Testament study among those preparing for or already engaged in church leadership, with emphasis on the preaching ministry. The thirty-four-hour program is offered through distance learning by videotape. It provides for communication with faculty by means of toll-free phone calls. Lectures are presented on videotape. Lessons are sent through the mail or by fax. Three short campus visits are required to complete the program.

Institutional Description

Johnson Bible College is a private, coeducational institution of higher learning offering associate's, bache- lor's, and master's degrees. Johnson Bible College educates students for specialized Christian ministries with emphasis on the preaching ministry. Because Christian ministry requires that students have a Christian world-view, understanding themselves as well as the Word of God and the world of people, the college stresses holistic education including spiritual, intellec- tual, professional, social, and physical development.

Tuition

$150 per credit hour

Denomination

None

Accreditation

Southern Association of Colleges and Schools

Web Address

http://www.jbc.edu
http://ashley.jbc.edu/mastersnt/

Liberty University

1971 University Blvd.
Lynchburg, VA 24502
804-582-2000
wcpenn@liberty.edu

Master of Arts in Counseling

Program Description

Liberty University provides master's level training to prepare persons for service as professional counselors within both the Christian and world communities. In addition, the M.A. program in professional counseling provides the foundational studies equipping students to pursue doctoral-level training in the field.

There are two tracks in the counseling program: a thirty-six-hour track and a forty-eight-hour track. Students who wish to become certified or licensed should enroll in the forty-eight-hour track. (Several states already require that candidates for licensure graduate from a forty-five- or forty-eight-hour program.)

The thirty-six-hour program is intended for those who use psychological information or do some counseling in their work but will not be seeking licensure as professional counselors. The core courses for the thirty-six-hour program are the first twelve courses in the forty-eight-hour program, so it is possible to transfer from the thirty-six- to the forty-eight-hour program at any time before graduation without losing any coursework. These courses adhere to the content requirements of CACREP and NBCC and of most states, so that by taking the forty-eight-hour program students will meet the academic licensing requirements for most states. There are a few states that require sixty hours of coursework, in which case twelve hours of postgraduate electives can be added to the program. Most states will also require two years of postgraduate experience under supervision before one can be licensed.

Institutional Description

Liberty University is a Christian academic community in the tradition of evangelical institutions of higher education. Liberty's mission is to produce Christ-centered men and women with the values, knowledge, and skills required to impact tomorrow's world. This mission is carried out for external students in a comparable academic program but without the structure of a resident community.

Tuition

$195 per semester hour

Denomination

None

Accreditation

Southern Association of Colleges and Schools

Web Address

http://www.liberty.edu
http://www.liberty.edu/admissions/distance/

Liberty University
1971 University Blvd.
Lynchburg, VA 24502
804-582-2000
wcpenn@liberty.edu

Master of Arts in Religion

Program Description

The Master of Arts in Religion degree is appropriate as an entry-level and general professional degree in religion. It is designed to give the student intensive study in the Scriptures and the essential truths of the Christian message. All courses offered through the external degree program are provided on standard VHS format T–120 videocassettes. The student will purchase a worktext and a textbook to accompany the lectures on videocassettes. Examinations for each course will be mailed to the faculty-approved proctor designated by the student. Each course has a specific examination schedule that is provided with the course materials.

Candidates for the Master of Arts in Religion degree must complete six hours on campus. Students may satisfy this requirement either by attending modular courses or by attending other regularly scheduled classes at Liberty University. Modular courses are one-week intensive sessions scheduled during summer and other selected times during the year. This forty-five-hour degree can be taken without specialization or can be pursued with a specialization in church growth, pastoral counseling, or worship studies.

Institutional Description

Liberty University is a Christian academic community in the tradition of evangelical institutions of higher education. Liberty's mission is to produce Christ-centered men and women with the values, knowledge, and skills required to impact tomorrow's world. This mission is carried out for external students in a comparable academic program but without the structure of a resident community.

Tuition

$195 per semester hour

Denomination

None

Accreditation

Southern Association of Colleges and Schools

Web Address

http://www.liberty.edu
http://www.liberty.edu/admissions/distance/

Liberty University
1971 University Blvd.
Lynchburg, VA 24502
804-582-2000
wcpenn@liberty.edu

Master of Business Administration

Program Description

The thirty-six-credit Master of Business Administration program provides master's level training to prepare people for business leadership. In accordance with the mission of Liberty University, the graduate faculty seeks to educate the whole person, developing the values, knowledge, and skills individuals need to have an impact on tomorrow's business world. Classroom instruction is sent to you on VHS videotapes that you can view and review. Course outlines and study notes are now available online. Students can enroll anytime and will have 120 days to complete each course. Students are also required to attend two weeklong modular seminars on the Liberty campus.

Institutional Description

Liberty University is a Christian academic community in the tradition of evangelical institutions of higher education. Liberty's mission is to produce Christ-centered men and women with the values, knowledge, and skills required to impact tomorrow's world. This mission is carried out for external students in a comparable academic program but without the structure of a resident community.

Tuition

$330 per semester hour

Denomination

None

Accreditation

Southern Association of Colleges and Schools

Web Address

http://www.liberty.edu
http://www.liberty.edu/admissions/distance/

Liberty University
1971 University Blvd.
Lynchburg, VA 24502
804-582-2000
wcpenn@liberty.edu

Master of Divinity

Program Description

The ninety-hour Master of Divinity degree is the program of study offered especially for persons who are called to be ministers, such as pastors, evangelists, missionaries, and chaplains. It may serve as the basis for future Th.M., D.Min., Ph.D., or Th.D. work. (Students having graduated with Liberty's M.A.R. degree may transfer all forty-five hours, as applicable, into the Master of Divinity program.) All courses offered through the External Degree Program are provided on standard VHS format T–120 videocassettes. The student will purchase a worktext and a textbook to accompany the lectures on videocassettes. Examinations for each course will be mailed to the faculty-approved proctor designated by the student. Each course has a specific examination schedule that is provided with the course materials.

Candidates for the Master of Divinity degree must complete sixteen hours on campus. Students may satisfy this requirement either by attending modular courses or by attending other regularly scheduled classes at Liberty University. Modular courses are one-week intensive sessions scheduled during summer and other selected times during the year.

Institutional Description

Liberty University is a Christian academic community in the tradition of evangelical institutions of higher education. Liberty's mission is to produce Christ-centered men and women with the values, knowledge, and skills required to impact tomorrow's world. This mission is carried out for external students in a comparable academic program but without the structure of a resident community.

Tuition
$195 per semester hour

Denomination
None

Accreditation
Southern Association of Colleges and Schools

Web Address
http://www.liberty.edu
http://www.liberty.edu/admissions/distance/

Liberty University

1971 University Blvd.
Lynchburg, VA 24502
804-582-2000
wcpenn@liberty.edu

Master of Education

Program Description

The thirty-six-credit Master of Education degree strives to produce educators who model high standards before their peers, and who have dedicated their lives to educational leadership. Concurrent with this goal, the graduate program offered by the School of Education is designed to prepare students for effective leadership in Christian, public, and private schools. Programs are available in elementary education, secondary education, administration and supervision, special education, school counseling, and reading specialist. All courses offered through the External Degree Program are provided on standard VHS format T–120 videocassettes. The student will purchase a worktext and a textbook to accompany the lectures on videocassettes. Examinations for each course will be mailed to the faculty-approved proctor designated by the student. Each course has a specific examination schedule that is provided with the course materials. Students are also required to attend required modular seminars on the Liberty campus.

Institutional Description

Liberty University is a Christian academic community in the tradition of evangelical institutions of higher education. Liberty's mission is to produce Christ-centered men and women with the values, knowledge, and skills required to impact tomorrow's world. This mission is carried out for external students in a comparable academic program but without the structure of a resident community.

Tuition

$195 per semester hour

Denomination

None

Accreditation

Southern Association of Colleges and Schools

Web Address

http://www.liberty.edu
http://www.liberty.edu/admissions/distance/

Nazarene Theological Seminary
1700 E. Meyer Blvd.
Kansas City, MO 64131
816-333-6254
enroll@nts.edu

In-Service Master of Divinity

Program Description

Nazarene Theological Seminary offers the Master of Divinity degree in a nontraditional format by utilizing a combination of intensive two-week modular sessions on the seminary campus, as well as cross-registration in graduate courses at regional Nazarene colleges and universities, individualized distance education, and advanced placement by assessment. This ninety-credit-hour program consists of courses in biblical studies, theology and philosophy, church history, foundations and practice of ministry, spiritual formation, and electives.

Institutional Description

Nazarene Theological Seminary prepares women and men for the practice of Christian ministry primarily in the Church of the Nazarene. The seminary is committed to the Wesleyan-Arminian theological tradition, grounded on faith in Christ and on Scripture as understood within that tradition, with special emphasis on the doctrine of entire sanctification, which leads to holiness of heart and life. The education offered stands in the context of classical theological education while incorporating engagement with applied disciplines for the practice of ministry.

Tuition

Varies by course

Denomination

Church of the Nazarene

Accreditation

Association of Theological Schools

Web Address

http://www.nts.edu

Oral Roberts University

7777 S. Lewis Ave.
Tulsa, OK 74171
888-900-4678
slle@oru.edu

Master of Divinity

Program Description

The Master of Divinity is an 88.5-semester-hour program that is the basic professional degree for ministry. It is a balanced program that integrates the fields of biblical literature, theological/historical studies, and the practices of ministry. As the foundational degree for ministry, this program prepares students for effective ministry as pastors, church associates, evangelists, chaplains, and a broad variety of ministries. Pastors and other leaders in ministry can pursue the Master of Divinity through the modular program. Students can take up to one-third of their program through distance education, including Internet courses, and complete the remainder through one-week modules that are offered monthly throughout the year.

Institutional Description

Oral Roberts University was founded as a result of the evangelist Oral Roberts obeying God's mandate to build a university on God's authority and the Holy Spirit. God's commission to Roberts was to "Raise up your students to hear My voice, to go where My light is dim, where My voice is heard small, and My healing power is not known, even to the uttermost bounds of the earth. Their work will exceed yours, and in this I am well pleased."

Oral Roberts University is a charismatic university founded in the fires of evangelism and upon the unchanging precepts of the Bible. The board of regents and the president and chief executive officer are dedicated to upholding the university's founding purpose.

Tuition

$225 per credit hour

Denomination

Nondenominational

Accreditation

North Central Association of Colleges and Schools

Web Address

http://www.oru.edu
http://www.oru.edu/university/departments/ALSCweb/htmlpages/dislo-t.htm
http://www.oruonline.org

Oral Roberts University

7777 S. Lewis Ave.
Tulsa, OK 74171
888-900-4678
slle@oru.edu

Master of Arts in Education

Program Description

For those called to teach or to educational administration, the Graduate School of Education offers eight M.A. degrees for public and Christian schoolteachers. M.A. students can earn half of their credit hours through distance education and the other half by coming on campus for two-week Summer Institute modules (three summers), allowing teachers or administrators to pursue an ORU education without relocating to Tulsa. ORU also offers a number of online courses that can be used to fulfill required and elective credits.

Institutional Description

Oral Roberts University was founded as a result of the evangelist Oral Roberts obeying God's mandate to build a university on God's authority and the Holy Spirit. God's commission to Oral Roberts was: "Raise up your students to hear My voice, to go where My light is dim, where My voice is heard small, and My healing power is not known, even to the uttermost bounds of the earth. Their work will exceed yours, and in this I am well pleased."

Oral Roberts University is a charismatic university founded in the fires of evangelism and upon the unchanging precepts of the Bible. The board of regents and the president and chief executive officer are dedicated to upholding the university's founding purpose.

Tuition

$225 per credit hour

Denomination

Nondenominational

Accreditation

North Central Association of Colleges and Schools

Web Address

http://www.oru.edu
http://www.oru.edu/university/departments/alscweb/htmlpages/
    dislo-e.htm
http://www.oruonline.org

Oral Roberts University

7777 S. Lewis Ave.
Tulsa, OK 74171
888-900-4678
slle@oru.edu

Master of Management in Nonprofit Management

Program Description

The Master of Management degree at the ORU School of Business provides a multidisciplinary course of study preparing students with leadership skills and advanced training in the management of the organization's most valuable asset—its human resources. The School of Business offers the thirty-five-credit Master of Management degree with a concentration in Nonprofit Management in a modular format that combines one-week intensive on campus modules with Internet courses. Campus sessions meet for one week in the fall, spring, and summer.

Institutional Description

Oral Roberts University was founded as a result of the evangelist Oral Roberts obeying God's mandate to build a university on God's authority and the Holy Spirit. God's commission to Roberts was to "Raise up your students to hear My voice, to go where My light is dim, where My voice is heard small, and My healing power is not known, even to the uttermost bounds of the earth. Their work will exceed yours, and in this I am well pleased."

Oral Roberts University is a charismatic university founded in the fires of evangelism and upon the unchanging precepts of the Bible. The board of regents and the president and chief executive officer are dedicated to upholding the university's founding purpose.

Tuition

$225 per credit hour

Denomination

Nondenominational

Accreditation

North Central Association of Colleges and Schools

Web Address

http://www.oru.edu
http://www.oru.edu/university/departments/ALSCweb/htmlpages/
    dislo-t.htm
http://www.oruonline.org

Pepperdine University

24255 Pacific Coast Hwy.
Malibu, CA 90263
310-456-4000
lpolin@pepperdine.edu

Master of Arts in Educational Technology

Program Description

The thirty-credit online M.A. takes thirteen months to complete, with only three face-to-face meetings: presession, midpoint, and end of the program. Face-to-face meetings have been carefully scheduled to require minimal absence from work and home. Instruction is learner-centered and real-world oriented. Courses require extensive project work. Students are expected to participate regularly online through synchronous and asynchronous forums. The program ends with a face-to-face juried exhibition of student work.

Coursework is more heavily weighted toward the integration of technology into teaching and curriculum. However, four of the ten courses (eleven of the thirty units) focus on teachers as leaders and agents of change. One course requires students to enter into a mentoring relationship with someone in their setting, for instance, a novice teacher or an administrator unfamiliar with technology or "new" ideas in teaching. A second introduces students to leadership styles and issues, and the special role technology can play as a catalyst for school reform.

Another focuses on human resource management issues of technology use as well as specific technology decisions site leaders must make, for instance, in setting up local networks. Applicants are expected to identify and articulate a personal vision, local problem/issue, or relevant topic of interest that they will "bring" to the program. Though it may evolve or otherwise change over the course of the program, this situated issue will be the focal point for much of the project work students will be asked to complete.

Institutional Description

Pepperdine is a Christian university committed to the highest standards of academic excellence and Christian values, where students are strengthened for lives of purpose, service, and leadership.

Tuition

$16,950 for the entire program

Denomination

None

Accreditation

Western Association of Schools and Colleges

Web Address

http://www.pepperdine.edu
http://moon.pepperdine.edu/gsep/programs/MAET/

Reformed Theological Seminary
2101 Carmel Rd.
Charlotte, NC 28226
800-227-2013
distance.education@rts.edu

Master of Arts (Religion)

Program Description

The Master of Arts in Religion is earned by completing formal academic advisement; establishing a regular local mentoring relationship; attending the on-campus introductory seminar; taking a series of distance courses in history, theology, New Testament, and Old Testament with mentored discussion and supervised teaching opportunities; writing an integrative academic thesis; composing an integrative portfolio; and participating in the summative integrative seminar including faculty and peer review of thesis and portfolio.

The church-based mentor is a key part of the program for academic progress and spiritual formation. This may be a pastor, elder, or other qualified person. Students meet regularly with the mentor to review course material and discuss application to personal growth and ministry opportunities. The mentor is invited to the on-campus seminars at RTS, discusses the lectures, proctors exams, reads the integration thesis, and evaluates the progress of the student throughout the program.

Institutional Description

The purpose of Reformed Theological Seminary is to serve the church in all branches of evangelical Christianity, especially the Presbyterian and Reformed family, by training its leaders (with a priority on pastors and including missionaries, educators, counselors, and others) through a program of theological education on the graduate level, based upon the authority of the inerrant Word of God and committed to the Reformed faith as set forth in the Westminster Confession of Faith and the Larger and Shorter Catechisms as originally adopted by the Presbyterian Church in the United States. This program shall be characterized by biblical fidelity, confessional integrity, and academic excellence.

Tuition

$220 per credit

Denomination

None

Accreditation

Southern Association of Colleges and Schools

Association of Theological Schools

Web Address

http://www.rts.edu
http://www.rtsvirtual.org

Reformed Theological Seminary
2101 Carmel Rd.
Charlotte, NC 28226
800-752-4382
admissions.orlando@rts.edu
Master of Arts (Summer/Winter M.A.)

Program Description

The program combines short, intensive residence study courses with audiotape and workbook external study courses. A fully-accredited master's degree in either biblical or theological studies is offered through this flexible study program. Students normally attend several one-week classes in January and again in the summer months. In addition, they typically complete two external courses during the fall and two more during the spring months. A minimum of thirty hours of residence study is required, with a total of sixty-six hours for completion of the Master of Arts degree.

Institutional Description

The purpose of Reformed Theological Seminary is to serve the church in all branches of evangelical Christianity, especially the Presbyterian and Reformed family, by training its leaders (with a priority on pastors and including missionaries, educators, counselors, and others) through a program of theological education on the graduate level, based upon the authority of the inerrant Word of God and committed to the Reformed faith as set forth in the Westminster Confession of Faith and the Larger and Shorter Catechisms as originally adopted by the Presbyterian Church in the United States. This program shall be characterized by biblical fidelity, confessional integrity, and academic excellence.

Tuition

$220 per credit

Denomination

None

Accreditation

Southern Association of Colleges and Schools

Association of Theological Schools

Web Address

http://www.rts.edu
http://www.rts.edu/degrees/ma/

Reformed Theological Seminary

2101 Carmel Rd.
Charlotte, NC 28226
800-752-4382
admissions.orlando@rts.edu

Master of Theology in Reformation Studies

Program Description

The Master of Theology (Th.M.) in Reformation Studies is now available in a modular format. In the modular format, students attend class on campus for eight one-week modules over a two-year term. A portion of the program is provided on the Internet and requires the student to have a computer and be proficient in its use.

This program has been designed to appeal to a wide range of interests, whether those interests are biblical, theological, or historical. The one-year Th.M. curriculum consists in six seminars (and a one-hour noncredit course in theological bibliography), of which two are required core seminars (on the Reformation and one on post-Reformation developments) and the remaining four are electives. Normally a working knowledge of ecclesiastical Latin is required before taking the fourth Th.M. seminar.

Institutional Description

The purpose of Reformed Theological Seminary is to serve the church in all branches of evangelical Christianity, especially the Presbyterian and Reformed family, by training its leaders (with a priority on pastors and including missionaries, educators, counselors, and others) through a program of theological education on the graduate level, based upon the authority of the inerrant Word of God and committed to the Reformed faith as set forth in the Westminster Confession of Faith and the Larger and Shorter Catechisms as originally adopted by the Presbyterian Church in the United States. This program shall be characterized by biblical fidelity, confessional integrity, and academic excellence.

Tuition

$220 per credit

Denomination

None

Accreditation

Southern Association of Colleges and Schools

Association of Theological Schools

Web Address

http://www.rts.edu
http://www.rts.edu/degrees/thm/thm-internet.html

Regent University
1000 Regent University Dr.
Virginia Beach, VA 23464-9800
800-373-5504
comcollege@regent.edu

Master of Arts in Communication

Program Description

The distance learning track of the master's degree in communication in the College of Communication and the Arts is designed to meet the needs of graduate students in eight areas of study: (1) rhetorical and communication studies, (2) organizational communication and development, (3) interpersonal/intercultural/international communication, (4) political communication, (5) professional writing/magazine journalism, (6) public relations, (7) script and screenwriting, and (8) critical studies in film/TV.

The required number of credits for the completion of an M.A. degree in the distance track is determined by the culminating option chosen by the student: the thesis option or the comprehensive examination option. The thesis option requires a minimum of forty graduate credits; the comprehensive examination option requires a minimum of forty-four credit hours. For students accepted into the distance track of the master's program without an adequate communication studies academic background, additional courses may be required beyond the degree minimum. All courses are delivered online.

Institutional Description

Regent University is the nation's premier Christian graduate university offering master's and doctoral degrees from a Judeo-Christian perspective. With a commitment to academic excellence and innovation, Regent prepares men and women to make a positive impact upon American society and the world. Twenty-two degree programs are offered on the Virginia Beach campus, and several are offered in the northern Virginia/Washington, D.C., area. Students may also pursue degree programs via the Internet. The eight graduate fields of study offered at Regent University include business, communication, counseling and psychology, divinity, education, government, law, and organizational leadership.

Tuition
$425 per credit

Denomination
Nondenominational

Accreditation
Southern Association of Colleges and Schools

Web Address

http://www.regent.edu
http://www.regent.edu/acad/schcom/ma/

Regent University

1000 Regent University Dr.
Virginia Beach, VA 23464-9800
800-373-5504
macmc@regent.edu

Master of Arts in Computer Mediated Communication

Program Description

The forty-credit cohort program features a common foundation of courses that combines theory and practice in areas including communication fundamentals, dynamics of computer mediated communication, social implications of the new media, virtual small groups, and the future of online communication. In addition, students have the option to select one of five concentrations: business, communication arts, divinity, education, and law. All courses are delivered online and no campus residency is required. The MA/CMC program can be pursued with either a thesis, portfolio, or comprehensive exam option. Students move through the program of studies as a cohort, to foster a sense of community as they become equipped to be leaders in online communication.

Institutional Description

Regent University is the nation's premier Christian graduate university offering masters and doctoral degrees from a Judeo-Christian perspective. With a commitment to academic excellence and innovation, Regent prepares men and women to make a positive impact upon American society and the world. Twenty-two degree programs are offered on the Virginia Beach campus, and several are offered in the northern Virginia/Washington, D.C., area. Students may also pursue degree programs via the Internet. The eight graduate fields of study offered at Regent University include business, communication, counseling and psychology, divinity, education, government, law, and organizational leadership.

Tuition

$425 per credit

Denomination

Nondenominational

Accreditation

Southern Association of Colleges and Schools

Web Address

http://www.regent.edu
http://www.regent.edu/acad/schcom/cmc/

Regent University
1000 Regent University Dr.
Virginia Beach, VA 23464-9800
800-373-5504
leadercenter@regent.edu

Master of Arts in Organizational Leadership

Program Description

The course structure for this thirty-three-credit-hour program is made up of three areas: multidisciplinary foundational courses, cognate specialty courses, and culminating activity. Students can specialize in business, communication, divinity, education, or create an individualized focus. All courses are delivered online.

Institutional Description

Regent University is the nation's premier Christian graduate university offering master's and doctoral degrees from a Judeo-Christian perspective. With a commitment to academic excellence and innovation, Regent prepares men and women to make a positive impact upon American society and the world. Twenty-two degree programs are offered on the Virginia Beach campus, and several are offered in the northern Virginia/Washington, D.C., area. Students may also pursue degree programs via the Internet. The eight graduate fields of study offered at Regent University include business, communication, counseling and psychology, divinity, education, government, law, and organizational leadership.

Tuition

$350 per credit hour

Denomination

Nondenominational

Accreditation

Southern Association of Colleges and Schools

Web Address

http://www.regent.edu
http://www.regent.edu/acad/cls/mol/

Regent University
1000 Regent University Dr.
Virginia Beach, VA 23464-9800
800-373-5504
govschool@regent.edu

Master of Arts in Political Management

Program Description

Mastering the fine points of political management requires practical learning experiences and mentoring by those who understand political systems firsthand. Designed for the development of skills and techniques to manage issues and individual campaigns for all levels of government, this degree emphasis gives students the benefit of learning from experienced practitioners. In the age of media-driven events and crisis, the M.A. in Political Management also provides those entering government with the skills necessary to handle a political or media crisis. This opportunity serves to provide career-boosting networking connections for talented students. Courses are delivered online.

Institutional Description

Regent University is the nation's premier Christian graduate university offering master's and doctoral degrees from a Judeo-Christian perspective.

With a commitment to academic excellence and innovation, Regent prepares men and women to make a positive impact upon American society and the world. Twenty-two degree programs are offered on the Virginia Beach campus, and several are offered in the northern Virginia/Washington, D.C., area. Students may also pursue degree programs via the Internet. The eight graduate fields of study offered at Regent University include business, communication, counseling and psychology, divinity, education, government, law, and organizational leadership.

Tuition

$340 per credit hour

Denomination

Nondenominational

Accreditation

Southern Association of Colleges and Schools

Web Address

http://www.regent.edu
http://www.regent.edu/acad/schgov/admissions/distance.html

Regent University

1000 Regent University Dr.
Virginia Beach, VA 23464-9800
800-373-5504
govschool@regent.edu

Master of Arts in Public Policy

Program Description

This program emphasizes law and action, examining social, family, and environmental issues from a legal and ethical perspective. Through a rigorous program of academic and practical training, students learn not only to analyze public policy but to create it as well. Philosophies of government are carefully studied in concert with practical skills, empowering students to make a difference in our nation as leaders who know how to get things done. Courses are delivered online.

Institutional Description

Regent University is the nation's premier Christian graduate university offering master's and doctoral degrees from a Judeo-Christian perspective. With a commitment to academic excellence and innovation, Regent prepares men and women to make a positive impact upon American society and the world. Twenty-two degree programs are offered on the Virginia Beach campus, and several are offered in the northern Virginia/Washington, D.C., area. Students may also pursue degree programs via the Internet. The eight graduate fields of study offered at Regent University include business, communication, counseling and psychology, divinity, education, government, law, and organizational leadership.

Tuition

$340 per credit hour

Denomination

Nondenominational

Accreditation

Southern Association of Colleges and Schools

Web Address

http://www.regent.edu
http://www.regent.edu/acad/schgov/admissions/distance.html

Regent University

1000 Regent University Dr.
Virginia Beach, VA 23464-9800
800-373-5504
busschool@regent.edu

Master of Business Administration
(Executive, Professional)

Program Description

The Regent University School of Business offers two distance M.B.A. degree programs: the Executive M.B.A. (E.M.B.A.) and the Professional M.B.A. (P.M.B.A.). Each provides you with the skills to lead organizations in changing times according to Christian values that have stood the test of time. The E.M.B.A. is for fast-track executives who need broad, strategic business education, but not any further specialization. The P.M.B.A. is for those with at least five years of business experience who want both broad business education and further specialization.

The E.M.B.A. is an eighteen-month, thirty-six-semester credit program designed for fast-track executives with seven or more years of focused, professional experience. The P.M.B.A. is a thirty-two-month, forty-eight-semester credit program designed for working business professionals with five or more years of experience. After an initial two-day orientation in Virginia Beach, students may customize their distance learning experience.

Institutional Description

Regent University is the nation's premier Christian graduate university offering master's and doctoral degrees from a Judeo-Christian perspective. With a commitment to academic excellence and innovation, Regent prepares men and women to make a positive impact upon American society and the world. Twenty-two degree programs are offered on the Virginia Beach campus, and several are offered in the northern Virginia/Washington, D.C., area. Students may also pursue degree programs via the Internet. The eight graduate fields of study offered at Regent University include business, communication, counseling and psychology, divinity, education, government, law, and organizational leadership.

Tuition

$325 per credit hour

Denomination

Nondenominational

Accreditation

Southern Association of Colleges and Schools

Web Address

http://www.regent.edu
http://www.regent.edu/acad/schbus/marketing/

Regent University
1000 Regent University Dr.
Virginia Beach, VA 23464-9800
800-373-5504
eduschool@regent.edu

Master of Education (Master Educator Program)

Program Description

This thirty-two- to thirty-four-credit-hour program offers courses in models of thinking, curriculum, instructional strategies, assessment research, character development, models of leadership, and more. The program culminates in a major project in which the learner demonstrates a synthesis of the knowledge and skills acquired in the program. The practitioner may produce a plan for the application of knowledge, strategies, and principles learned in the program. The leader may develop a systematic professional development program in a particular area. The scholar/consultant may write an article, chapter in a book, or thesis for future publication. All courses are delivered online.

Institutional Description

Regent University is the nation's premier Christian graduate university offering master's and doctoral degrees from a Judeo-Christian perspective.

With a commitment to academic excellence and innovation, Regent prepares men and women to make a positive impact upon American society and the world. Twenty-two degree programs are offered on the Virginia Beach campus, and several are offered in the northern Virginia/Washington, D.C., area. Students may also pursue degree programs via the Internet. The eight graduate fields of study offered at Regent University include business, communication, counseling and psychology, divinity, education, government, law, and organizational leadership.

Tuition

$295 per semester hour

Denomination

Nondenominational

Accreditation

Southern Association of Colleges and Schools

Web Address

http://www.regent.edu
http://www.regent.edu/acad/schedu/distance/

Regent University
1000 Regent University Dr.
Virginia Beach, VA 23464-9800
800-373-5504
llm@regent.edu
Master of Laws in International Taxation

Program Description

The Regent University School of Law LL.M. graduate program in International Taxation is designed for the practitioner who wishes to satisfy this need rapidly and through a state-of-the-art, user-friendly curriculum. In each course, students are able to analyze assigned reading material through a series of carefully crafted lesson plans accompanied by weekly online lectures. Electronic chat rooms and e-mail facilitate interaction between faculty and fellow students. Each course is constructed of a number of modules the student must complete in a specified period of time. Each student may progress at his or her own speed within predetermined time frames. Progress is assessed through periodic online examinations.

The program consists of both required and elective coursework designed to provide a sophisticated background in the general principles of international taxation and global and offshore tax planning, as well as the opportunity for students to examine areas of particular interest. Under the supervision of a full-time faculty member the latter is accomplished through a regimen of independent research and writing, which culminates with the submission of a master's thesis.

Institutional Description

Regent University is the nation's premier Christian graduate university offering master's and doctoral degrees from a Judeo-Christian perspective. Regent prepares men and women to make a positive impact upon American society and the world. Twenty-two degree programs are offered on the Virginia Beach campus, and several are offered in the northern Virginia/Washington, D.C., area. Students may also pursue degree programs via the Internet. The eight graduate fields of study offered at Regent University include business, communication, counseling and psychology, divinity, education, government, law, and organizational leadership.

Tuition

$15,000 for the entire program for U.S. nationals

$20,000 for the entire program for non–U.S. nationals

Denomination

Nondenominational

Accreditation

Southern Association of Colleges and Schools

American Bar Association

Web Address

http://www.regent.edu
http://www.regent.edu/acad/schlaw/llm/

Regent University
1000 Regent University Dr.
Virginia Beach, VA 23464-9800
800-373-5504
govschool@regent.edu

Masters in Public Administration

Program Description

The management of state and local government involves organizational skills as well as wisdom in the application of political theory and philosophy. The master's degree program in public administration provides preparation in these areas for solid careers in government. The program offers both academic preparation and practical training for management positions at state and local levels of government, as well as nongovernmental organizations involved in public policy. Courses are delivered online.

Institutional Description

Regent University is the nation's premier Christian graduate university offering master's and doctoral degrees from a Judeo-Christian perspective. With a commitment to academic excellence and innovation, Regent prepares men and women to make a positive impact upon American society and the world. Twenty-two degree programs are offered on the Virginia Beach campus, and several are offered in the northern Virginia/Washington, D.C., area. Students may also pursue degree programs via the Internet. The eight graduate fields of study offered at Regent University include business, communication, counseling and psychology, divinity, education, government, law, and organizational leadership.

Tuition

$340 per credit hour

Denomination

Nondenominational

Accreditation

Southern Association of Colleges and Schools

Web Address

http://www.regent.edu
http://www.regent.edu/acad/schgov/admissions/distance.html

Seattle Pacific University

3307 Third Ave. W.
Seattle, WA 98199
206-281-2378
rmlong@spu.edu

Master of Education in Curriculum and Instruction

Program Description

This two-year master's degree in curriculum and instruction is geared for certified teachers who want to develop their leadership skills and improve their instructional abilities. Under this umbrella master's degree, the online degree program offers you the opportunity to focus on teaching and learning concepts and strategies.

The Master of Education in Curriculum and Instruction is designed to help teachers strengthen their instructional skills while developing their leadership abilities for such roles as department chair, staff development leader, or curriculum coordinator. There are four components in the curriculum and instruction degree: a research core, a curriculum/instruction core, an elective sequence, and a comprehensive examination.

Institutional Description

With a long and distinguished history in Christian higher education, Seattle Pacific University approaches the new century positioned to serve and to lead in the city, the world, and the church. At a time when the legacy of the secularized modern university is under scrutiny, Seattle Pacific provides more than 3,300 students with a high-quality, comprehensive education grounded on the gospel of Jesus Christ. This combination of vital scholarship and thoughtful faith is a powerful one that brings about lasting change in the lives of our graduates, and in the people and communities they serve.

Tuition

$288 per credit

Denomination

Free Methodist

Accreditation

Northwest Association of Schools and Colleges

Web Address

http://www.spu.edu
http://www.spu.edu/online

Southern Christian University

P.O. Box 240240
Montgomery, AL 36124-0240
800-351-4040
onlinecourses@southernchristian.edu

Master of Arts in Religious Studies

Program Description

The Master of Arts is designed to provide a high level of preparation for ministry and/or preparation for advanced graduate study. This degree program is strongly academic in nature and concentrates primarily on biblical studies, including exegesis of Scripture in at least one of the original languages in which it was written. Some electives may be taken in areas other than textual biblical studies. Students who complete this degree may enter or continue careers in ministry, may transfer to another graduate program to pursue a Ph.D., or may enter the Master of Divinity program at Southern Christian University. The M.A. program is open to applicants who hold the B.A. or B.S. degree. The major for this program is religious studies. A student may acquire an area of concentration by earning twelve semester hours of non-required courses in foundation studies, Old Testament studies, New Testament studies, professional studies, theological and historical studies, missions studies, or counseling studies.

Institutional Description

Southern Christian University offers upper-level undergraduate programs, master's programs, and a doctoral program that are designed to train Christian ministers, missionaries, counselors, and other church workers. Admission is open to all persons of good character and good reputation whose backgrounds and abilities qualify them for undergraduate or graduate education. Southern Christian University does not discriminate on the basis of race, color, national or ethnic origin, religion, sex, or handicap in the administration of its educational policies, programs, and activities except where necessitated by the specific religious tenets held by the institution. Southern Christian University is a private religious school affiliated by common purpose and cooperative effort with the Churches of Christ, an undenominational fellowship of independent congregations that strive to reproduce New Testament Christianity today.

Tuition

$230 per semester hour

Denomination

Churches of Christ

Accreditation

Southern Association of Colleges and Schools

Web Address

http://www.southernchristian.edu

Southern Christian University

P.O. Box 240240
Montgomery, AL 36124-0240
800-351-4040
onlinecourses@southernchristian.edu

Master of Divinity

Program Description

The ninety-credit Master of Divinity is generally considered to be the basic professional degree in ministry. The curriculum, which takes the equivalent of three years of full-time work to complete, requires both extensive studies in the biblical text and thorough preparation in theology and various areas of practical ministry. Because of the practical emphasis of this program, students normally enter or continue careers in full-time ministry.

The M.Div. program is open to applicants who hold the B.A. or B.S. degree. A student may elect to earn the Master of Science or Master of Arts degree on the way to the Master of Divinity degree. The major for this program is Christian ministry or family therapy. A student may acquire an area of concentration by earning eighteen semester hours of non-required courses in foundation studies, Old Testament studies, New Testament studies, professional studies, theological and historical studies, missions studies, or counseling studies. A thesis is not required for this program.

Institutional Description

Southern Christian University offers upper-level undergraduate programs, master's programs, and a doctoral program that are designed to train Christian ministers, missionaries, counselors, and other church workers. Admission is open to all persons of good character and good reputation whose backgrounds and abilities qualify them for undergraduate or graduate education. Southern Christian University does not discriminate on the basis of race, color, national or ethnic origin, religion, sex, or handicap in the administration of its educational policies, programs, and activities except where necessitated by the specific religious tenets held by the institution. Southern Christian University is a private religious school affiliated by common purpose and cooperative effort with the Churches of Christ, an undenominational fellowship of independent congregations that strive to reproduce New Testament Christianity today.

Tuition

$230 per semester hour

Denomination

Churches of Christ

Accreditation

Southern Association of Colleges and Schools

Web Address

http://www.southernchristian.edu

Southern Christian University

P.O. Box 240240
Montgomery, AL 36124-0240
800-351-4040
onlinecourses@southernchristian.edu

Master of Science in Family Therapy

Program Description

The Master of Science is designed to provide a high level of preparation for ministry. The Master of Science program is open to applicants who hold the Bachelor of Arts or Bachelor of Science degree. The forty-five-credit marriage and family degree is designed to train therapists to diagnose and treat mental and emotional disorders and other behavioral problems. This discipline also addresses a wide array of relationship issues within the context of the family. Individuals, couples, and families benefit from the unique perspective and skills of marriage and family therapists. They practice in many health and mental health settings in both the public and private sectors.

Institutional Description

Southern Christian University offers upper-level undergraduate programs, master's programs, and a doctoral program that are designed to train Christian ministers, missionaries, counselors, and other church workers. Admission is open to all persons of good character and good reputation whose backgrounds and abilities qualify them for undergraduate or graduate education. Southern Christian University does not discriminate on the basis of race, color, national or ethnic origin, religion, sex, or handicap in the administration of its educational policies, programs, and activities except where necessitated by the specific religious tenets held by the institution. Southern Christian University is a private religious school affiliated by common purpose and cooperative effort with the Churches of Christ, an undenominational fellowship of independent congregations that strive to reproduce New Testament Christianity today.

Tuition

$230 per semester hour

Denomination

Churches of Christ

Accreditation

Southern Association of Colleges and Schools

Web Address

http://www.southernchristian.edu

Southern Christian University

P.O. Box 240240
Montgomery, AL 36124-0240
800-351-4040
onlinecourses@southernchristian.edu

Master of Science in Ministry

Program Description

The Master of Science is designed to provide a high level of preparation for ministry. The Master of Science program is open to applicants who hold the Bachelor of Arts or Bachelor of Science degree. The emphasis in ministry requires the completion of thirty-six semester hours including courses in Bible, homiletics, and ministry. The program, while giving considerable emphasis to biblical studies, is more oriented toward practical ministry than is the Master of Arts. A student who takes the ministry option may acquire an area of concentration by earning twelve semester hours of non-required courses in New Testament studies, Old Testament studies, theological and historical studies, or missions studies.

Faculty members establish telephone hours for off-campus students to call with any questions or problems. Students may also submit questions or comments by mail or e-mail when they return the tapes. Professors typically start each lecture by restating and answering questions received since the last class. Class content may be adjusted to meet the needs and interests of extended learning students.

Institutional Description

Southern Christian University offers upper-level undergraduate programs, master's programs, and a doctoral program that are designed to train Christian ministers, missionaries, counselors, and other church workers. Southern Christian University does not discriminate on the basis of race, color, national or ethnic origin, religion, sex, or handicap in the administration of its educational policies, programs, and activities except where necessitated by the specific religious tenets held by the institution. Southern Christian University is a private religious school affiliated by common purpose and cooperative effort with the Churches of Christ, an undenominational fellowship of independent congregations that strive to reproduce New Testament Christianity today.

Tuition

$230 per semester hour

Denomination

Churches of Christ

Accreditation

Southern Association of Colleges and Schools

Web Address

http://www.southernchristian.edu

Southern Christian University

P.O. Box 240240
Montgomery, AL 36124-0240
800-351-4040
onlinecourses@southernchristian.edu

Master of Science in Organizational Leadership

Program Description

The Master of Science in Organizational Leadership is a forty-credit program that addresses the needs of leaders in a rapidly changing world. Set within a biblical worldview, course topics include leadership foundations, building effective organizations, leadership visualization and values, systems for today's leaders, strategies for organizational change, organizational communication, negotiation and conflict resolution, and spiritual leadership within the organization. Campus classes are recorded on videotape and mailed to the students or delivered via the Web. In effect, distance learning students are in the same class and receive the same quality of instruction as on-campus students. They are encouraged to interact with the instructor by toll-free telephone. They must complete the same assignments, meet the same deadlines, and take the same tests. They are graded on the same basis.

Institutional Description

Southern Christian University offers upper-level undergraduate programs, master's programs, and a doctoral program that are designed to train Christian ministers, missionaries, counselors, and other church workers. Admission is open to all persons of good character and good reputation whose backgrounds and abilities qualify them for undergraduate or graduate education. Southern Christian University does not discriminate on the basis of race, color, national or ethnic origin, religion, sex, or handicap in the administration of its educational policies, programs, and activities except where necessitated by the specific religious tenets held by the institution. Southern Christian University is a private religious school affiliated by common purpose and cooperative effort with the Churches of Christ, an undenominational fellowship of independent congregations that strive to reproduce New Testament Christianity today.

Tuition

$230 per semester hour

Denomination

Churches of Christ

Accreditation

Southern Association of Colleges and Schools

Web Address

http://www.southernchristian.edu

Southwestern Assemblies of God University

1200 Sycamore
Waxahachie, TX 75165
888-937-7248
info@sagu.edu

Master of Education

Program Description

Southwestern offers a graduate program that focuses on administration as well as classroom management and instruction, preparing administrators and educators to face the educational challenges of the twenty-first century. This thirty-six-hour degree examines finance, legal issues, and administration in the Christian school, and gives attention to educational leadership and supervision. Courses are delivered via audio- and videotaped lectures, and students have the option of telephone or e-mail interaction with their instructors. Full Internet courses are also available.

Students enrolling for graduate distance education will attend a first-semester orientation that enables them to function well with distance education processes at SAGU, and that provides appropriate academic and financial counseling. This visit to campus combines with the opportunity to register for courses and take initial course seminars. During these opening seminars students meet instructors and receive an introduction to the course(s) in which they've enrolled. Each semester thereafter, distance education students return to campus for their course seminars, then do follow-up work from home.

Institutional Description

Southwestern Assemblies of God University understands that every person has a divine destiny that can be realized if God-given endowments are trained for optimum performance. This premise is held to be the primary justification for institutional education by the Assemblies of God, the parent body of Southwestern Assemblies of God University.

Southwestern is committed to the task of contributing to the training of Christian individuals to carry the gospel to the ends of the earth while fulfilling their divinely approved place in the kingdom of God.

Tuition

None

Denomination

Assemblies of God

Accreditation

Southern Association of Colleges and Schools

Web Address

http://www.sagu.edu
http://www.sagu.edu/sde/graduate/

Southwestern Assemblies of God University
1200 Sycamore
Waxahachie, TX 75165
888-937-7248
info@sagu.edu

Master of Science/Arts in Practical Theology

Program Description

The Masters in Practical Theology is a Bible-based program that will prepare students for ministry in the local church and society at large; provide intensive training in persuasive preaching, effective teaching, and Christ-centered counseling; develop administrative skills that will empower local congregations to fulfill their redemptive roles in society; and ensure academic excellence that will lead to advanced or terminal degrees. Courses are delivered via audio- and videotaped lectures and students have the option of telephone or e-mail interaction with their instructors. Full Internet courses are also available.

Students enrolling for graduate distance education will attend a first-semester orientation that enables them to function well with distance education processes at SAGU, and that provides appropriate academic and financial counseling. This visit to campus combines with the opportunity to register for courses and take initial course seminars. During these opening seminars students meet instructors and receive an introduction to the course(s) in which they've enrolled. Each semester thereafter, distance education students return to campus for their course seminars, then do follow-up work from home.

Institutional Description

Southwestern Assemblies of God University understands that every person has a divine destiny that can be realized if God-given endowments are trained for optimum performance. This premise is held to be the primary justification for institutional education by the Assemblies of God, the parent body of Southwestern Assemblies of God University.

Southwestern is committed to the task of contributing to the training of Christian individuals to carry the gospel to the ends of the earth while fulfilling their divinely approved place in the kingdom of God.

Tuition
None

Denomination
Assemblies of God

Accreditation
Southern Association of Colleges and Schools

Web Address
http://www.sagu.edu
http://www.sagu.edu/sde/graduate/

Texas Christian University

2800 S. University Dr.
Fort Worth, TX 76129
817-257-7000
frogmail@tcu.edu

Master of Liberal Arts

Program Description

The Master of Liberal Arts program is designed to offer graduate level education in the broad areas of liberal studies. It is a multidisciplinary, non-career oriented program that seeks to offer a wide range of educational opportunities to students of diverse educational backgrounds. The intent of the program is to make available to all college graduates an opportunity to satisfy their intellectual curiosity and to broaden their knowledge. The MLA degree requires successful completion of thirty hours of coursework. Twelve of the thirty hours must be in MLA courses designated "Perspectives on Society." Courses so designated will relate a liberal arts discipline to (a) issues of contemporary American society, (b) issues of culture or cultural diversity in America, and (c) other world cultures and societies. No thesis is required. Most students complete the program in two to three years. However, it is possible to finish in less time with a heavier course load. All courses are delivered online and no campus residency is required.

Institutional Description

TCU maintains the highest of academic traditions with a faculty brought together from institutions throughout the world. Yet the university is influenced by other roots as well. Born on the American frontier, it respects the ideals of self-reliance, lack of pretension, and belief in hard work that have branded the Southwest. Its association with the Christian Church (Disciples of Christ) places prime importance on the individual as part of community, and encourages open inquiry, be it toward a reasoned faith or a career path. As an independent, self-governing university, it exercises the freedom to set the goals and objectives that best serve its students and society at large in a constantly changing world.

Tuition

$320 per semester hour

Denomination

Christian Church (Disciples of Christ)

Accreditation

Southern Association of Colleges and Schools

Web Address

http://www.tcu.edu
http://www.tcuglobal.edu

12

DOCTORAL DEGREE PROGRAMS

The doctoral degree is the pinnacle of formal education. The research-oriented Ph.D., or Doctor of Philosophy, is the most common degree pursued by individuals interested in becoming college professors. However, there are other doctoral degrees, such as the Doctor of Education (Ed.D.), that are designed for the active practitioner rather than someone interested in doing theoretical research. Distance doctoral programs are relatively rare and, given the small number of Christian institutions that offer any Ph.D. and Ed.D. degree programs, the number of Christian distance doctoral options are rarer still.

The following list doesn't include Doctor of Ministry (D.Min.) programs because most of them are designed for the active pastor using modular courses on campus. Therefore, since most D.Min. programs are nonresidential, a catalog of distance programs would basically result in a listing of all of them.

You'll notice that virtually every doctoral program listed in this chapter requires some on-campus residency time. Accrediting agencies require that. That may change in the future, but you should expect to spend some time on campus if you want to earn an accredited doctoral degree.

Baptist Bible College and Seminary
538 Venard Rd.
Clarks Summit, PA 18411
570-586-2400
info@bbc.edu

Ph.D. in Biblical Studies

Program Description

The Ph.D. in Biblical Studies is designed to meet the learning needs of those who are called of God to a teaching ministry in the disciplines of Bible and theology. While the Ph.D. degree is considered to be the terminal degree for those who teach at the college, graduate school, or seminary level, pastors desiring a strong teaching ministry in their church will also find this program ideally designed.

The Ph.D. may be earned in-service, allowing students to maintain current ministry and place of residence while in the program. This is accomplished through a twelve-week "external residency" and a one-week "internal residency" for each course. The degree may be earned in less time by living in the area and carrying a larger load of courses. A student may enroll after completing either an M.Div. degree or a Th.M. degree. Those possessing a Th.M. degree (or its 120-credit-hour equivalent) will enroll in thirty-seven additional credit hours to earn the Ph.D. Those with an M.Div. degree will take sixty credit hours for this Ph.D.

Institutional Description

The Baptist Bible Seminary experience stresses scholarship for the student. Minds sharpened by the scholarly study of the Word of God are foundational for significant, life-changing ministry. But scholarship alone is not enough—the Baptist Bible Seminary experience cultivates passion for ministry. People who make a difference are people who care. Passion is not so much a discipline that is taught as it is a life-motivating zeal that is caught. The Baptist Bible Seminary experience develops passion for ministry in the hearts of students. A heart consumed by godly passion is the fuel that drives significant, life-changing ministry. Service is the outcome of combining leadership and passion. In ministry, service should be a lifelong process. Hands that work to serve are the means of significant, life-changing ministry.

Tuition
$370 per credit hour

Denomination
General Association of Regular Baptist Churches

Accreditation
Middle States Association of Colleges and Schools

Web Address
http://www.bbc.edu
http://seminary.bbc.edu/phd/

George Fox University
414 N. Meridian St.
Newberg, OR 97132-2697
503-538-8383
sheadly@georgefox.edu

Ed. D. (Doctor of Education)

Program Description

George Fox University offers a doctoral program that prepares educators to be leaders in their chosen specialties at the K–20 levels. The Doctor of Education (Ed.D.) program focuses on qualities of cultural, moral, and organizational leadership for leading complex education organizations. This professionally oriented program is designed to maximize accessibility for full-time educators. Students will have an opportunity to complete the degree in approximately four years through Internet-based courses, independent study, and summer sessions on campus.

The Doctor of Education program is comprised of fifty-five semester units of coursework and a minimum of eight semester units of dissertation. Students will fulfill these requirements by transferring up to seventeen semester units appropriate to the curriculum past the master's degree, taking thirty-six core semester hours in leadership, foundational perspectives, and research, and nineteen elective hours (through transfer and coursework) in a chosen specialty.

Institutional Description

George Fox University is Christ-centered. Our heritage as a Quaker-founded institution gives us distinctives common to the Friends Church, such as a concern for social justice, a commitment to peace and nonviolence, and a belief in the equality of all people. While approximately 9 percent of our undergraduate students are Friends, more than fifty denominations are represented on campus, the largest being Baptist. Students of all faiths are welcome. While we don't require a signed statement of faith, we are a Christian community, and as such, ask and expect our students and employees to abide by the university's community responsibilities and expectations. In keeping with our mission of Christian higher education, all employees—faculty, administration, and staff—are committed evangelical Christians.

Tuition

$355 per credit hour

Denomination

Evangelical Friends

Accreditation

Northwest Association of Schools and Colleges

Web Address

http://www.georgefox.edu
http://voyager.georgefox.edu/edd/

Liberty University
1971 University Blvd.
Lynchburg, VA 24502
804-582-2000
soe@liberty.edu

Ed.D. in Educational Leadership

Program Description

The Doctor of Education in Educational Leadership is designed to prepare competent effective leaders with a Christian worldview who will model high standards and assume a leadership role in the field of education. Leaders in the field of education are seen as those who assume a facilitating role in accomplishing the goals and objectives of an education system whether it be as a superintendent, principal, curriculum director, instructional supervisor, or university administrator.

The sixty-credit Ed.D. program consists of twelve hours of leadership core courses, twenty-four hours of concentration courses (eight courses in either administration, curriculum, or instruction), twelve hours from a cognate area (administration, curriculum, instruction in higher education, foundations, reading, school counseling, or special education), six credits in educational research, and six credits of dissertation. The student is also required to pass a comprehensive examination and successfully defend a dissertation. Twelve hours must be completed on campus to meet the residency requirements.

Institutional Description

Liberty University is a Christian academic community in the tradition of evangelical institutions of higher education. Liberty's mission is to produce Christ-centered men and women with the values, knowledge, and skills required to impact tomorrow's world. This mission is carried out for external students in a comparable academic program but without the structure of a resident community.

Tuition

$195 per semester hour

Denomination

None

Accreditation

Southern Association of Colleges and Schools

Web Address

http://www.liberty.edu
http://www.liberty.edu/admissions/distance/

Pepperdine University

24255 Pacific Coast Hwy.
Malibu, CA 90263
310-456-4000
mniese@pepperdine.edu

Ed. D. in Educational Technology

Program Description

The doctoral concentration in Educational Technology is designed to prepare leaders in the field of technological applications and innovation in the world of education and business. Students attend class in a mix of face-to-face and Internet sessions, creating a truly distributed learning environment. In addition, students and faculty communicate asynchronously through e-mail and newsgroups.

Concentration courses focus on advanced learning theory as it relates to product design, the relationship between humans and computers, and the special management issues that surround technology. Core courses are geared toward the technological environment where appropriate. All students will complete a five-unit consultancy, and as part of the policy development course, will spend several days in Washington, D.C., discussing technology and education policy with national leaders.

All applicants should have at least five years of work experience in a technology-rich environment. Management experience is a plus. Online classes are conducted on the Internet, and all face-to-face classes are offered at Pepperdine University Plaza in West Los Angeles. To facilitate online communication and assignment completion, all students are required to purchase a laptop computer. The program begins with a one-week technology camp. Attendance in West Los Angeles is required for four weeks and six weekends each year. In addition to the twenty-three units of core courses, students enroll in twenty-one units of concentration courses.

Institutional Description

Pepperdine is a Christian university committed to the highest standards of academic excellence and Christian values, where students are strengthened for lives of purpose, service, and leadership.

Tuition

$690 per credit hour

Denomination

None

Accreditation

Western Association of Schools and Colleges

Web Address

http://www.pepperdine.edu
http://moon.pepperdine.edu:80/gsep/programs/et/

Regent University

1000 Regent University Dr.
Virginia Beach, VA 23464-9800
800-373-5504
eduschool@regent.edu

Ed.D. (Doctor of Education)

Program Description

The Doctor of Education is a sixty-credit program conducted entirely online, with dispersed residencies in one of four cities. The Ed.D. program features concentrations in K–12 School Leadership, Higher Education Administration, Staff Development/Adult Education, Educational Psychology, Special Education, Distance Education. The program combines both interactive Web-based courses and dispersed residency requirements in one of four cities. Learning activities are designed to meet specific competencies, facilitate the learning styles of adults, and provide a collaborative community for the purposes of higher-level thinking and problem solving. The problem-based curriculum, practical dissertation projects, and individually designed cognates allow for a tailor-made program.

Institutional Description

Regent University is the nation's premier Christian graduate university offering master's and doctoral degrees from a Judeo-Christian perspective. With a commitment to academic excellence and innovation, Regent prepares men and women to make a positive impact on American society and the world. Twenty-two degree programs are offered on the Virginia Beach campus, and several are offered in the northern Virginia/Washington, D.C., area. Students may also pursue degree programs via the Internet. The eight graduate fields of study offered at Regent University include business, communication, counseling and psychology, divinity, education, government, law, and organizational leadership.

Tuition

$325 per credit

Denomination

Nondenominational

Accreditation

Southern Association of Colleges and Schools

Web Address

http://www.regent.edu
http://www.regent.edu/acad/schedu/edd/

Regent University

1000 Regent University Dr.
Virginia Beach, VA 23464-9800
800-373-5504
comcollege@regent.edu

Ph.D. in Communication

Program Description

The Ph.D. degree generally serves three purposes: teaching, research, and administration. The doctoral studies program in the College of Communication and the Arts at Regent University meets the needs of doctoral students seeking a career in one of the three areas. The program prepares a select number of students to enter the college workforce, to fill research positions, or to function in top-level administrative positions within research firms, businesses of various types, non-profit organizations, parachurch ministries, and other types of organizations in need of highly skilled communication and/or arts professionals.

Chosen distance doctoral applicants must attend an on-campus admissions orientation scheduled during a two-week summer session as the final screening step to formal acceptance into the program. Each subsequent summer session following any semester with required coursework, the distance doctoral student must attend a two-credit summer doctoral seminar. The program consists of a minimum of forty-two credits of coursework, comprehensive examinations, and a dissertation.

Institutional Description

Regent University is the nation's premier Christian graduate university offering master's and doctoral degrees from a Judeo-Christian perspective. With a commitment to academic excellence and innovation, Regent prepares men and women to make a positive impact upon American society and the world. Twenty-two degree programs are offered on the Virginia Beach campus, and several are offered in the northern Virginia/Washington, D.C., area. Students may also pursue degree programs via the Internet. The eight graduate fields of study offered at Regent University include business, communication, counseling and psychology, divinity, education, government, law, and organizational leadership.

Tuition

$400 per credit

Denomination

Nondenominational

Accreditation

Southern Association of Colleges and Schools

Web Address

http://www.regent.edu
http://www.regent.edu/acad/schcom/phd/

Regent University
1000 Regent University Dr.
Virginia Beach, VA 23464-9800
800-373-5504
leadercenter@regent.edu

Ph.D. in Organizational Leadership

Program Description

At the heart of the Center for Leadership Studies is its doctoral program in organizational leadership. This Ph.D. program is aimed at immediately facilitating the leadership abilities and roles of strategic mid-career professionals. The doctoral program accomplishes this by incorporating rigorous critical thinking and scholarly research grounded in a biblical worldview. A primary distinctive of the organizational leadership program is its utilization of Computer Mediated Learning.

Ordinarily, sixty semester hours is required beyond the master's degree to complete the doctor of philosophy degree. Each learner will designate a cognate from either business, divinity, education, or government. With permission of the faculty advisor, a learner with a focused objective may select an independent cognate that draws from two or more of the foregoing areas. The program is designed to be completed in three years (including dissertation), with three summer residencies to be held at our Virginia Beach campus.

Institutional Description

Regent University is the nation's premier Christian graduate university offering master's and doctoral degrees from a Judeo-Christian perspective. With a commitment to academic excellence and innovation, Regent prepares men and women to make a positive impact upon American society and the world. Twenty-two degree programs are offered on the Virginia Beach campus, and several are offered in the northern Virginia/Washington, D.C., area. Students may also pursue degree programs via the Internet. The eight graduate fields of study offered at Regent University include business, communication, counseling and psychology, divinity, education, government, law, and organizational leadership.

Tuition
$2,200 per term

Denomination
Nondenominational

Accreditation
Southern Association of Colleges and Schools

Web Address
http://www.regent.edu
http://www.regent.edu/acad/cls/olphd/

Southern Baptist Theological Seminary

2825 Lexington Rd.
Louisville, KY 40280
800-626-5525
eddlead@sbts.edu

Ed.D. in Leadership

Program Description

The Ed.D. in Leadership is designed to meet the learning needs of educational ministry professionals with substantive full-time ministry experience who are unable to relinquish or suspend their full-time employment or change locations to attend Southern Baptist Theological Seminary. The primary educational objective of the degree is the development of leadership, advanced research, and critical-thinking and problem-solving skills in persons continuing in full-time practitioner status in local church, denominational, or higher education leadership positions in the field of Christian education.

The Ed.D. in Leadership will consist of forty-eight semester hours (two years; twelve courses) of seminar research followed by sixteen hours (one year; four courses) of dissertation research. Participants enter the program as a cohort of twenty-five to thirty students who complete each course in the prescribed sequence.

Courses will be offered in an accelerated instructional format consisting of a research triad: (1) a foundational research component; (2) a research seminar component; and (3) an advanced research component.

Institutional Description

The mission of the Southern Baptist Theological Seminary is to be totally committed to the Bible as the Word of God and to be a servant of the churches of the Southern Baptist Convention by training, educating, and preparing ministers of the gospel for more faithful service.

The seminary's programs focus on development of ministerial competencies at the pre-baccalaureate, baccalaureate, basic professional postbaccalaureate, advanced professional, and advanced research levels. The seminary also offers programs of continuing education for ministry.

Tuition

$8,500 for the whole program for a Southern Baptist student

$17,000 for the whole program for a non–Southern Baptist student

Denomination

Southern Baptist Convention

Accreditation

Southern Association of Colleges and Schools

Association of Theological Schools

Web Address

http://www.sbts.edu
http://www.sbts.edu/celead/edd/edd.html

13

CUSTOM PROGRAMS

By eliminating the need to attend classes at fixed times throughout the week, distance programs offer students increased flexibility over traditional campus-based courses. However, almost all of the distance programs listed to this point still use a fixed curriculum of required courses, specialization tracks, and elective credits. This chapter contains a list of programs—associate's level through doctoral level—lacking even that level of rigidity. These programs permit you to design your own degree curriculum and are particularly useful if you haven't yet found a program that meets your needs. Before profiling such custom programs, though, let's examine a few of the unique issues related to individualized degrees: transfer credits, credit by examination, prior learning assessment, portfolios, degree committees, and learning contracts.

INDIVIDUALIZED UNDERGRADUATE STUDY

On the undergraduate level, it is actually possible to earn a degree based completely on prior learning. Graduate degrees, on the other hand, are based almost entirely on new learning. In other words, if you're someone with a lot of academic or life experience, you may be able to earn an associate's or bachelor's degree without taking any new courses. For example, if you started college a few years ago but never completed your degree, you may be able to transfer those credits into a program and apply them toward a B.A. Some of the programs in this chapter, such as the bachelor's degree from Thomas Edison State College, function like a credit bank where you can deposit all of the college credits you've earned through the years and parlay them into advanced standing or even a complete degree. Many undergraduate and graduate programs do permit students to transfer some credits earned at other institutions, but the institutions listed in this chapter have much more generous limits (and sometimes no limits) on the number of transfer credits that can be applied toward undergraduate degrees.

Credit by examination is another option for earning credit at the undergraduate level. If you feel confident in your knowledge of a particular subject and are comfortable taking tests, you may be able to earn college credit by passing various subject tests. For example, if you score above the eightieth percentile on one of the GRE Advanced Subject Tests (offered in areas such as biology, economics, English, and history), Regents College will grant you thirty credits toward an undergraduate degree. Earning one-fourth of a bachelor's degree in one sitting is a pretty impressive feat. Other subject-oriented tests (e.g., Regents College Examinations, CLEP Subject Examinations, and DANTES Subject Standardized Tests) can also be used to earn credit.

Portfolios, or prior learning assessment, represent another option for earning credits without taking new courses. Using this approach, you can earn credit by developing a portfolio of your prior learning experiences and demonstrating that they correspond to accepted coursework. For example, suppose you taught yourself how to design Web pages and want credit for that. Your first step would be to find a college that offered a similar course, such as a three-credit Introduction to Web Page Design course. You then assemble a portfolio of your Web work that clearly demonstrates your mastery of the material taught in the Web design course (based on the course summary and/or syllabus) and submit it for review. If your portfolio is convincing, a school such as Charter Oak State College will grant you three credits for your effort. Such prior learning assessment is an excellent way to earn credits for what you already know, regardless of how you learned it.

INDIVIDUALIZED GRADUATE STUDY

As I mentioned earlier, credit for prior learning is largely limited to undergraduate programs. However, on the graduate level you have the opportunity to custom-design a curriculum that draws from any number of learning sources—courses from a variety of schools, tutorial sessions with faculty, and independent study. And unlike undergraduate degrees, which require coursework in a broad array of fields, you can focus all of your graduate efforts in a single area of study. Generally such individualized graduate programs involve the development of a degree committee and a learning contract.

A degree committee typically consists of a faculty advisor plus one or more additional professors. Your faculty advisor is generally someone in your field of study who works for the university at which you're enrolled. Additional faculty members on your committee can usually be selected from other professors at your institution and/or faculty from other universities. Your advisor and committee will help you develop your individualized curriculum, monitor your progress along the way, and ultimately sign off on your efforts and authorize the institution to grant your degree.

The creation of your individualized curriculum in graduate programs such as the ones found in this chapter usually involves the development of a learning contract. This document outlines the specific learning experiences you will undertake in pursuit of your degree. Such learning experiences might be courses from that institution, on-campus or distance courses from other institutions, one-on-one tutorials with professors in your field, independent studies incorporating reading lists and research papers, field experience projects, conferences, and any other form of new learning accepted by your committee. Once you've developed such a contract, you follow it the same way more traditional students follow a fixed degree plan. And when you're done, you've earned your degree. Don't expect that such individualized degree plans will be easy—your committee will make sure that it's suitable for the graduate degree that you're pursuing—but they do enable you to study exactly what you want.

In this chapter you'll find a number of secular institutions that offer individualized degree programs for degrees ranging from a B.A. to a Ph.D.

California State University, Dominguez Hills

Humanities External Degree Program
1000 E. Victoria St.—SAC2-2126
Carson, CA 90747
310-243-3743
huxonline@dhvx20.csudh.edu

Master of Arts in the Humanities

Program Description

California State University, Dominguez Hills offers a Master of Arts in the Humanities degree. It is a fully-accredited correspondence program that does not require on-campus attendance of any kind. Students can specialize in one of five areas: art, music, literature, philosophy, or history, or they can do a generalized or interdisciplinary study in all five areas. Students must complete thirty units (up to nine graduate-level units in humanities can be transferred in) and finish within five years to earn the degree. At present, introductory level courses and selected core courses are available with a computer online instruction option, so that students can do assignments and correspond with their instructors and other students via the Internet.

The Master of Arts in the Humanities offers broad interdisciplinary exposure to all areas of the humanities—history, literature, philosophy, music, and art—and the establishment of an integrated perspective that emphasizes their interrelating effects and influences.

The Master of Arts degree is offered as an external degree program for any-one presently holding a bachelor's degree and preferring an individualized approach to advanced education rather than traditional classroom courses on college campuses. Achievement of the degree emphasizes independent study guided by qualified faculty. An undergraduate concentration in the humanities is not a prerequisite for this master's degree program.

Institutional Description

California State University, Dominguez Hills is a 346-acre campus situated on what was formerly Rancho San Pedro, the oldest Spanish land grant in the Los Angeles area. It is situated close to many of Southern California's cultural centers, attractions, and business and industrial centers. Founded in 1960, the university served its first students in 1965. It is a contemporary four-year public university, one of twenty-two California State University campuses.

Tuition

$140 per unit

Accreditation

Western Association of Schools and Colleges

Web Address

http://www.csudh.edu
http://www.csudh.edu/hux/

Charter Oak State College
55 Paul J. Manafort Dr.
New Britain, CT 06053-2142
860-832-3800
info@mail.cosc.edu

Bachelor of Arts/Science in General Studies

Program Description

Charter Oak holds no classes. Instead, students earn credits through the following sources: college courses, university correspondence courses, nationally accredited noncollegiate courses, Military Service School courses, noncollegiate courses/programs evaluated by Charter Oak State College, Charter Oak State College Testing Program, nationally standardized public testing programs, distance learning (including independent guided study [IGS] and online courses), portfolio review, and contract learning. One hundred twenty credits are required for the bachelor's degree. All students must complete distributive requirements, which include general education requirements as well as a minimum number of credits in the liberal arts. Achievement in these areas demonstrates breadth of learning. Each candidate for the bachelor's degree must establish and complete a faculty-approved concentration of thirty-six credits or more in a single subject or combination of subjects through which they demonstrate in-depth knowledge within one or more fields of study.

You can complete your degree program by combining prior learning with the acquisition of new knowledge in a manner that best suits your needs and inclination. Charter Oak recognizes that college-level learning can take place in a variety of settings outside the traditional college classroom, but it does not grant credit for "life experience," per se. Rather, it evaluates learning acquired informally through a variety of life experiences, including employment, military service, and volunteer-, travel-, recreational-, and family-related activities as well as through noncollegiate sponsored instruction.

Institutional Description

Charter Oak State College is the external degree program of the State of Connecticut. We offer adult learners anytime, anywhere, the opportunity to earn credits, an array of methods to assess learning acquired through experience, cost-effective alternatives for earning credits to acquiring a degree, and a college with no residency requirement and no limit on the number or age of transfer credits.

Tuition

Varies by learning effort

Accreditation

New England Association of Schools and Colleges

Web Address

http://www.cosc.edu
http://www.cosc.edu/dl/dl.htm

Goddard College
123 Pitkin Rd.
Plainfield, VT 05667
800-468-4888
admissions@earth.goddard.edu

Bachelor of Arts in Individualized Studies

Program Description

This 120-credit low-residency liberal arts degree program requires a seven-day residency prior to each semester to meet with other students and to collaborate with a faculty advisor in planning undergraduate work. The rest of the time is spent in a student's own home or community doing independent study in collaboration with a faculty advisor. Students may bring with them up to ninety approved credits through a combination of transfer credits and credits earned through assessment of prior learning.

With the help of a faculty mentor or advisor, a student creates a study plan each semester. The plan states what the student intends to learn, in what group studies the student will be involved, and where and how he or she will secure the basic resources needed for the study. It also states his or her approach to learning: to defining and dealing with the problem or coming to terms with the issues, to seeking meaningful order, to analyzing and evaluating the learning experiences, and finally, to making the whole process part of his or her life.

Institutional Description

Founded in 1863, Goddard is recognized for innovation in education. Our mission is to advance the theory and practice of learning by undertaking new experiments based upon the ideals of democracy and the principles of progressive education first asserted by John Dewey. Goddard's students are regarded as unique individuals who take charge of their own learning. Through collaboration with faculty and staff, Goddard encourages students to become creative, passionate, lifelong learners, working and living with an earnest concern for others and for the welfare of the earth.

Tuition

Varies by learning effort

Accreditation

New England Association of Schools and Colleges

Web Address

http://www.goddard.edu
http://www.goddard.edu/indexoffcampus.htm

Goddard College
123 Pitkin Rd.
Plainfield, VT 05667
800-468-4888
admissions@earth.goddard.edu

Master of Arts in Individualized Studies

Program Description

This thirty-six-credit low-residency graduate degree program requires a seven-day residency prior to each semester to meet with other students and to collaborate with a faculty advisor in planning one's graduate work. Throughout the week, students meet in work groups designed to orient them to graduate study and to help develop the critical and creative thinking tools necessary for the study.

With the help of a faculty mentor or advisor, a student creates a study plan each semester. The plan states what the student intends to learn, in what group studies the student will be involved, and where and how he or she will secure the basic resources needed for the study. It also states his or her approach to learning: to defining and dealing with the problem or coming to terms with the issues, to seeking meaningful order, to analyzing and evaluating the learning experiences, and finally, to making the whole process part of his or her life. During the semester, the student fulfills the goals of the individual study plan through regular correspondence with advisors.

The fruit of this synthesis, the thesis, demonstrates understanding of the issues and ideas that have guided the graduate inquiry as well as a student's unique interpretation of or personal contribution to these issues. Final products are of two types: a written thesis or a primary product that is practical or creative in nature (e.g., a body of artwork, a manual, a field project) accompanied by an interpretive process paper.

Institutional Description

Founded in 1863, Goddard is recognized for innovation in education. Our mission is to advance the theory and practice of learning by undertaking new experiments based upon the ideals of democracy and the principles of progressive education first asserted by John Dewey. Goddard's students are regarded as unique individuals who take charge of their own learning. Through collaboration with faculty and staff, Goddard encourages students to become creative, passionate, lifelong learners, working and living with an earnest concern for others and for the welfare of the earth.

Tuition

Varies by learning effort

Accreditation

New England Association of Schools and Colleges

Web Address

http://www.goddard.edu
http://www.goddard.edu/indexoffcampus.htm

The McGregor School of Antioch University
800 Livermore St.
Yellow Springs, OH 45387
937-767-6325
admiss@mcgregor.edu

Individualized Master of Arts Program

Program Description

The sixty-credit Individualized Master of Arts (I.M.A.) program offers a unique opportunity for students to build on a solid structure for both the process and content of graduate study, and at the same time design learning that fulfills both personal and professional goals. Students pursue their studies via a combination of intensive seminar attendance and distance education, making it possible to combine graduate education with work and family commitments. All tracks lead to a Master of Arts degree. The I.M.A. offers you the opportunity to study in your own community, arrange portions of your learning to fit your schedule, communicate with faculty via a range of distance learning technologies, including e-mail, fax, and phone. The I.M.A. helps you to identify meaningful educational and professional goals, integrate theory with practice, and conceptualize and write a thesis relevant to your interests.

The self-designed study concentration builds on two brief seminars for which students are residents on the Antioch campus in Yellow Springs. All learning experiences are designed by the student under the guidance of Antioch faculty and experts who are knowledgeable in the student's field and possess appropriate academic credentials and interests. The average amount of time necessary for students to complete the requirements for the degree is two to two-and-a-half years (eight to ten quarters). The minimum time is one-and-a-half years (six quarters). The program *must* be completed within five years.

Institutional Description

The McGregor School of Antioch University offers adults who are interested in furthering their education a diverse range of graduate and undergraduate programs that are responsive to emerging societal needs. The McGregor School is imbued with an entrepreneurial spirit and strives to provide high quality, socially responsible, flexible, and innovative educational programs.

Tuition

$1,486 per quarter

Accreditation

North Central Association of Colleges and Schools

Web Address

http://www.mcgregor.edu
http://www.mcgregor.edu/imaself.html

Regents College
7 Columbia Circle
Albany, NY 12203-5159
888-647-2388
admissions@regents.edu

Bachelor of Arts

Program Description

This 120-credit liberal arts degree can be earned through a combination of prior and new learning. Regents College uses team advising to support you in your educational progress. After you enroll, Regent will assign you an advising team based on your degree program. A team member will review your transcripts and other educational documents and prepare a status report that will indicate how all your previous education and learning will apply to your Regents College degree.

The three main sources of credit used by Regents College students are traditional college classes or correspondence courses; proficiency examinations, special assessment, and portfolio assessment; and military or business/industry training. Regents currently provides access to over ten thousand distance courses and for-credit examination programs offered by more than a hundred accredited institutions. Courses and examinations provide a means for you to study at your own pace, when and where you can, while continually moving toward the college degree you have always wanted.

Institutional Description

Founded on the belief that what someone knows is more important than where and how the knowledge was acquired, Regents College provides opportunity for motivated adult learners to obtain recognition of their college-level educational achievement. In the past twenty-five years, more than eighty thousand individuals have earned accredited associate and baccalaureate degrees in business, liberal arts, nursing, and technology from this unique college.

Originally founded in 1971 by the New York State Board of Regents as the external degree program of the University of the State of New York, Regents College is a private, independently chartered institution based in Albany, New York. It is governed by a board of trustees comprised of a national group of prominent leaders in education, business, and the professions.

Tuition

Varies by learning effort

Accreditation

Middle States Association of Colleges and Schools

Web Address

http://www.regents.edu

Regents College

7 Columbia Circle
Albany, NY 12203-5159
888-647-2388
admissions@regents.edu

Master of Arts in Liberal Studies

Program Description

The Master of Arts in Liberal Studies (M.L.S.) program allows for interdisciplinary study in the arts and sciences through a flexible program of study delivered at a distance via assessment, guided learning packages, and Web-based technology. It is designed for highly motivated working adults who desire more than vocational training or discipline-specific study. The M.L.S. degree program requires thirty-three credits of interdisciplinary study in the arts and sciences. There are no on-campus residency requirements for the program.

The program is divided into three tiers. Tier I requires the completion of a common core of two six-credit courses that introduce you to interdisciplinary study through the consideration of selected topics in Western civilization. Tier II requires the completion of fifteen credits in two or more disciplines. These credits can be earned from a variety of sources and through a variety of learning modes such as your choice of coursework taken at other institutions, independent learning contracts with Regents College faculty, and assessments of graduate-level learning you have acquired through nontraditional means. Tier II will prepare you for writing the thesis in Tier III, which requires the completion of a six-credit thesis.

Institutional Description

Founded on the belief that what someone knows is more important than where and how the knowledge was acquired, Regents College provides opportunity for motivated adult learners to obtain recognition of their college-level educational achievement. In the past twenty-five years, more than eighty thousand individuals have earned accredited associate and baccalaureate degrees in business, liberal arts, nursing, and technology from this unique college.

Originally founded in 1971 by the New York State Board of Regents as the external degree program of the University of the State of New York, Regents College is a private, independently chartered institution based in Albany, New York. It is governed by a board of trustees comprised of a national group of prominent leaders in education, business, and the professions.

Tuition

Varies by learning effort

Accreditation

Middle States Association of Colleges and Schools

Web Address

http://www.regents.edu

Thomas Edison State College
101 W. State St.
Trenton, NJ 08608-1176
609-984-1150
info@tesc.edu
Bachelor of Arts/Science Programs

Program Description

Adults may earn a 120-credit Bachelor of Arts or Bachelor of Science degrees through testing, portfolios demonstrating knowledge, credit for courses taken at work or in the military, and credit for certain licenses and certificates. Students also may earn credit through Thomas Edison's Distance & Independent Adult Learning (DIAL) program, which includes the online computer classroom, guided study (mentored courses taken at home or work), and contract learning. Other options such as approved telecourses and correspondence courses also are available.

In addition to a general B.A. degree, TESC offers Bachelor of Science in business administration, applied science and technology, human services, and in nursing. Credit distribution requirements vary by program.

Institutional Description

Thomas Edison State College is a state college of the New Jersey system of higher education. A national leader in distance education, Thomas Edison State College enables adult learners to complete baccalaureate and associate's degrees wherever they live and work. At Thomas Edison, students in any state or nation earn credit for college-level knowledge acquired outside the classroom (such as knowledge gained on the job or through volunteer activities). There are no residency requirements.

Tuition

Varies by learning effort

Accreditation

Middle States Association of Colleges and Schools

Web Address

http://www.tesc.edu
http://www.tesc.edu/degree_programs/bachelors.html

The Union Institute
440 E. McMillan St.
Cincinnati, OH 45206-1925
800-486-3116
tmott@tui.edu
Bachelor of Arts or Bachelor of Science

Program Description

The Union Institute's College of Undergraduate Studies offers a unique opportunity to the highly motivated, mid-career adult who seeks to complete a bachelor's degree—the B.A. or B.S. Most students have had some prior college or learning experiences at the college level. The Union Institute provides one-on-one guidance and counseling to learners in planning and developing their program of study and flexible scheduling through both tutorial study options and course meeting times scheduled at the learner's convenience. The Institute also looks at the learner's past educational endeavors to assess and incorporate learning experiences regardless of where that learning has taken place. The baccalaureate degree requires the completion of 128 semester credits, of which at least thirty-two credits must be from sponsored learning at The Union Institute.

Because the Institute's approach to education is individualized and interdisciplinary, the faculty uses the term "area of concentration" rather than "major" when referring to the focus of a learner's curriculum. Many learners focus on the same types of subjects pursued by students in traditional colleges: psychology, social work, business administration, management, criminal justice, health care administration, communications, education, etc. Some learners, however, develop areas of concentration that are highly personalized, reflecting their own unique educational goals. In either case, learners have considerable latitude to shape their degree plans according to individual needs, interests, and abilities.

Institutional Description

The Union Institute is a unique university within American higher education. Union students are highly motivated, mid-career adults whose needs and interests determine the pace and breadth of their learning experience. The Union Institute's tutorial-based studies lead either to the baccalaureate B.A. or B.S. degree or the doctoral Ph.D. degree. Current enrollment is approximately twenty-two hundred. The Union Institute has nearly six thousand alumni.

Tuition

$262 per semester credit hour

Accreditation

North Central Association of Colleges and Schools

Web Address

http://www.tui.edu/
http://www.tui.edu/programs/undergrad/undergrad.html

The Union Institute
440 E. McMillan St.
Cincinnati, OH 45206-1925
800-486-3116
jhill@tui.edu

Ph.D. Program in Interdisciplinary Arts and Sciences

Program Description

The graduate school of The Union Institute has been called the university for people whose life experience has educated them beyond the limits of traditional doctoral programs. The Union Institute does not impose a fixed curriculum to which everyone is expected to conform. Rather, the shape of the doctoral program emerges from the needs, interests, and background of each individual learner.

All doctoral work at The Union Institute rests on four cornerstones: it is interdisciplinary; it incorporates an awareness of its social impact; it fosters a mingling of theory and practice; and it includes formal considerations of personal growth. The doctoral program has three basic components: new learning, internship, and original research. All components are carried out under the guidance of a doctoral committee.

The program requires periods of intense residence including a ten-day entry colloquium, three seminars of five days each, and ten peer days. All residency events are scheduled at the convenience of the learner with numerous options for both time and site. After matriculation, each learner forms a doctoral committee. The committee includes two of our core faculty members plus two adjunct faculty members and two peer members. The first major document produced in the program is the learning agreement, a document that specifies all of the activities and resources that will be engaged to fulfill the new learning, internship, and research program requirements.

Institutional Description

The Union Institute is a unique university within American higher education. Union students are highly motivated, mid-career adults whose needs and interests determine the pace and breadth of their learning experience. The Union Institute's tutorial-based studies lead either to the baccalaureate B.A. or B.S. degree or the doctoral Ph.D. degree. Current enrollment is approximately twenty-two hundred. The Union Institute has nearly six thousand alumni.

Tuition

$4,300 per semester

Accreditation

North Central Association of Colleges and Schools

Web Address

http://www.tui.edu/
http://www.tui.edu/programs/graduate/graduate.html

Vermont College of Norwich University

36 College St.
Montpelier, VT 05602
800-336-6794
vcadmis@norwich.edu

Bachelor of Arts in Liberal Studies

Program Description

Study in the adult degree program leads to the Bachelor of Arts degree in Liberal Studies and is based on the classical English model of learning that offers adults a unique approach to college study. This 120-credit undergraduate program features one-to-one study with a faculty mentor, completion of a college degree in four years or less, and studies that are relevant to personal and professional goals, including preparation for graduate school, and study from the convenience of your own home or office.

Students attend either a weekend residency once a month or a nine-day residency every six months. Academic residency activities include selecting a faculty mentor, planning the study project, faculty and student presentations, seminars, readings and exhibitions, and guest presentations. Off-campus components include completion of reading, research, and writing; sustained dialogue with a faculty mentor at least once a month; and internships, field research, artwork, local courses, seminars, and workshops as applicable.

Working closely with a faculty mentor, students draft a semester study plan. You'll also meet regularly with an academic advisor. You'll need to meet certain degree criteria (study in liberal arts areas) to satisfy requirements for the B.A. degree. Your academic advisor will keep you on track, making sure that you're aware of these as you design your general education and concentration studies to earn the 120 credits required for the B.A.

Institutional Description

Steeped in the traditions of Oxford and American Progressive Education, Vermont College offers undergraduate, graduate, and fine arts programs, awarding bachelor's degrees in liberal studies, master's degrees, and Master of Fine Arts degrees. The school also offers one of the oldest Master of Arts in Art Therapy programs in the United States. All programs allow students to incorporate life experience and previous education into self-designed studies that are guided by outstanding faculty mentors.

Tuition

$4,310 per six-month term

Accreditation

New England Association of Schools and Colleges

Web Address

http://www.norwich.edu/vermontcollege/
http://www.norwich.edu/vermontcollege/adp/

Vermont College of Norwich University

36 College St.
Montpelier, VT 05602
800-336-6794
vcadmis@norwich.edu

Master of Arts (Humanities or Social Sciences)

Program Description

Study in the adult degree program leads to the Master of Arts degree with concentrations in the humanities and social sciences. Students design their own program of study under the guidance of experienced faculty advisors. These individualized studies build on academic, work, and life experiences. The graduate program features individually-tailored study plans, convenient home study with access to a dynamic learning community, one-to-one study with two experienced faculty advisors, and the completion of a Master of Arts degree in one and a half to three years.

There are three options for enrollment. The online option requires you to attend one colloquium on the Montpelier, Vermont, campus during your first month of enrollment, then continue studies largely via e-mail and conferencing. The regional option combines independent study with periodic regional seminars held at selected sites in North America, as well as in Zurich, Switzerland. These seminars are conveniently scheduled on weekends. Students in the regional option must attend one brief colloquium either on our Montpelier, Vermont, campus or in California. In the weekend option, students take part in a one-day seminar held once a month at either Montpelier or Brattleboro, Vermont. During the length of your enrollment, you will attend one five-day colloquium in Montpelier.

Institutional Description

Steeped in the traditions of Oxford and American Progressive Education, Vermont College offers undergraduate, graduate, and fine arts programs, awarding bachelor's degrees in liberal studies, master's degrees, and Master of Fine Arts degrees. The school also offers one of the oldest Master of Arts in Art Therapy programs in the United States. All programs allow students to incorporate life experience and previous education into self-designed studies that are guided by outstanding faculty mentors.

Tuition

$4,723 per six-month term (online option)

$4,575 per six-month term (regional option)

$4,770 per six-month term (weekend option)

Accreditation

New England Association of Schools and Colleges

Web Address

http://www.norwich.edu/vermontcollege/
http://www.norwich.edu/grad/

BAKER'S GUIDE ONLINE

I hope that this book has opened your eyes to the multitude of opportunities available to you through distance education. Since institutions are adding programs on a regular basis, I encourage you to visit the *Baker's Guide to Christian Distance Education* Web site at http://www.bakersguide.com. Baker's Guide Online serves as an online counterpart to this book and as a central repository for information related to Christian distance education. Although it doesn't feature the in-depth program profiles found in this print edition, it does contain links to many of the institutions that offer distance education opportunities. You can also register for a free newsletter that offers monthly e-mail updates about current happenings in Christian distance education.

I pray that this book proves beneficial for you as you consider furthering your education through online and distance learning opportunities. If you have any additional questions or comments about distance education, or are interested in further consultation, please visit http://www.bakersguide.com or e-mail me at jason@bakersguide.com.

Have fun embarking on your own Christian distance learning journey!

Jason D. Baker is an assistant professor of communication at Regent University, working primarily with the online M.A. in computer-mediated communication program. He holds an M.A. in education from The George Washington University and is a Ph.D. candidate at Regent University, where his research focuses on online communication and distance learning. He has written and spoken extensively on the use of online communication for the building of God's kingdom, and his earlier books include *Parents' Computer Companion* and *Christian Cyberspace Companion*. Jason, his wife Julianne, and their two sons live in Baltimore.

You can contact Jason via e-mail at jason@bakersguide.com or at the *Baker's Guide to Christian Distance Education* Web site at http://www.bakersguide.com

Consejos y datos

✔ Distintas investigaciones indican que entre cinco y nueve miligramos de cafeína por cada 2.2 libras de peso corporal pueden reducir la fatiga muscular respiratoria y el estrechamiento de las vías respiratorias inducido por el ejercicio.

Ver el remedio en la página · 174

Compresas de col

Seguramente te ha pasado que, después de un largo viaje, tus tobillos parecen regresar de la guerra. En algunas ocasiones, se inflaman tanto que se deforman y no hay manera de calzarlos nuevamente si nos quitamos los zapatos al comenzar el viaje. Se trata de un edema, una acumulación de líquido anormal

• Reducir la hinchazón de pies, tobillos, piernas y manos hinchadas (edema en las extremidades)

en los tejidos y músculos de las extremidades. Puede que se inflamen los tobillos, los pies completos e incluso las piernas, desde los muslos. O bien, las manos. Puede ser producto de una lesión, una cirugía, una infección no detectada o un coágulo en la pierna, que debe ser revisado. Pero, en ocasiones, se trata de cansancio, exceso de actividad, sobrepeso, uso de algunas medicinas, entre otros. Y en esos casos, se puede recurrir a algunos métodos naturales para ayudar a que ese líquido acumulado se elimine.

Por qué sí funciona

♦ Las hojas de col ayudan a absorber el exceso de líquido de la zona afectada, disminuyendo la inflamación. Un estudio realizado entre varios centros de investigación coreanos en 2014 demostró que el compuesto Berteroin (5-methylthiopentyl isothiocyanate), presente en vegetales como col regular, col china, rucola y aceite de mostaza, entre otros, tiene potentes propiedades antiinflamatorias.

Contribuye a cualquier tratamiento natural bebiendo mucho líquido, especialmente agua pura, y manteniendo los pies elevados, al menos cada cierto tiempo.

Ver el remedio en la página 174

Fresas y bicarbonato

Según la Academia Americana de Odontología Cos-
mética, en Estados Unidos más del 92% de los adultos
cree que contar con una sonrisa blanca y llamativa es
un recurso importante a nivel profesional y personal.

• Blanquear los dientes

Pero solo la mitad de la población cree que cumple con este requisito. Y en eso, el
color amarillento o manchado de los dientes tiene mucho que ver.

Lamentablemente, la superficie de los dientes es porosa y absorbe muchas de las
sustancias que ingresan por nuestra boca: café, té, frutas, colorantes, vino, cigarrillo,
etcétera. Así como también la edad, malos hábitos de higiene y medicamentos, entre
otros, pueden ayudar a mancharlos y quitarles el brillo natural.

Es importante tener en cuenta que el ácido cítrico no debe ser utilizado en exceso,
ya que reduce la dureza de los dientes debido a su efecto erosivo.

Por qué sí funciona

♦ En la reunión anual de la Asociación
Americana para la Investigación Dental
realizada en Tampa, Florida, en el 2012,
se presentó la opción natural para
blanqueamiento de dientes basada
en la mezcla de fresas y bicarbonato.
De acuerdo con algunos expertos,
el ácido cítrico y el ácido málico que
contienen las fresas ayudan a eliminar
las manchas de café, té, cigarrillo y vino
tinto que se adhieren al esmalte de los
dientes, ya que las disuelven. Además,
el bicarbonato funciona como un
abrasivo que ayuda a pulir la superficie
del diente. De hecho, es un ingrediente
activo en muchas pastas dentales.

Ver el remedio en la página
175

Hisopo o cotoneta

En la antigua Roma, tener hipo era una señal inequívoca de un castigo de Júpiter, mientras que para los nobles ingleses de la Edad Media, si una persona sufría de hipo era calificada de inmediato como mentirosa.

• Detener el hipo

El nombre científico del hipo es singulto y proviene del latín *singultus*, que significa "jadeo" o "suspiro". Es una contracción repentina e incontrolable del diafragma y de los músculos del pecho. De inmediato se produce el cierre de una zona de las cuerdas vocales llamada glotis, lo que genera ese sonido que suena como ¡hip!

Por lo general, los episodios de hipo son esporádicos y no pasan de durar unos minutos. Pero existe un caso que ¡duró 68 años! Lo padeció un estadounidense entre 1922 y 1991, y terminó apenas un año antes de que él muriera.

ESTE ES EL REMEDIO:
Cosquillas en el paladar con algodón

1 hisopo de algodón (*cotton swab*) o una bola de algodón

Simplemente, abre la boca y pasa rozando el hisopo o la bola de algodón repetidamente por tu paladar para generar cosquillas en esa zona.

También se recomienda respirar en series de 15 o 10 repeticiones dentro de una bolsa de papel colocada alrededor de la nariz y la boca. Esto se debe a que los ejercicios de respiración consciente ayudan a aumentar la cantidad de dióxido de carbono en la sangre, restablecen el ritmo y ayudan a relajarse, recuperando la normalidad.

Por qué sí funciona

♦ No hay total certeza acerca del origen del hipo, pero una de las explicaciones más confiables es que se produce por la irritación del nervio vago, que va desde el cerebro hasta el abdomen. Este nervio modera a su vez al nervio frénico, el cual activa el diafragma, que es un músculo ubicado debajo de los pulmones y que, al contraerse, controla la respiración de manera automática y rítmica. Cuando esa contracción rítmica involuntaria se altera, se produce el hipo.

♦ Al hacer cosquillas en el área del paladar con un hisopo o con una bola de algodón, se activa el nervio vago, relajando el diafragma, que suele retomar de inmediato su ritmo natural.

Lengua

Seguramente te ha pasado en más de una ocasión, cada vez que comes helado, un batido con mucho hielo picado, una bebida extremadamente fría o una margarita congelada... Y es ese súbito dolor de cabeza que parece partirla, producto del frío. Es un mal

• Cerebro congelado (esfenopalatino ganglioneuralgia o *brain freeze*)

universal y tan común que, en 1988, la Sociedad Internacional del Dolor de Cabeza (International Headache Society) lo reconoció, denominándolo cefalea por estímulo frío.

Se debe a que, al pasar el líquido frío por el paladar y luego por la faringe, la sangre se enfría y los vasos se abren y se cierran, haciendo que la sangre fluya rápidamente, generando el dolor. Apenas los vasos sanguíneos retoman la normalidad se quita ese malestar. Pero eso demora unos minutos.

ESTE ES EL REMEDIO:
Usa tu lengua

Apenas sientas algo tan helado que amenaza con congelar tu cerebro, pon tu lengua en el paladar superior, o techo hueco de tu boca.

Por qué sí funciona

♦ En 2012, el doctor Jorge Serrador, instructor en neurología del Brigham and Women's Hospital e investigador de la Universidad de Harvard, decidió estudiar por qué se produce este fenómeno. En su experimento con 13 personas descubrió que la sensación fría aumenta la rapidez y fuerza del flujo sanguíneo al cerebro a través de la dilatación de la arteria cerebral anterior, activando el dolor mediante el nervio trigeminal, que es el que envía las señales de dolor a la parte frontal de la cabeza. En otras palabras, apenas

detecta el frío, nuestro organismo responde enviando más sangre caliente al cerebro. Ese cambio de flujo sanguíneo genera el dolor. Frente a eso, el calor de la lengua calma los nervios y reduce el dolor más rápidamente.

♦ Un investigador del Centro Médico Olímpico del Reino Unido aseguró, en una carta al editor de la *British Medical Journal*, en 1997, que los surfistas también experimentan este tipo de dolor cuando se sumergen en una ola a punto de romperse, así como los patinadores de hielo al inhalar aire frío.

Miel, aceite de oliva y cera de abejas

Se dice que unos labios hermosos pueden doblegar la voluntad de cualquiera. No en vano muchas de las famosas más envidiadas por millones deben su fama a unos la-

- Labios partidos, irritados, secos

bios impactantes o, al menos, saludables. Pero en el mundo real eso parece no ser tan fácil, pues a pesar de la infinidad de productos disponibles, los labios resecos, rotos, enrojecidos, quemados o escamosos son algo normal.

Nuestros labios están cubiertos por distintas capas. Sin embargo, el aire seco, el frío, el aire acondicionado, los productos químicos de algunos labiales y pastas dentales, e incluso la propia acidez de la saliva van eliminándolas, dejándolos desprotegidos y, por lo tanto, frágiles.

La manera de cuidar de esta parte vital para nuestro buen funcionamiento es curándolos y protegiéndolos para evitar que vuelvan a dañarse.

Evita morderte los labios o mojarlos con saliva si los sientes resecos. No te quites los pedacitos de piel que comienzan a desprenderse: usa alguna mascarilla y humecta los labios hasta que los pedacitos se desprendan solos. Mantén siempre un bálsamo natural en tu bolso o en el automóvil para humectar los labios constantemente, especialmente si están deteriorados.

Por qué sí funciona

- ◆ Infinidad de estudios confirman las propiedades antibacteriales y antioxidantes de la miel, que ayudan a reparar y proteger los finos tejidos de los labios. Lo mismo ocurre con la cera de abejas, con propiedades antioxidantes, curativas y humectantes.
- ◆ El aceite de oliva contiene tres antioxidantes principales: vitamina E, polifenoles y fitoesteroles. Estos protegen la piel del envejecimiento prematuro. La vitamina E ayuda a restaurar la suavidad de la piel y protege contra los rayos ultravioleta. Contiene también hidroxitirosol, un compuesto bastante escaso en otros productos, que previene el daño de los radicales libres y restaura. Este compuesto fue ampliamente investigado en Italia en 2005.

Ver el remedio en la página 175

Pelota de tenis

Más de algún amigo o paciente en la consulta, especialmente mujeres, me han contado, medio en broma, medio en serio, que están a punto de divorciarse por culpa de los ronquidos de su pareja.

• Evitar los ronquidos

El ronquido se produce cuando el tejido de la parte superior de la garganta se relaja al dormir y el viento que entra al respirar produce una vibración sonora. Ese ruido llega a ser tan molesto que se convierte en uno de los principales trastornos del sueño.

De acuerdo con datos recientes publicados en la revista *Prevention*, se estima que en Estados Unidos unos 90 millones de adultos ven afectados sus hábitos de vida y sus relaciones por este problema. Dormir mal por el ronquido ajeno causa cansancio, mal humor, falta de productividad y concentración y, con esto, mayor probabilidad de accidentes, entre una larga lista de problemas.

Si roncas, mantén un peso adecuado. La relación de libras extra y ronquidos es proporcional. Apenas un poco de sobrepeso suele incrementar los ronquidos, ya que la grasa acumulada en la zona de la garganta aumenta, obstruyendo el paso del aire.

ESTE ES EL REMEDIO:
"Molestador" nocturno automático

1 pelota de tenis	1 camiseta de pijama	Hilo de coser
1 trozo de tela	1 aguja	

Envuelve la pelota en un trozo de tela, como si fuera un bolsillo o bolso pequeño. Fija este bolso con la pelota a la parte de atrás de la camiseta, por dentro o por fuera, a la altura de la espalda, y cósela. Si no tienes una pelota de tenis, puedes usar algo similar, no demasiado blando, pues la idea es que te incomode.

Por qué sí funciona

♦ La mayor parte de los ronquidos ocurren cuando dormimos de espalda, ya que la posición impide que el aire fluya naturalmente. De acuerdo con expertos del sueño, este sencillo y económico truco hace que la posición de espalda sea incómoda. De esa manera te obliga a acomodarte de lado sin necesidad de despertarte o de que alguien te mueva.

♦ Otra manera de ayudarse es manteniendo el torso más elevado al dormir, lo cual puedes lograr con una almohada extra.

Sopa de pollo

Mi abuela y mi madre pertenecen al club universal de "mujeres sabias" que entienden que una sopa de pollo bien calientita, hecha en casa, es capaz de quitar ¡hasta el mal de amor! No hay lugar en el mundo donde las matriarcas no conozcan este secreto milenario que parece curarlo todo, mientras acaricia nuestra alma, dejándonos una sensación de calma y de que "mañana todo estará bien".

• Combatir gripes y resfrío
• Levantar el ánimo
• Despejar las vías respiratorias

Los registros indican que entre los pioneros en mezclar pollo y agua se encuentran los griegos. Se cuenta que el filósofo y médico judío Moisés Maimónides ya conocía las propiedades "terapéuticas" de la sopa en pleno Medievo. En sus escritos llamados *Sobre la causa de los síntomas*, recomendaba el caldo de gallina y otras aves para distintos propósitos, como curar la lepra y el asma, entre otros.

Los chinos han consumido la sopa de pollo por siglos y siglos con un toque de jengibre, mientras que en México le dan un saborcito picante, como puede esperarse por las decenas de variedades de chile con que cuenta su cocina.

Por qué sí funciona

♦ Un estudio realizado por el Centro Médico de la Universidad de Nebraska confirmó que ayuda al organismo a sentirse mejor frente a los síntomas de resfrío o gripe. Los investigadores descubrieron que los aminoácidos que se producen al preparar el caldo de pollo reducen la inflamación en el sistema respiratorio, mejoran la digestión, reducen la congestión y lubrican la garganta, aliviando la irritación. Además, contiene compuestos químicos semejantes a los antigripales, que ayudan a sanar más rápidamente.

♦ Puede apoyar el sistema inmunológico y curar trastornos como las alergias, el asma y la artritis.

♦ El vapor de la sopa de pollo caliente mejora la manera en que algunos filamentos ubicados en el interior de la nariz protegen del ingreso de bacterias y virus y acelera el movimiento de la mucosa nasal, dilatando los vasos sanguíneos y aumentando el flujo sanguíneo. Esto permite expulsar mucosidades y aliviar la congestión.

Consejos y datos

✔ Los efectos de la sopa de pollo se dan cuando se cocina pollo de verdad y no al utilizar saborizantes o caldos concentrados, como los que vienen en la mayoría de las sopas previamente preparadas o envasadas. Ese caldo es una concentración de sodio y una sustancia llamada glutamato monosódico (MSG), que tiene el sabor, pero es una neurotoxina.

Ver el remedio en la página 175

Té negro

Conozco personas que afirman que "el olor a queso" de sus pies les ha hecho pasar más de un momento embarazoso, así como otras que han estado a punto de dejar a sus parejas por culpa de este problema.

• Mal olor en los pies (bromhidrosis)

La bromhidrosis o mal olor en los pies es un problema más frecuente de lo que quisiéramos. Se estima que cerca del 15% de la población la padece al menos temporalmente. Nuestros pies, especialmente en la planta, tienen una gran cantidad de glándulas sudoríparas que transpiran naturalmente y que aumentan su actividad por el calor ambiental, el material con que son fabricadas las medias y zapatos que usamos, estrés, alimentación, medicamentos, cambios hormonales, etcétera. Esa humedad excesiva provoca que se generen microorganismos como hongos y una bacteria conocida como *Kytococcus sedentarius*. Al descomponerse estos hongos y bacterias, empiezan a generar ácidos orgánicos y sustancias como metilmercaptano, que son las que huelen fatal.

Lavar los pies en té negro, puede aliviar el mal olor. Si esta molestia persiste y se vuelve crónico, puede que se deba a alguna alteración a causa de algún medicamento, o sea, un síntoma de otro problema. Visita a tu dermatólogo o a tu médico general para una evaluación más completa.

Por qué sí funciona

♦ El té negro es rico en unas sustancias llamadas taninos, que le dan ese saborcito amargo y la capacidad de ser astringente, es decir, de secar. Estas propiedades, a su vez, son las que combaten el mal olor, ya que alteraran el pH de la piel de los pies. Se ha probado que los astringentes pueden contraer los tejidos del cuerpo, incluyendo las glándulas sudoríparas, que, como ya sabes, son las que los hacen sudar.

Consejos y datos

✔ Utiliza un buen calzado y medias de algodón, ventila los pies y sécalos bien después del baño.

✔ Evita caminar descalzo en zonas húmedas, especialmente duchas de hoteles, piscinas y gimnasios.

Ver el remedio en la página · 176

Uvas

Hoy más que nunca, todos parecemos encontrarnos en una lucha contra el reloj, tratando de que nada en nosotros delate el número de años que lleva nuestra cédula de identidad. Es un mal de los tiempos. Lamentablemente, por más *millennial* que tratemos de vernos, vestirnos, peinarnos,

• Nutrir, humectar y rehidratar la piel
• Mejorar su textura
• Combatir signos de envejecimiento (manchas, líneas, etcétera)

etcétera, la piel siempre nos delata y revela esa edad que queremos esconder.

Es cierto que hay infinidad de productos, tratamientos, inyecciones, rellenos... ¡Lo que quieras! (seguramente lo sabes mejor que yo). Todos prometen batallar contra las arrugas, las manchas, la decoloración de la piel, y algunos lo logran, pero tienen su "letra chica" o efectos secundarios.

Muchos elementos químicos nos pueden causar reacciones alérgicas o tener riesgos mayores para nuestra salud. Por eso, en general, soy partidario de volver al estilo de cuidado y belleza de nuestras abuelas, buscar en la naturaleza aquellas fórmulas sencillas que nos ayuden.

Por qué sí funciona

♦ Las uvas contienen polifenoles, potentes antioxidantes. Las oscuras contienen, además, resveratrol, una sustancia altamente estudiada, ya que activa la enzima sirtuina, que retrasa el envejecimiento de la piel y aumenta la vitalidad celular de los tejidos. Las semillas tienen vitaminas C, D y E, betacarotenos, ácido linoleico y ácidos grasos omega 3 y 6, que regeneran, aportan elasticidad y suavizan la piel.

Ver el remedio en la página 176

Vinagre de Marsella

Cuenta la leyenda que, en plena Edad Media, cuando Europa sucumbía al embate de la peste bubónica provocada por las pulgas de las ratas, hubo un grupo de hombres en Marsella, Francia, que logró salvarse gracias a una mezcla secreta. Algunas versiones dicen que una banda de cuatro ladrones desnudaba y robaba los cuerpos de las víctimas de la peste sin infectarse, gracias a un compuesto de hierbas que usaban. Cuando la policía los capturó, negociaron la libertad a cambio de la fórmula, que llevaba, entre otras cosas: vinagre blanco, ajenjo, salvia, clavo de olor, tomillo y romero. Por eso también conocido como vinagre de los cuatro ladrones y remedio de Marsella.

- Combatir virus, hongos y bacterias
- Apoyar el sistema inmune
- Prevenir y curar infecciones de la piel
- Repeler insectos y parásitos (piojos, liendres, pulgas, etcétera)

Lo puedes usar diariamente en un proceso de recuperación tras una gripe o un resfrío y, como repelente tópico, antes de una actividad al aire libre. También lo puedes usar para prevenir un contagio o, si ya has contraído una dolencia, para recuperarte, agregando una taza de vinagre al baño de tina, o como *spray*, para usarlo en las habitaciones, la ropa de cama, etcétera.

Por qué sí funciona

♦ Todas las hierbas y especias usadas en esta mezcla están validadas científicamente por sus propiedades antibacteriales, en contra de hongos y virus. Algunos, como el vinagre, se usan desde la época de Hipócrates, inhibe el crecimiento de bacterias como *E. coli*, por ejemplo.

♦ El poder antimicrobiano del clavo puede combatir la *E. coli*, la *Staphylococcus aureus*, que causa el acné, y la *Pseudomonas aeruginosa*, que causa neumonía.

♦ El tomillo puede acabar con diferentes bacterias, gérmenes y hongos, entre ellas *Staphylococcus aureus*, *Bacillus subtilis*, *E. coli* y *Shigella sonnei*, entre otros.

♦ El aceite esencial de salvia tiene propiedades carminativas, antiespasmódicas, antisépticas y astringentes.

Ver el remedio en la página 176

Remedios para preparar en casa

Aceite de ricino

Laxante de ricino para limpiar el organismo

1   cucharada de aceite de ricino
1   taza de agua
1   cucharada de jugo de limón

Mezcla muy bien los ingredientes y bébelo con el estómago vacío. Espera al menos unas tres o cuatro horas antes de comer. De preferencia, que esa primera comida sea jugo de frutas natural, sopas o cremas de vegetales. Luego comienza a comer de manera normal.

Mascarilla de aceite de ricino

1½ cucharadas de aceite de ricino
1   yema de huevo

Mezcla una cucharada de aceite de ricino con una yema de huevo hasta que quede una pasta homogénea.

Aplícala en tu rostro y déjala reposar durante algunos minutos. Retírala con agua tibia. Seca tu rostro con una toalla de papel. Luego, aplica el resto del aceite de ricino puro sobre la piel y déjalo toda la noche.

Máscara de aceite de ricino para las pestañas

1   cucharadita de aceite de ricino
⅓   de cucharadita de aceite de almendra
⅓   de cucharadita de gel de aloe vera natural

Mezcla muy bien los ingredientes y pon la mezcla en un recipiente de máscara de pestañas que esté completamente limpio. Aplica la mezcla en las pestañas por la noche, después de quitarte el maquillaje, utilizando el cepillo de la máscara o rímel para aplicarlo.

Ajo

Jugo de ajo y manzana

2   dientes de ajo
1   manzana cortada en trozos
    Jugo de un limón
1   trocito de jengibre fresco
⅓   de taza de menta fresca
10 onzas de agua
    Stevia al gusto

Licúa los ingredientes hasta que queden bien disueltos. Bébelo de inmediato, en ayunas. La manzana, el limón, la menta y el jengibre ayudan a atenuar y disipar el intenso olor del ajo.

Jugo verde "al ajillo"

2   dientes de ajo pelados
1   taza de espinaca
½   taza de perejil fresco
½   pepino
    Jugo de un limón
1   trocito de jengibre fresco
10 onzas de agua

Procesa todos los ingredientes y bébelo de inmediato. Si gustas, agrégale un par de cubos de hielo.

La clorofila de las espinacas y el perejil ayudan a disminuir un poco el olor intenso del ajo.

Pasta de ajo

4   dientes de ajo pelados y picados
    Aceite de oliva
1   cucharada de jugo de limón
    Sal y pimienta

Tritura el ajo en un procesador, mortero o sobre la tabla de picar. Ponlo en un recipiente y añade lentamente el aceite. Mezcla hasta obtener una pasta de consistencia espesa. Agrégale el jugo de limón, la sal y la pimienta. Disfrútala untando la pasta en pan, papas, apio, zanahoria o lo que desees.

Si tienes una reunión o una cena especial, prepárala el día anterior para que su sabor decante y se sienta más intenso.

Crema de ajo

3   dientes de ajo medianos
1   taza de yogur griego, sin sabor
¼   de taza de perejil fresco picado
    finamente

Pon todos los ingredientes en un procesador de alimentos y mezcla hasta que queden bien incorporados. Acompaña tus legumbres, vegetales al vapor, carnes o papas untados con esta deliciosa crema.

Albahaca

Pesto hecho en casa

1   taza de albahaca fresca
2   dientes de ajo
1   cucharada de piñones (*pine nuts*)
1   cucharada de nueces de la India
    (*cashews*)
1 o 2 cucharadas de aceite de oliva

Pon los ingredientes en un procesador y mézclalos hasta obtener una crema suave. Mezcla bien y úsala para acompañar tus platillos favoritos. Pon el resto en un recipiente de vidrio y guárdalo en la nevera.

Té de albahaca

4   hojas de albahaca fresca
1   taza de agua recién hervida
    Stevia al gusto

Pon las hojas en el agua y deja reposar por 10 minutos. Disfrútalo.

Batido verde con albahaca

½   taza de albahaca fresca
1   manzana verde cortada en trocitos
½   pepino cortado en trocitos
8   onzas de agua fría
    Stevia, si lo deseas

Pon todos los ingredientes en una licuadora y procésalos. Bébelo de inmediato.

Alcachofa

Alcachofas hervidas

2   alcachofas frescas cocidas al vapor
    Sal
1   cucharadita de jugo de limón
2   cucharadas de aceite de oliva

Prepara una vinagreta con limón, aceite y sal. Mezcla muy bien. Quítale las hojas y remueve con una cuchara cada pulpa de estas adherida al corazón de la alcachofa. Desprende los pelillos del corazón. Pon toda la pulpa obtenida en la mezcla. Disfrútala sola o como acompañante.

Té de hojas de alcachofa

3   hojas de alcachofa
2   tazas de agua

Pon a hervir el agua con las hojas de alcachofa. Deja que hiervan por unos cinco minutos. Apaga y deja reposar por 10 minutos. Endulza al gusto y bébela después de comer.

También puedes usar té de alcachofas en bolsita. En ese caso, solo agrega agua hirviendo y deja reposar unos minutos.

Alcachofas en salsa de vino blanco con queso gratinado

2   alcachofas hervidas o al vapor
½   cebolla cortada en cuadritos
2   dientes de ajo picados finamente
2   cucharadas de albahaca picada
    finamente
½   taza de vino blanco
    Sal
    Pimienta
    Aceite de oliva
1   lámina de queso mozzarella (o del
    queso de tu preferencia)

Pon en una sartén el aceite, la cebolla, el ajo, la albahaca, la sal y la pimienta. Sofríe por unos minutos hasta que se doren levemente. Agrega el vino y deja en el fuego la mezcla por un par de minutos hasta que se evapore el alcohol. No cocines en exceso la cebolla. Luego apaga. Precalienta el horno a temperatura media. Pon las alcachofas en un recipiente que puedas llevar al horno. Agrega por encima la mezcla de cebolla y ajo. Coloca el queso sobre las alcachofas. Ponlas al horno por unos 10 a 15 minutos (hasta que veas que el queso se derrita y dore levemente). Disfrútalas solas o como acompañamiento.

Alfalfa

Bebida fría de alfalfa

⅓   de taza de alfalfa fresca (ya lavada)
    o seca
1   kiwi
    Jugo de un limón
1   rodaja de limón, naranja o
    mandarina
8   onzas de agua fría
    Hielo (opcional)
1   cucharadita de miel, agave u otro
    endulzante (opcional)

Pon los ingredientes (excepto la rodaja de limón o cítrico) en la licuadora. Procésalos y sírvelos. Agrega más hielo, si gustas, y la rodaja de limón, naranja o mandarina.

Infusión de alfalfa y menta

⅓ de taza de alfalfa fresca o seca
2 o 3 hojitas frescas o una cucharadita de menta seca
1½ tazas de agua caliente

Pon las hierbas en una taza y agrega el agua caliente. Deja reposar por unos cinco minutos. Cuélala y bébela.

Jugo verde con alfalfa

1 taza de alfalfa
½ taza de perejil
½ pepino
½ manzana verde
 Jugo de un limón
8 onzas de agua

Licúa todos los ingredientes y listo.

Aloe vera o sábila

Licuado de gel de aloe vera para problemas estomacales y mejorar la digestión

1 penca de aloe vera
1 cucharada de miel (si no tienes diabetes o prediabetes)
1 limón (jugo)
8 onzas de agua

Quita con una cuchara el gel del interior y ponlo en una licuadora. Agrega el agua, la miel y el jugo de un limón. Licúa muy bien y, cuando esté listo, bébelo.

Tintura de gel de aloe vera para distintos usos

Sirve para desinfectar heridas, como enjuague bucal, para masajes en zonas del cuerpo con dolor, para usarse en compresas o para agregarla a un baño de tina, entre otros usos externos.

1 penca de aloe vera
2 onzas de alcohol medicinal de 96º
1½ onzas de agua destilada

Utensilios
1 frasco de vidrio limpio y con tapa hermética
1 colador de tela o un trozo de tela limpia
1 frasco de vidrio opaco o pintado (que no le entre luz externa)

Con una cuchara, quita el gel del interior y ponlo en una licuadora. Licúalo muy bien. Agrega el alcohol y el agua destilada. Vuelve a licuar muy bien hasta que quede homogéneo. Pon la mezcla en el frasco y déjala reposar por al menos 20 días en un lugar fresco (en la alacena de la cocina, por ejemplo). Agita la mezcla de vez en cuando. Idealmente, una vez al día. Pasado el tiempo de reposo, filtra la mezcla a través de un colador de tela o un trozo de tela limpio. Ponla en el frasco opaco o pintado para que no se oxide tan rápidamente. Guárdala en la nevera.

Para usarla en un baño de tina, pon la penca en el agua y deja reposar por 10 minutos. Disfrútalo.

Cataplasma de gel de aloe vera

1 penca de aloe vera

Quita con una cuchara el gel del interior y ponlo en un recipiente. Trata de dejar los trozos enteros para que sea fácil aplicarlos sobre la piel.

Pon una capa sobre la herida, picadura o quemadura. Guarda el resto en la nevera y úsalo dos o tres veces al día. Puede durar entre siete y diez días bien cerrado.

Mascarilla de gel de aloe, pepino y limón para mejorar textura de la piel

1 penca de aloe vera
½ pepino pelado y cortado en cubos
1 limón (jugo)

Quita con una cuchara el gel del interior y ponlo en una licuadora. Agrega el pepino y el jugo de limón. Licúa muy bien. Aplica la mezcla en el rostro, el cuello y el escote. Déjalo que actúe por unos 30 minutos. Retírala enjuagándote con agua tibia.

También puedes hacer la mascarilla usando solo aloe vera y pepino, y dejarla sobre el rostro como si fuera crema, sin enjuagar. La puedes dejar durante el día, si estás en tu casa, o durante la noche, mientras duermes.

Arándanos agrios

Jugo de arándanos

4 tazas de agua
1 taza de arándanos agrios frescos
1 rodaja de naranja

Pon a hervir los arándanos en el agua. Déjalos hervir por 20 minutos. Luego, apaga y deja que repose al menos una hora. Puedes ponerlo en la nevera si te gusta frío o beberlo a temperatura ambiente, o caliente. Agrega la rodaja de naranja y bébelo a lo largo del día.

Salsa de arándanos agrios

3 tazas de arándanos agrios
3 tazas de agua
1 taza de jugo de naranja fresco
1 cucharada de ralladura de cáscara de naranja
1 raja de canela
1 taza de azúcar morena o stevia, al gusto

Pon en una olla el jugo de naranja y el azúcar o stevia. Prende el fuego y revuelve hasta disolver el azúcar. Agrega los arándanos, la canela y el agua. Deja que hiervan hasta que los arándanos se abran (aproximadamente 10 minutos). Apaga el fuego y agrega la cucharada de cáscara de naranja rallada. Deja reposar.

Si te gusta la salsa con trocitos, déjala como está. Pero si la prefieres cremosa, pon todo en la licuadora y ya está. Guárdala en la nevera hasta que la uses para acompañar carnes, ensaladas, papas, etcétera.

Avena

Porridge

1 taza de leche (animal o vegetal)
2 cucharadas de avena entera
1 taza de agua
   Azúcar morena o stevia (opcional)
1 cucharada de uvas pasas
½ cucharadita de canela molida
½ banana
½ manzana en cuadritos

Mezcla y cocina la avena con el agua y la leche. Agrégale la canela y el azúcar. Cuando esté lista, apaga y sírvela. Agrega las pasas, la manzana y la banana.

Batido de avena

2 cucharadas de avena cruda
1 taza de agua
1 taza de leche de tu preferencia
   (de vaca, de almendra, de avena, de coco, de soya)
½ cucharadita de canela en polvo
2 cucharadas de dátiles sin semilla
   (o puedes usar uvas pasas)
   Stevia al gusto

Pon a remojar la avena en la taza de agua durante la noche anterior. Por la mañana, pon el contenido del agua y la avena remojada en una licuadora. Agrega la leche, la canela, los dátiles y la stevia (si te hace falta). Pon a licuar y disfruta.

Loción de avena para el baño

2 cucharadas de avena
1 taza de agua tibia
1 trozo de tela de algodón (o una media de algodón que no uses)

Pon la avena dentro de la tela y arma una bolsita, atándola con una liga. Si usas una media, pon la avena y luego anuda la media para que no se salga. Ponla a remojar en la taza de agua, al menos por un par de horas; se obtiene un mejor resultado si la dejas toda la noche o todo el día. Usa el agua gelatinosa que se forma como jabón para la cara y para el cuerpo. Puedes apretar un poco la bolsa para obtener más gelatina. Aplícala especialmente en las zonas donde tienes reseca la piel o alguna erupción.

Azafrán

Batido con azafrán

8 onzas de té de albahaca frío, preparado previamente
1 pera madura
2 cucharadas de avena cruda molida
¼ de cucharadita de azafrán (0.5 mg aproximadamente)
1 cucharada de miel o agave (opcional)

Licúa todo y disfrútalo.

Té de azafrán

¼ de cucharadita de azafrán (0.5 mg aproximadamente)

1 cucharada de miel o agave (opcional)
1 taza de agua recién hervida

Pon el azafrán y la miel en el agua. Revuelve y bébelo dos veces al día.

Aromaterapia de azafrán para combatir la ansiedad

1 incienso de azafrán o ¼ de cucharadita de azafrán

Enciende el incienso o bien pon el azafrán en un quemador de aceites esenciales, para perfumar el área donde estás.

Bicarbonato de sodio

Enjuague bucal de bicarbonato para combatir el mal aliento

¼ de taza de bicarbonato de sodio
¼ de cucharadita de sal de mar
2 gotas de extracto de menta
½ cucharadita de agua

Mezcla muy bien los ingredientes en una taza hasta obtener una pasta. Unta un cepillo de dientes de cerdas muy suaves con la mezcla o bien utiliza tu dedo índice. Pasa suavemente el cepillo o el dedo por tus dientes, especialmente por las encías, tanto en la parte interna como la externa. Luego pásalo por la lengua. Escupe cuando lo necesites. Deja actuar la mezcla por unos 10 minutos y luego enjuaga con agua tibia.

Bebida de bicarbonato, agua y limón para el dolor de estómago y gastritis

1 litro de agua
1 cucharadita de bicarbonato
Jugo de ½ limón

Mezcla los ingredientes y bébelo durante el día.

Compresas de bicarbonato para picaduras de insectos

1 cucharada de bicarbonato
½ taza de agua tibia
Toalla pequeña de algodón o un trozo de algodón

Mezcla bien el agua y el bicarbonato. Humedece la toalla o el algodón con la mezcla y ponla sobre la piel irritada. Repite cuantas veces sea necesario hasta que sientas alivio.

Exfoliante de bicarbonato para la piel

1 cucharada de bicarbonato de sodio
1 cucharada de aceite de coco

Mezcla bien los ingredientes. Aplica la mezcla sobre el rostro con movimientos circulares y suaves. Ponla especialmente en zonas como la nariz, la barbilla y la frente, o donde veas mayor porosidad de la piel o se acumule más grasa. Enjuaga con agua tibia y seca con una toalla de papel desechable.

Cacao

Leche con cacao crudo

- 2 cucharaditas de cacao crudo en polvo
- 2 cucharadas de agua caliente
- 1 taza de leche de tu preferencia (de vaca, de almendra, de soya, de coco, etcétera)
- ½ cucharadita de esencia de vainilla natural o en vainas
  Stevia al gusto

Disuelve el chocolate en una o dos cucharadas de agua caliente. Calienta la leche. Mezcla el cacao disuelto con la leche. Agrega la vainilla y stevia. Disfrútala.

Batido de cacao

- 2 cucharaditas de cacao crudo en polvo
- 8 onzas de leche de coco o almendra bien fría
- ½ cucharadita de canela en polvo
  Stevia al gusto

Mezcla todos los ingredientes en la licuadora y procésalos. Disfrútalo de inmediato.

Brownie de cacao crudo

- ½ taza de cacao crudo en polvo
- 2 cucharadas de virutas de cacao (*cacao nibs*)
- 1 taza de almendras o nueces (pueden ser mezcladas)
- 1 taza de dátiles sin semilla, picados
- 2 o 3 cucharadas de miel o agave

Mezcla en un procesador las almendras o nueces hasta que queden en trocitos pequeños. Si te gusta sentirlas con más textura, déjalas en trozos más grandes. Colócalas en un recipiente. Pon los dátiles en el procesador junto al cacao. Procésalos hasta que se forme una pasta. Si está muy dura, agrégale la miel o el agave, de a poco, para que vaya incorporándose y ayude a mezclar. Pon la mezcla en el recipiente junto a las nueces y almendras. Mezcla y dale la forma en un molde que puedas poner en la nevera. Espolvoréalo con las virutas de cacao. Ponlo en la nevera por un par de horas y luego disfrútalo.

Caléndula

Compresa de caléndula

- 2 cucharadas de caléndula deshidratada
- 1½ tazas de agua caliente

Remoja las hojas en el agua hasta que esta se enfríe. Cuélala y pon las hojas directamente sobre la zona afectada. Envuélvela con gasa o tela de algodón suave. No botes el agua, ya que puedes usarla para mojar la tela y mantenerla húmeda sobre la piel, o para beberla.

Infusión de caléndula

- 1 cucharadita de caléndula deshidratada (o un sobre)
- 1½ tazas de agua caliente

Remoja las flores deshidratadas en el agua durante 10 minutos. Cuélalas (no las botes, úsalas para el remedio de compresa) y endulza la infusión si deseas. Bébela. (También puedes usar esa infusión para la piel inflamada: rostro, extremidades, hemorroides, etcétera.)

Aceite concentrado de caléndula

1 taza de caléndula deshidratada
2 tazas de aceite de oliva extravirgen

Pon la caléndula en un frasco o una botella y agrega el aceite. El aceite debe cubrir todas las hojas. Tapa bien el frasco o la botella y déjala macerar por al menos un mes en un lugar oscuro y fresco (dentro de alguna gaveta de la cocina). Revisa a diario y muévela para que se impregnen completamente. Si las hojas absorben demasiado aceite, agrega un poco más de este.

Cuela el aceite para que te sea más fácil usarlo (o bien deja la mezcla). De preferencia, úsalo dentro de los siguientes 12 meses sobre la piel.

Canela

Bebida caliente de canela

1½ tazas de agua
1 varita de canela
½ cucharadita de jengibre fresco rallado (o ⅓ de polvo)
½ cucharadita de cúrcuma rallada (o ⅓ en polvo)
Cáscara de naranja
1 cucharada de jugo de limón
Miel o stevia

Pon a hervir el agua con la canela por unos cinco minutos. Apaga y agrega la cúrcuma, la cáscara de naranja y el jengibre. Deja que se enfríe hasta que esté tibia. Agrega el limón y la miel o stevia al gusto. Revuelve bien. Disfrútala de inmediato.

Café con canela

1 taza de leche de tu preferencia (de vaca, de soya, de almendra, de coco, etcétera)
Café colado
½ cucharadita de canela en polvo
1 pizca de nuez moscada en polvo
Stevia al gusto

Mezcla en la licuadora la leche, el café, la canela, la nuez moscada y la stevia. Sirve y disfruta de inmediato.

Postre de chía y canela

8 onzas de leche de vaca, de almendra, de coco o de soya
½ taza de semillas de chía
1 cucharadita de canela en polvo
Stevia al gusto

Mezcla los ingredientes en un recipiente de vidrio. Ponlo en el congelador por al menos dos horas hasta que la chía se vuelva gelatinosa y se expanda. Luego sírvelo, espolvoreando un poco más de canela si gustas. Disfrútalo.

Cardamomo

Chai latte

8 onzas de leche vegetal
1 sobre de té negro
1 varita de canela
1 trocito de jengibre
1 clavo de olor molido
1 pizca de nuez moscada molida
1 vaina de cardamomo molida
   Stevia o agave

Pon a hervir la leche con las especias por cinco minutos. Apaga y agrégale la bolsa de té. Deja reposar por 10 minutos. Cuélalo. Endúlzalo y disfruta tu *chai latte*.

Semillas de cardamomo para el mal aliento

1 o 2 vainas de cardamomo

Mastica por unos minutos las semillas. Escupe de vez en cuando si te parece demasiado fuerte, aunque también, sin problema, puedes tragar el jugo que genera al mezclarse con la saliva.

Té de cardamomo

2 vainas de cardamomo
1½ tazas de agua
   Stevia al gusto

En una olla pequeña, pon a hervir el agua con las vainas de cardamomo por unos cinco minutos. Apaga y deja reposar 10 minutos. Endulza con stevia y disfruta tu té caliente o frío.

Batido de chocolate con cardamomo

8 onzas de leche de coco o almendra bien fría
½ banana
2 vainas de cardamomo
1 pizca de canela molida
1 cucharadita de cacao puro en polvo sin endulzante
   Stevia al gusto

En una licuadora pon la leche, la banana, la canela, el cacao y la stevia. Abre las vainas de cardamomo, quítales las semillas cuidadosamente y ponlas en la mezcla de ingredientes. Licúa todo y disfruta de inmediato.

Ensalada de tubérculos con cardamomo

1 papa pequeña hervida, sin piel, cortada en cuadritos
1 zanahoria ligeramente hervida, sin piel, cortada en cuadritos
½ remolacha ligeramente hervida, sin piel, cortada en cuadritos
½ cebolla ligeramente hervida, cortada en cuadritos
1 cucharada de perejil fresco picado
1 cucharada de albahaca fresca picada
   Sal
   Aceite de oliva
   Vinagre balsámico
3 vainas de cardamomo

Mezcla todos los ingredientes en una ensaladera, menos el cardamomo. Muele cuidadosamente las vainas de cardamomo en un mortero y agrégalas a la mezcla de ingredientes. Disfruta tu ensalada como acompañamiento de alguna carne o pescado.

Cebada

Infusión caliente de cebada para relajarse

1   taza de cebada
5   tazas de agua

Remoja la cebada por al menos un par de horas. Luego, hiérvela en una olla hasta que esté blanda. No dejes que baje el nivel de agua. No le agregues sal para que puedas usarla en platillos salados o dulces, según prefieras. Cuela la cebada, pero no botes el agua. Una hora antes de dormir, bebe una taza del agua en que se cocinó. Pon el resto del agua en un recipiente de vidrio en la nevera para beberla con miel o usarla de base para tus batidos. En tanto, usa la cebada cocida para preparar un *porridge*, en ensalada o para acompañar la carne.

Porridge de cebada para el desayuno

½   taza de cebada preparada como se hace con el arroz, pero sin sal
1   cucharada de almendras en lascas
1   cucharada de nueces
1   taza de bayas frescas mezcladas (fresas, frambuesas, moras y arándanos azules)
1   taza de leche descremada o leche vegetal
1   cucharada de miel o agave

Pon la cebada y la leche en un recipiente y mezcla bien. Agrégale las bayas, luego las almendras y las nueces. Mezcla. Termina agregándole la miel por encima, y a disfrutar.

Ensalada de cebada y vegetales

½   taza de cebada preparada como se hace con el arroz
½   taza de tomates cereza cortados por la mitad
1   taza de hojas de espinaca
⅓   de taza de zanahoria cruda rallada
⅓   de taza de pepino cortado en cuadritos
⅓   de taza de garbanzos cocidos
1   cucharada de semillas de girasol
Sal
Pimienta
Aceite de oliva
Vinagre balsámico

Mezcla todos los ingredientes en un recipiente. Sazónalos con aceite de oliva, vinagre balsámico, sal y pimienta al gusto. Disfrútala.

Cerezas

Jugo de cerezas para mejorar el ciclo de sueño

½   taza de cerezas sin semilla (regulares o cerezas agrias)
1   taza de agua

Licúa muy bien y bébelo.

Postre de cerezas para dormir mejor

½ taza de cerezas agrias

Cómelas después de cenar, o como colación, una hora antes de ir a dormir.

Ensalada para cenar y dormir como un bebé

½ taza de cerezas sin semilla
1½ tazas de lechuga
4 a 6 onzas de pechuga de pavo cocida
    o a la plancha
¼ de taza de semillas de calabaza
1 taza de vinagre balsámico dulce
    de cereza
    Sal rosada
    Aceite de oliva

Pon las cerezas al fuego en una sartén, con unas gotas de aceite. Dora levemente y agrega el vinagre balsámico. Deja un par de minutos, revolviendo constantemente. Apaga y quita del fuego. Deja enfriar. En un recipiente, pon la lechuga, el pavo cortado en cuadritos y las semillas de calabaza, sal, aceite y la salsa de cerezas. Disfrútala.

Citronela

Desodorante natural de citronela

10 cucharadas de aceite esencial
    de citronela
10 cucharadas de aceite de coco
    líquido
2 cucharaditas de bicarbonato

En un recipiente para mezclar, incorpora el bicarbonato con el aceite de coco hasta que se disuelva por completo. Agrégale el aceite de citronela. Mezcla bien. Guarda la mezcla en una botella de plástico limpia.

Para usarla, puedes aplicar unas gotas de la mezcla directamente sobre la piel utilizando una bolita de algodón.

Aceite de citronela para ayudar a la concentración

4 gotas de aceite de citronela

Pon las gotas en un pañuelo de tela y déjalo cerca, donde puedas olerlo.

Repelente para insectos de uso en la piel

20 gotas de aceite esencial de citronela
½ onza de crema hidratante neutra (20 cucharadas aproximadamente)

Mezcla la crema con el aceite esencial en una botella plástica limpia o en cualquier otro recipiente. Úsala sobre la piel antes de salir al aire libre.

Clavo de olor

Infusión de clavo de olor para tratar inflamación, flatulencia, dolor de estómago y náuseas

3 clavos de olor
1½ tazas de agua
    Miel o stevia al gusto

Pon a hervir el agua con los clavos en una olla pequeña. Hierve por cinco minutos. Apaga y deja reposar.

Endulza con miel o stevia. Disfrútalo.

Clavo de olor para el mal aliento

1 clavo de olor

Mastica el clavo de olor por unos minutos. Poco a poco irá soltando su aceite, combatiendo los gérmenes que causan el mal aliento.

Ungüento para el dolor de cabeza y jaqueca

3 clavos de olor
¼ de taza de agua
1 cucharadita de sal

Pon a hervir el agua con los clavos de olor por cinco minutos. Apaga y deja reposar. Toma una cucharada de agua y mézclala con la sal hasta formar una pasta. Aplícala alrededor de la frente y las sienes, masajeando suavemente (cuidado con los ojos). Déjala por 15 minutos. Luego, enjuaga con agua fría.

Crema para el dolor de muelas, dientes y encías

1 cucharada de aceite esencial de clavo de olor
1 cucharada de aceite de coco o de oliva

Mezcla bien ambos aceites en un recipiente de cristal limpio y luego pásalo por tus encías suavemente con una bolita de algodón o con tu dedo. Déjalo ahí por unos minutos. Escupe lo que te sobre. No es necesario enjuagar.

Loción limpiadora de la piel contra el acné

3 gotas de aceite de clavo de olor
1 cucharada de miel cruda de abeja

Mezcla muy bien el aceite y la miel. Aplícala sobre las zonas afectadas. Déjala actuar por 15 minutos. Enjuaga con agua tibia.

Cúrcuma

Infusión de cúrcuma

1 raíz pequeña de cúrcuma
¼ de cucharadita de pimienta negra (o tres semillas de canela negra)
½ cucharadita de canela en polvo (o una varita)
4 tazas de agua
Stevia al gusto

Pon a hervir en un recipiente el agua con todos los ingredientes. Deja hervir por dos minutos y luego apaga. Deja reposar por unos 10 minutos y luego comienza a beber la infusión.

Batido de cúrcuma

1 cucharadita de cúrcuma
¼ de cucharadita de canela
¼ de cucharadita de pimienta negra
1 taza de papaya picada

8 onzas de leche de coco o de almendra bien fría
Stevia al gusto

Licúa todos los ingredientes y bébelo de inmediato.

Batido verde antiinflamatorio

1 cucharadita de cúrcuma en polvo
½ cucharadita de jengibre en polvo
¼ de cucharadita de pimienta negra
Jugo de un limón
½ taza de pepino
½ taza de apio
8 onzas de agua

Licúa los ingredientes y bébelo de inmediato. Hazlo diariamente como merienda por, al menos, una semana, para ver resultados.

Crema de zanahoria y calabaza con cúrcuma

1 cucharada de cúrcuma en polvo
2 tazas de calabaza picada
1 diente de ajo
½ taza de cebolla picada
2 zanahorias limpias
4 tazas de agua
1 cucharada de semillas de calabaza horneadas
Sal
Pimienta negra
Aceite de oliva

Pon a cocinar la calabaza, la cebolla, la zanahoria y el ajo con el agua. Sazona con sal, pimienta negra y la cúrcuma.

Cuando los vegetales estén blandos, retíralos del fuego. Deja enfriar un poco y procésalos hasta que quede una crema suave. Sirve rociando con aceite de oliva y las semillas de calabaza.

Diente de león

Infusión de diente de león para desintoxicar el hígado, la vesícula y los riñones

30 g de raíz de diente de león (¼ de taza)
30 g de hojas de diente de león (¼ de taza)
4 tazas de agua

Pon a hervir la raíz y las hojas durante cinco minutos. Deja reposar unos 10 minutos. Cuélala y bebe una taza antes de cada comida, tres o cuatro tazas durante el día.

Té de diente de león

1 cucharadita de hojas, flores o raíz, o una bolsita de estos
1 taza de agua caliente

Deja reposar la hierba en el agua por unos cinco minutos. Cuélala, endúlzala si deseas y bébela.

Equinácea

Té de equinácea y propóleo para la gripe y el resfriado

1½ tazas de agua
½ cucharada de equinácea en polvo

1 cucharada de propóleo
½ cucharadita de miel

Hierve el agua con la equinácea por cinco minutos. Apaga y déjala reposar por unos minutos. Agrégale el propóleo y la miel. Bebe de inmediato. Toma tres o cuatro tazas al día.

Infusión de equinácea para fortalecer el organismo

1½ tazas de agua
½ cucharada de equinácea en polvo

Hierve el agua con la equinácea durante cinco minutos. Apágala y déjala reposar. Bébela por la mañana y la noche (una taza), durante al menos un mes.

Flor de Jamaica

Bebida fría

¼ de taza de flor de Jamaica
16 onzas de agua
4 rodajas de naranja o limón
1 varita de canela
Hielo
Stevia (opcional)

Pon a hervir la mitad del agua y la canela. Apaga, espera cinco minutos y agrega las flores de Jamaica. Deja reposar. Agrega el resto del agua y las rodajas de naranja o limón. Ponla en la nevera por al menos una hora. Disfrútala con hielo y unas gotas de stevia, si lo deseas.

Paletas heladas de flor de Jamaica

½ taza de flor de Jamaica
1 taza de jugo de naranja fresca, colada, sin pulpa
8 onzas de agua
Stevia líquida

Pon a hervir el agua. Quítala del fuego y déjala reposar por unos minutos. Agrégale las hojas de flor de Jamaica y déjalas reposar hasta que se enfríe. Luego, cuela la infusión. Agrégale el jugo de naranja y, si lo quieres más dulce, unas gotitas de stevia. Viértela en moldes plásticos de paleta helada o en recipientes pequeños, como vasos plásticos. Ponla en el congelador por un par de horas. Si utilizas vasos plásticos, ponlos en el congelador por 40 minutos y luego inserta un palito de madera para helado en el medio. Vuelve a congelar por un par de horas. Disfrútalas cuando quieras.

Bebida de flor de Jamaica con jengibre

¼ de taza de té de flor de Jamaica
16 onzas de agua
¼ de taza de jengibre fresco picado (o triturado)
1 varita pequeña de canela (o media cucharadita de canela en polvo)
4 clavos de olor

Pon a hervir el agua con la canela y los clavos de olor. Apaga el fuego y deja que la cocción repose unos minutos. Agrega el té de Jamaica, el jengibre y deja reposar por unos 15 minutos más. Antes de servirlo, cuélalo. Puedes disfrutarlo caliente, a temperatura ambiente o ponerlo en la nevera para beberlo bien frío. Agrega hielo y unas gotas de stevia, si lo prefieres.

Si tienes gripe o sientes algún malestar en la garganta, puedes agregarle una cucharadita de miel de abejas (si padeces de diabetes no uses miel).

Postre saludable de gelatina de flor de Jamaica

½ taza de flor de Jamaica
2 tazas de agua recién hervida
1 paquete de gelatina sin sabor
½ taza de arándanos azules
Stevia líquida

En un molde de vidrio resistente al calor y al frío, pon a remojar la flor de Jamaica con una taza de agua caliente durante 20 minutos. Cuela la infusión. Luego, disuelve la gelatina en otra taza de agua caliente. Agrégale la taza de infusión concentrada de té de Jamaica. Agrégale stevia al gusto. Añade los arándanos. Pon todo en el molde y déjalo en el refrigerador por una hora. Disfruta de tu gelatina.

Salsa o aderezo de flor de Jamaica

½ taza de flor de Jamaica
½ taza de agua recién hervida
2 cucharadas de vinagre balsámico
4 cucharadas de aceite de oliva
1 cucharada de miel (si no padeces de diabetes)
1 pizca de sal rosada
1 pizca de pimienta negra

Pon a remojar durante una noche la flor de Jamaica en el agua hervida. Al día siguiente, cuela la mezcla de infusión muy concentrada. Ponla en un frasco de vidrio y agrégale el resto de los ingredientes. Mezcla muy bien antes de usar sobre tu ensalada favorita.

Frambuesas

Ensalada con frambuesas

1 taza de rúcula
4 tomates cereza cortados en gajos
½ taza de frambuesas frescas
½ pepino cortado en cuadritos
1 cucharada de almendras en lascas
Sal
Aceite de oliva
Vinagre balsámico

Mezcla la rúcula, el pepino y los tomates en un recipiente. Alíñalos con sal, vinagre y aceite de oliva. Revuelve bien. Agrega las frambuesas y las almendras al final. Disfrútala.

Batido multivitamínico con frambuesas

8 onzas de agua fría
1 taza de frambuesas frescas o congeladas
1 pera
½ pepino verde

Mezcla todos los ingredientes en una licuadora y disfrútalo de inmediato.

Yogur, granola y frambuesas

½ taza de frambuesas frescas
1 taza de yogur
⅓ de taza de granola
1 cucharada de semillas de chía
1 cucharadita de miel, si gustas

Pon el yogur en un recipiente, agrega la granola, las frambuesas y encima la chía. Termina rociando la miel por encima y disfrútalo.

Ginseng

Té de ginseng

1 raíz de ginseng rojo (o 4 g de ginseng rojo en polvo)
2 tazas de agua

Hierve el agua en una olla con el ginseng. Déjalo hervir por 15 minutos. Apaga y deja reposar. Cuélalo y sírvelo. Puedes tomar hasta tres tazas al día.

Extracto de ginseng rojo

25 gotas de extracto de ginseng
8 onzas de agua

Revuélvelo y tómatelo. Puedes agregar el extracto a un jugo de frutas o un té si prefieres.

Tómalo de una a tres veces al día.

Grosella negra

Batido púrpura

4 onzas de jugo de uva negra (sin azúcar)
4 gramos de jugo de grosella negra (sin azúcar)
1 taza de grosellas negras frescas, congeladas o deshidratadas
½ taza de frambuesas
½ taza de cerezas sin semilla
½ taza de fresas

Mezcla todos los ingredientes en una licuadora y disfrútalo. Puedes agregarle un par de cubos de hielo si te gusta bien frío.

Concentrado de vitamina C

8 onzas de jugo de manzana sin azúcar
1 taza de grosellas negras frescas, congeladas o deshidratadas
⅓ de taza de tomillo fresco
⅓ de taza de perejil fresco

Mezcla todos los ingredientes en una licuadora y disfruta.

Batido de grosellas negras rico en calcio

1 taza de yogur griego de vainilla
8 onzas de jugo de grosellas negras (también puedes usar jugo de manzana)
1 taza de grosellas negras frescas, congeladas o deshidratadas

Si utilizas grosellas deshidratadas, déjalas remojando en el jugo al menos por un par de horas. Pon todos los ingredientes en una licuadora, licúa y disfruta.

Hierba de San Juan

Macerado de San Juan para lesiones de la piel, hemorroides y dolores musculares

- 4 cucharadas de hierba de San Juan
- 2 cucharadas de aceite de oliva

Muele bien la hierba y agrégale el aceite. Déjala macerar en una botella de vidrio cerrada y guardada en un lugar oscuro y fresco por al menos 24 horas. Cuélala y aplícala sobre la zona que necesites.

Aceite esencial de hierba de San Juan o "aceite hipérico" para dolores menstruales, depresión, síntomas de menopausia, etcétera

- 1 botellita de aceite esencial

Toma una cucharadita de aceite hipérico tres veces al día.

Té de hierba de San Juan para dolores menstruales, cólicos estomacales y para dormir

- 1 o 2 cucharadas de hierba seca de San Juan (o una bolsita de té)
- 1 taza de agua recién hervida

Deja reposar la hierba en el agua por 10 minutos, cuela y bébela, especialmente antes de dormir. Puedes tomar dos o tres tazas al día.

Hinojo

Infusión de hinojo para cólicos, gases, presión alta y mala visión

- 1 cucharada de hojas de hinojo deshidratadas o un ramito de hojas frescas
- 1 taza de agua caliente

Deja remojando las hojas en el agua caliente por 10 minutos. Luego endúlzala si deseas y bébela.

Infusión de raíz de hinojo para eliminar líquido del cuerpo, bajar la presión y apoyar la salud ocular

- 2 onzas de raíz (tubérculo)
- 4 tazas de agua

Hierve el agua con la raíz por al menos 10 minutos. Apaga y deja reposar otros 10 minutos. Cuela y bebe dos tazas al día.

Cataplasma de hinojo para calmar cólicos estomacales

- Hojas de hinojo
- 4 tazas de agua

Hierve por 10 minutos las hojas en el agua. Deja que se enfríen y ponlas directamente sobre el vientre o estómago. Déjalas que actúen por unos 20 minutos.

Jengibre

Té de jengibre para dolores menstruales, inflamación estomacal, náuseas y vómitos

½ pulgada de jengibre fresco pelado y picado
1 taza de agua caliente

Muele el jengibre en un mortero pequeño o con un triturador. Ponlo en una taza y agrégale el agua.
Deja reposar por 10 minutos. Bebe el té.

Jengibre fresco con manzana y miel para combatir mareos, vómitos, náuseas y dolores de articulaciones

1 trocito de jengibre fresco, pelado y picado en pedacitos pequeños
1 manzana pelada y cortada en trocitos
½ cucharadita de miel

Unta el jengibre con la miel (si no padeces de diabetes y si te parece demasiado picante). Mézclalo con la manzana. Disfrútalo, masticando despacio.

Extracto de jengibre para combatir mareos, vómitos, náuseas y dolores de articulaciones

20 gotas de extracto de jengibre fresco o envasado
1 taza de agua

Mezcla el jengibre con el agua y bébelo.

Lavanda

Sobres de lavanda para combatir el insomnio

4 cucharadas de flores y hojas de lavanda secas

Pon la lavanda dentro de una bolsita de tela pequeña (puedes elaborar esta con un pañuelo de tela, una toalla delgada, una camiseta vieja de algodón, etcétera) y cósela para que no se salga. Pon la bolsita debajo de tu almohada, sobre la mesa de noche o donde puedas olerla.

Té de lavanda para relajarse y dormir

1 cucharada de lavanda seca (o una bolsa de té)
1 taza de agua recién hervida

Deja reposar la lavanda en el agua por 10 minutos y luego bébela. Hazlo al menos una hora antes de ir a la cama.

Aceite esencial para tratar heridas y dolor de cabeza

3 o 4 gotas de aceite esencial de lavanda

Aplica el aceite esencial de lavanda en la herida, corte o picadura. Hazlo dos veces al día. Si tienes dolor de cabeza, unta tus sienes con el aceite y masajea suavemente.

Baño de lavanda

4 cucharadas de lavanda seca

Pon la lavanda en media tina con agua caliente. Deja que se remoje al menos media hora, hasta que el agua esté tibia. Sumérgete y relájate un rato antes de ir a dormir.

Limón

Agua con limón y miel para combatir un proceso infeccioso intestinal o de garganta

½ taza de jugo de limón
1 taza de agua
1 cucharada de miel

Agrega el jugo recién exprimido y la miel al agua y bébela de inmediato.

Infusión antiséptica con limón

½ taza de jugo de limón
1 taza de agua recién hervida
4 hojas de menta o romero

Pon las hojas de menta o romero en el agua caliente. Deja reposar cinco minutos. Agrega el limón y bébela.

Aromaterapia de limón para mejorar el ánimo

4 gotas de aceite esencial de limón

Enciende un quemador de aceite y agrega la esencia de limón. Ponla en un lugar cercano a donde estés para disfrutar de su aroma.

Manzanilla

Té de manzanilla

1 cucharada de manzanilla seca (o una bolsita de té)
1 taza de agua recién hervida

Deja reposar la bolsita en el agua caliente por 10 minutos. Luego bébela después de comer algo pesado, o una hora antes de ir a la cama, para que te ayude a relajarte y dormir como un bebé.

Lavado de manzanilla para deshinchar los pies y las piernas

4 cucharadas de manzanilla seca (o cuatro bolsitas de té)
4 taza de agua recién hervida

Deja reposar las bolsitas en el agua por unos 15 minutos. Pon el agua en un recipiente donde puedas poner los pies. Si no tienes un recipiente apropiado, empapa una toalla con el agua y envuelve tus pies y piernas con esta. Hazlo durante unos 20 minutos.

Compresas de manzanilla para bajar la inflamación de los ojos

2 bolsas de té de manzanilla
½ taza de agua caliente

Humedece las bolsas de té en el agua. Déjalas que se enfríen. Luego, ponlas media hora en la nevera para que estén lo más frías posible. Sácalas de la nevera y ponlas sobre tus párpados cerrados por unos 20 minutos.

Infusión de manzanilla para cicatrizar brotes de acné y quitar exceso de grasa de la piel

- 1 cucharada de manzanilla seca o una bolsa de té
- ½ taza de agua caliente

Deja reposar la manzanilla en el agua hasta que esta se enfríe. Empapa una bolita de algodón con la infusión y aplícala sobre tu rostro, especialmente en las zonas que concentran la grasa o donde tengas brotes. Hazlo dos veces a la semana si tienes demasiados brotes, pero no te excedas para no resecar mucho la piel.

Maracuyá

Infusión de maracuyá

- ¼ de taza de hojas secas de maracuyá (o una bolsita de té de maracuyá)
- 1 taza de agua recién hervida

Vierte el agua en una taza con las hojas o té de maracuyá. Deja reposar 10 minutos. Cuela las hojas y bebe el té.

Baño de maracuyá y lavanda para relajarse antes de ir a la cama o calmar dolores menstruales y musculares

- ½ taza de hojas secas de maracuyá (o dos bolsitas de té de maracuyá)

- ½ taza de hojas de lavanda (o esencia de lavanda)
- 1 galón de agua

Pon a hervir el agua y agrega las hojas o té de maracuyá. Si tienes lavanda en hojas, agrégalas también. Deja que hierva durante 10 minutos. Retira del fuego. Déjalas reposar por 10 minutos. Cuela. Si tienes lavanda en esencia, agrégala. Llena la bañera de agua caliente y agrégale la infusión. Disfruta de tu baño antes de ir a la cama.

Infusión de maracuyá y valeriana para dormir

- ¼ de taza de hojas secas de maracuyá (o una bolsita de té de maracuyá)
- ¼ de taza de valeriana en hojas o una bolsita de té
- 1 ½ tazas de agua
  Stevia si lo deseas

Pon a hervir el agua por cinco minutos y agrega las hojas o té de maracuyá. Retira del fuego. Agrega la valeriana y déjalas reposar por 10 minutos. Puedes agregarle unas gotas de stevia. Cuela las hojas y bebe el té unos 30 minutos antes de ir a dormir.

Menta

Té de menta estilo marroquí

- 1 ½ tazas de agua recién hervida
- 1 cucharadita de té verde
- 4 hojas de menta fresca
  Endulzante
  Jugo de limón

En un recipiente, pon las hojas de menta y agrega el agua hirviendo sobre estas. Déjala por unos cinco minutos. Luego agrega el té verde y deja reposar un par de minutos más. Endulza y agrega el limón. Lo puedes tomar frío o caliente.

Loción casera de menta para quemaduras de sol, refrescante de la piel, enjuague bucal

2 tazas de agua recién hervida
⅓ de taza de menta fresca o 3 bolsitas de té
1 botellita con atomizador

Pon el agua caliente sobre la menta y deja que repose hasta enfriar. Quedará bastante concentrado. Pon la mezcla en la botellita con atomizador y déjala en la nevera para que quede bien fría. Aplícala en las zonas afectadas o en el rostro para refrescar. También puedes usarla como enjuague bucal, después del cepillado. Si no tienes atomizador, usa una bolita de algodón para aplicarla o en compresas, empapando una toalla.

Descongestionante nasal de menta

2 cucharadas de aceite esencial de menta
4 taza de agua caliente

Pon el aceite en un recipiente resistente al calor. Agrégale el agua. Ponlo sobre una mesa o lugar donde esté firme y seguro. Aspira el vapor que despide. También podrías empapar una esponja o toalla con el aceite esencial y ponerlo en la tina al momento de bañarte. El agua caliente que le caiga generará el mismo efecto.

Aceite de menta para dolores de cabeza, energizarte y mejorar la concentración

2 gotas de aceite esencial de menta

Ponte las gotas sobre la frente y sienes, masajeando suavemente. Ten cuidado de que no entre en los ojos.

Moringa

Batido verde con moringa

1 cucharada de moringa en polvo
8 onzas de agua
1 taza de vegetales verdes (espinaca, rúcula, col rizada)
1 manzana
Hielo, si gustas

Licúa los ingredientes y tómalo de inmediato.

Vinagreta con aceite de semilla de moringa

¼ de taza de aceite de semilla de moringa
¼ de taza de vinagre balsámico
1 cucharada de jugo de mandarina
Sal al gusto

Mezcla bien los ingredientes y agrégala a cualquier ensalada para sazonarla.

Aceite de semilla de moringa para la piel

1 cucharada de aceite de semilla de moringa

Aplícalo directamente en la piel para curar picaduras, acné, brotes o resequedad.

Té antioxidante de moringa

1 cucharada de hojas de moringa seca o una bolsa de té de moringa
1 taza de agua hervida, no muy caliente
1 cucharadita de agave

Pon las hojas en la taza con el agua. Deja reposar 10 minutos. Agrégale agave, revuelve y bébelo.

Nimba

Infusión para tratar caspa, piojos, bacterias bucales o piel

2 tazas de hojas de nimba
4 tazas de agua caliente

Hierve las hojas de nimba hasta que el agua se ponga verde. Déjala enfriar. También puedes usar agua muy caliente y dejarla reposar por al menos 30 minutos. Cuélala y úsala como enjuague final de tu cabello después de lavarlo.

Aceite de nimba para tratar problemas de la piel y usar como repelente natural

1 cucharadita de aceite de nimba

Aplica el aceite sobre las zonas afectadas de la piel o cuando estés expuesto a picaduras de insectos.

Pasta de nimba y albahaca para tratar caspa, piojos y problemas en la piel

1 taza de hojas de nimba
1 taza de hojas de albahaca

Muele las hojas en un mortero o en un procesador de alimentos hasta formar una pasta fina. Aplícala sobre el cuero cabelludo con masajes suaves. Déjala actuar por una hora y luego enjuaga con agua tibia. La misma pasta la puedes aplicar sobre la piel, en zonas con hongos o picazón.

Baño caliente de hojas de nimba para calmar alergias, picazón, hongos y problemas menores de la piel

1 taza de hojas frescas de nimba
Tina o recipiente grande con agua caliente

Pon las hojas en el agua y deja que se remojen unos 15 minutos, mientras se enfría un poco. Cuando esté a una temperatura adecuada, sumérgete y disfruta de un baño relajante. Sécate con una toalla limpia o una desechable, especialmente las zonas afectadas.

Nopal

Batido verde con nopal

- 1 taza de nopal fresco o congelado picado o dos cucharadas en polvo
- ½ taza de acelga picada
- ½ remolacha (betabel, betarraga)
- ½ manzana verde
- 1 rama de apio
- 8 onzas de agua
- 1 pizca de pimienta (opcional)
  Hielo (opcional)

Procesa todos los ingredientes y bébelo bien frío.

Batido de nopal, limón y semillas de chía

- 1 penca de nopal fresco
- 1 limón exprimido (jugo)
- 1 cucharada de semillas de chía
- 8 onzas de agua
  Stevia líquida para endulzar

Licúa todos los ingredientes durante un par de minutos. Bebe el batido.

Batido de nopal, zanahoria y alfalfa

- 1 penca de nopal
- 8 onzas de jugo fresco de zanahoria, recién preparado
- 1 taza de alfalfa

Procesa todos los ingredientes y bébelo.

Batido de nopal, perejil y semillas de chía

- 1 penca de nopal fresco
- ⅓ de taza de perejil fresco picado (una o dos ramitas)
- 1 cucharada de semillas de chía
- 8 onzas de agua
  Stevia líquida para endulzar

Procesa todos los ingredientes y bébelo lentamente.

Sopa de nopal

- 3 o 4 pencas de nopal fresco
- 1 taza de cebolla picada
- 1 taza de espinaca picada
- ¼ de taza de cilantro fresco picado
- 1 diente de ajo picado
- 4 tazas de agua
  Pimienta
- 1 pizca de sal
- 1 cucharadita de aceite de oliva

Lava y corta las pencas de nopal en cuadritos. Luego, pon el nopal junto a la cebolla, el ajo y la sal en una olla, con el agua. Cubre y deja hervir durante 10 minutos. Apaga y deja que repose unos minutos. Agrega la espinaca, el cilantro y la pimienta al gusto. Licúa la mezcla y sírvela agregándole la cucharada de aceite por encima.

Orégano

Adobo curativo para carnes

- ½ taza de orégano molido
- 1 cucharada de canela molida

1 cucharada de clavo de olor molido
1 cucharada de romero
1 cucharada de jengibre en polvo
1 cucharada de ajo en polvo
½ cucharadita de pimienta negra en polvo
½ cucharadita de pimienta roja en polvo

Mezcla los ingredientes y adoba con esto la carne, especialmente la roja, antes de cocinarla.

Inhalaciones de vapor de orégano para problemas respiratorios

1 rama de orégano
2 tazas de agua

Pon a hervir el agua con el orégano. Una vez que hierva, apágala y ponla en algún lugar en el que puedas aspirar el vapor. Cerciórate de que esté en un lugar seguro para evitar accidentes.

Té de orégano

1 ramita de orégano
1 taza de agua caliente

Deja reposar el orégano en el agua por unos cinco minutos y luego bébela. También puedes usarla para hacer gárgaras.

Aceite esencial de orégano para eliminar bacterias bucales

1 gota de aceite esencial de orégano
1 gota de aceite de oliva

Mézclalos y póntelos debajo de la lengua por unos minutos. Luego, trágalos. Repite esta operación hasta cuatro veces al día.

Ortiga

Algodón con esencia natural de ortiga para detener una hemorragia nasal o bucal

6 hojas de ortiga

Aplasta las hojas en un mortero hasta conseguir su jugo y aceites. Empapa una bolita de algodón con ese jugo e introdúcelo en la entrada de la nariz. Déjalo ahí por unos minutos hasta que deje de sangrar.

Infusión de ortiga como diurético

½ cucharada de hojas secas
1 taza de agua caliente

Deja reposar las hojas en el agua caliente, endulza (opcional) y bébela.

Infusión de raíz de ortiga para alergias y para eliminar líquido

1 raíz de ortiga
4 tazas de agua

Hierve la raíz en el agua durante 10 minutos. Luego deja reposar. Cuélala y bébela durante el día. También puedes aplicarla directamente en la piel.

Perejil

Batido de perejil

1 taza de perejil fresco
1 manzana verde
   Jugo de un limón
½ pepino
8 onzas de agua fría

Licúa todo y disfrútalo.

Té de perejil

1 ramita de perejil fresco
1 taza de agua caliente

Remoja el perejil en el agua por unos cinco minutos y luego bébela.

Pasta de perejil para desinflamar piernas, pies, manos, etcétera

1 taza de hojas de perejil
   Un par de gotas de agua (opcional)

Aplasta las hojas en un mortero (o procésalas) y luego aplica la pasta que queda en las zonas afectadas. Cubre con una tela o gasa y deja que actúe por una hora. Hazlo dos veces al día.

Psyllium (cáscara)

Batido con psyllium

2 cucharadas de psyllium en polvo sin azúcar
12 onzas de agua

1 manzana
1 cucharada de uvas pasas

Mezcla todos los ingredientes en una licuadora y bébelo de inmediato.

Panquecas con psyllium

2 cucharadas de pysllium en polvo sin sabor
1 huevo
2 claras de huevo
½ taza de leche descremada o vegetal
½ taza de avena molida
1 cucharada de sirope, miel o agave
   Frutas de tu elección
1 cucharada de nueces molidas
   Aceite de oliva o coco

Procesa el huevo, las claras, la avena, la leche, el pysillium y el sirope hasta que quede cremoso. En una sartén antiadherente vierte unas gotas de aceite y calienta. Agrega una cantidad de mezcla suficiente para una panqueca delgada. Voltea para dorar por ambos lados. Sírvela con la fruta que gustes y nueces por encima.

Regaliz

Infusión de regaliz

¼ de taza de regaliz (o una cucharada de esencia)
⅓ de taza de hojas de eucalipto (o dos cucharadas de esencia)
3 varitas de canela
2 tazas de agua

Pon a hervir todos los ingredientes por un par de minutos. (Si el regaliz y eucalipto son esencia, no los hiervas. Agrégalos cuando esté reposando.) Deja reposar por 10 minutos. Cuélala y bébela.

Té de regaliz

¼   de taza de raíz de regaliz
1½ tazas de agua

Pon a hervir el agua con la raíz. Deja que hierva un par de minutos. Luego apaga y deja reposar. Bébelo.

Infusión combinada para problemas intestinales, gastritis y úlceras

½   cucharadita de regaliz
½   cucharadita de melisa
½   cucharadita de poleo
½   cucharadita de milhojas
     (milenrama o *yarrow*)
2   tazas de agua

Pon a hervir las hierbas por un par de minutos. Apaga y deja reposar. Cuélala y bébela.

Salvia

Infusión de salvia

1   cucharadita de hierba seca o fresca de salvia
1   taza de agua caliente

Deja reposar la hierba en el agua por unos minutos. Cuélala. Endulza si deseas

y bébela. También puedes usar este té como enjuague bucal y para gárgaras.

Tinte de salvia para tratar afecciones de la piel

¼   de cucharadita de salvia seca
¼   de taza de agua caliente

Pon la salvia seca en una taza y agrégale el agua caliente. Deja reposar hasta que el agua se enfríe. Cuélalo y mézclalo con más agua para lavados de zonas con infecciones.

Aromatizante y repelente de salvia

10 gotas de aceite esencial de salvia
4   cucharaditas de aceite de oliva
     (puedes reemplazarlo con agua)

Mezcla los ingredientes en una botella de vidrio y aplícalo directamente en la piel. Si usas agua, puedes rociarlo en el ambiente.

Semillas de calabaza

Batido de calabaza

1   taza de leche vegetal
1   taza de té de caléndula
1   taza de calabaza cruda cortada en trozos
2 o 3 cucharadas de semillas de calabaza frescas
     Miel o stevia al gusto

Procesa primero las semillas y la leche hasta que queden bien molidas. Agrega luego la pulpa, el té y la miel, y vuelve a procesar hasta que quede cremoso. Disfrútalo de inmediato.

Crema de calabaza

1 calabaza mediana, sin cáscara, cortada en trozos
2 zanahorias
1 taza de puerros
½ taza de cebolla picada
2 cucharaditas de cúrcuma
Sal
Pimienta negra
⅓ de taza de albahaca fresca picada
⅓ de taza de perejil fresco picado
4 tazas de agua
3 cucharadas de las semillas de calabaza frescas
Aceite de oliva

Separa las semillas de calabaza para prepararlas aparte. Pon a hervir la calabaza, la cebolla y las zanahorias hasta que estén blandas. Apaga y agrégale el puerro. Deja reposar por unos 20 minutos. Agrega sal, pimienta, cúrcuma, albahaca y perejil. Licúa. Pon las semillas de calabaza en una sartén con unas gotas de aceite. Deja que se doren un poco y retíralas. Sirve la crema con unas gotas de aceite de oliva y las semillas. Disfrútala.

Postre de frutas y mermelada de calabaza

½ calabaza sin cáscara, cortada en rodajas
2 cucharadas de canela en polvo
Azúcar morena (o stevia)
2 cucharadas de semillas de calabaza frescas o deshidratadas, sin sal
1 cucharada de nueces picadas
½ banana
1 manzana

En una sartén antiadherente, pon a dorar la calabaza, espolvoreándola con la canela y el azúcar (o stevia), a fuego suave. Voltéala constantemente para que no se queme: la idea es suavizarla sin quemarla. Cuando esté lista, deja que se enfríe. Procesa hasta que quede cremosa. Pon la mezcla en un frasco de vidrio y guarda en la nevera lo que no utilices. Corta el banano y la manzana en rodajas y sírvelos.

Pon en un procesador las semillas de calabaza y las nueces hasta que queden del tamaño que te gusta para espolvorearlas sobre tu postre.

Agrega unas cucharadas de mermelada de calabaza sobre tu fruta y espolvorea las semillas. Disfrútalo.

Semillas negras

Tónico para la tos y el sistema inmune

½ taza de aceite de semillas negras
3 cucharadas de miel
3 dientes de ajo triturados

Mezcla todos los ingredientes en un recipiente de vidrio o en un procesador pequeño. Toma una cucharada de la mezcla cada seis horas para disminuir la tos. Si lo usas solo como prevención, una o dos cucharadas al día bastan.

Té de semilla negra

1 cucharada de semillas negras
1 taza de agua recién hervida
  Stevia al gusto

Agrega las semillas a la taza de agua. Deja reposar por 10 minutos. Luego endúlzala al gusto y disfrútala.

Ensalada con semillas negras

1 taza de rúcula
1 tomate cortado en cuadritos
½ pepino cortado en cuadritos
½ taza de garbanzos cocidos
  Sal
  Vinagre balsámico
  Aceite, a tu elección
1 cucharada de semillas negras

Mezcla los ingredientes en un recipiente y disfrútala como almuerzo o cena.

Té verde matcha

Té verde matcha *latte*

1 cucharada de té verde matcha en polvo
½ taza de agua hervida
½ taza de leche de tu elección
  Stevia al gusto

Disuelve el polvo matcha en el agua caliente. Utiliza un batidor manual o ponlo en la licuadora para disolverlo mejor.

Agrega la leche y la stevia. Vuelve a batir. Disfrútalo.

Batido de frutas y matcha

1 cucharada de té verde matcha en polvo
4 onzas de agua fría
4 onzas de leche vegetal fría (almendras, soya, coco, etcétera)
1 manzana cortada en trozos
1 kiwi
  Stevia

Licúa todos los ingredientes. Disfrútalo a media mañana o antes de hacer ejercicio.

Batido verde con matcha

1 cucharada de té verde matcha en polvo
8 onzas de agua fría
1 rama de apio
1 taza de espinacas
1 manzana verde
1 cucharadita de jugo de limón

Licúa todos los ingredientes. Disfrútalo como merienda de media mañana o tarde.

Tilo

Té de tilo

1 cucharada de hierba de tilo seca
1 taza de agua recién hervida

Pon la hierba en una taza y agrega el agua. Deja reposar por unos 15 minutos y luego bébelo, sorbo a sorbo.

Baño de tilo para relajarse y descansar los pies

1 taza de flores de tilo
8 tazas de agua hirviendo

Pon las flores en un recipiente donde puedas poner los pies o en la bañera. Agrégale el agua y déjala reposar unos 15 minutos, hasta que se entibie. Pon los pies adentro o agrega más agua y toma un baño de cuerpo entero.

Tomillo

Jarabe natural de tomillo para la garganta

½ taza de hierba fresca de tomillo
½ taza de miel

Muele la hierba en un mortero para extraer sus aceites y jugos. Cuélalo y mezcla ese líquido con la miel. Toma una cucharadita de jarabe tres veces al día. Guarda el resto en un lugar oscuro, en un frasco de vidrio bien sellado.

Infusión de tomillo para problemas de la garganta, enjuagues bucales e infecciones

1 cucharadita de hierba seca o de hojas frescas de tomillo
1 taza de agua caliente

Deja reposar la hierba en el agua caliente unos minutos. Luego bébela. Esa misma infusión la puedes usar para enjuagarte la boca.

Compresas de tomillo para problemas de la garganta

1 taza de hojas y flores frescas o deshidratadas de tomillo
1 taza de agua caliente

Remoja el tomillo en el agua por unos minutos, hasta que se enfríe. Luego, cuélalo y pon la hierba sobre una tela o gasa limpia. Aplícala directamente en la zona del cuello, alrededor de las amígdalas o en donde tengas dolor. Deja que actúe por unos 20 minutos. Agrégale unas gotas del líquido restante para refrescarla, si lo necesitas.

Repelente casero de tomillo

16 gotas de aceite esencial de tomillo
4 cucharaditas de aceite de oliva (puedes reemplazarlo con agua)

Mezcla los ingredientes en una botella de vidrio y aplícalo directamente en la piel.

Loción astringente y antibacterial de tomillo para el acné

1 taza de tomillo seco o fresco
1 taza de vinagre de manzana

Pon el tomillo en un frasco o botella de vidrio y agrega el vinagre de tal manera que lo cubra por completo. Puedes añadir un poco más de vinagre si hace falta. Ponle la tapa al frasco y déjalo en un lugar oscuro durante dos semanas. Agítalo de vez en cuando para que se empape por completo. Pasado el tiempo, cuélalo y guárdalo en una botella o frasco de vidrio, siempre en un sitio oscuro. Empapa un algodón con esta loción y úsala cuando lo necesites (dura un año).

Verbena de limón

Té de verbena de limón

¼ de taza de hojas de verbena de limón
1 taza de agua caliente
½ cucharadita de jugo de limón (opcional)
Endulzante (opcional)

Pon las hojas en un recipiente resistente al calor. Agrega el agua caliente. Deja reposar por cinco minutos. Agrega el endulzante y limón, si gustas. Disfrútala.

Sorbete de verbena de limón

½ taza de verbena de limón fresca o 1 cucharadita de hierba seca
½ cucharadita de hibisco seco
1 taza de agua caliente
1 taza de hielo
1 cucharada de miel, agave o stevia
1 cucharadita de jugo de limón

Pon las hojas de verbena de limón e hibisco en un recipiente resistente al calor. Agrega el agua caliente. Deja reposar hasta que se enfríe. Luego cuélalo.

Pon el té, que debe estar muy cargado, en una licuadora o máquina de hacer helado. Agrégale el hielo, el jugo de limón y el endulzante, si lo deseas. Bate hasta que quede muy suave. Sírvelo con un pitillo o popote y disfrútalo.

Aceite aromático a verbena de limón

2 tazas de aceite de oliva extravirgen
1 taza de hojas frescas de verbena de limón

Aplasta suavemente en un mortero (o con una cuchara de madera) las hojas de verbena, para que suelten sus aceites naturales.

Aparte, en una sartén, calienta el aceite hasta que casi comience a humear, con cuidado de no quemarlo. Quítalo del calor. Añádele las hojas aplastadas, cuidando que queden cubiertas por el aceite. Cúbrelo con una tapa o plato y deja que reposen al menos un par de horas. Cuela y utiliza el aceite para aliñar ensaladas, carnes, patatas, etcétera.

Vinagre de sidra de manzana

Vinagre de sidra de manzana para regular el azúcar en la sangre

1 cucharada de vinagre de sidra de manzana
½ taza de agua

Diluye el vinagre en el agua y bébela. Tómalo dos veces al día, 30 minutos antes de comer.

Loción astringente de vinagre de sidra de manzana para la piel

1 cucharada de vinagre de sidra de manzana
2 cucharadas de agua

Mezcla el vinagre con el agua. Aplica con una bolita de algodón sobre la piel, después de haber quitado el maquillaje.

Lavado de vinagre para desinflamar los pies y eliminar hongos

1 taza de vinagre de sidra de manzana
1 galón de agua tibia

Mezcla el vinagre con el agua en un recipiente grande. Pon los pies en el recipiente y déjalos reposar ahí por unos 20 minutos. Seca muy bien con toalla de papel.

Zanahoria

Sopa de zanahoria

1 libra de zanahorias sin piel y rallada
4 tazas de agua
Sal
Aceite de oliva

Cocina la zanahoria en la mitad del agua por no más de 15 a 20 minutos. No necesita estar demasiado blanda. Cuando esté lista, procésala y agrégale la sal y el resto del agua previamente hervida, hasta completar un litro. Puedes disfrutarla con unas gotas de aceite de oliva.

Jugo de zanahoria y espinaca para el estreñimiento

8 onzas de jugo de zanahoria fresca y cruda
1 taza de espinaca fresca

2 cucharadas de jugo de limón

Pon todos los ingredientes en la licuadora. Procésalos. Bébelo de inmediato.

Batido de frutas y zanahorias

1 taza de jugo de zanahoria fresca y cruda
1 taza de jugo de naranja fresca
1 taza de jugo de toronja fresca
1 manzana

Pon todos los ingredientes en una licuadora y procésalos. Disfrútalo de inmediato.

Ensalada de zanahoria y pasas

3 zanahorias peladas
1 cucharada de uvas pasas
1 cucharada de grosellas negras deshidratadas (*black currant*)
1 cucharadita de piñones (*pine nuts*)
Sal
Aceite de oliva
Jugo de limón

Cocina levemente las zanahorias al vapor durante no más de 15 minutos para que no se ablanden demasiado. Luego ponlas en agua fría por unos minutos. Corta las zanahorias en rodajas y ponlas en una ensaladera. Agrégales las uvas pasas, las grosellas negras y los piñones. Sazona con sal, limón y aceite. Disfrútala durante el almuerzo o cena para acompañar cualquier proteína.

Brócoli crudo

Ensalada de brócoli crudo

1 taza de flores de brócoli separadas
½ cucharadita de jugo de limón
   Sal
   Aceite de oliva

Sazona las flores de brócoli con aceite, limón y sal. Puedes mezclarlas con otros vegetales si gustas.

Café

Café negro para combatir un ataque de asma

1½ tazas de agua hervida
2 cucharadas de café molido

Cuela el café en la cafetera que usas regularmente y bebe el café de inmediato. No le agregues azúcar. Es conveniente beberlo amargo. Bebe una o dos tazas.

Café estilo árabe para la fatiga, dolor de cabeza y problemas respiratorios

½ taza de agua
1 cucharada de café árabe
1 cucharada de cardamomo
1 trocito pequeño de jengibre
1 clavo de olor
¼ de cucharadita de azafrán en polvo

Pon a hervir el agua en un recipiente. Apenas comience a hervir, baja el calor al mínimo y agrega el café. Déjalo por un par de minutos y luego apaga. Agrega el cardamomo, jengibre, clavo de olor y azafrán. Vuelve a ponerlo al fuego por un par de minutos. Saca y cuela. Sírvelo de inmediato y disfrútalo.

Café con ginkgo biloba para abrir las vías respiratorias

1½ tazas de agua
2 cucharadas de café
2 hojitas de ginkgo biloba

Cuela el café en la cafetera que usas regularmente. Cuando esté listo, agrégale el ginkgo biloba y déjalo reposar por 10 minutos. Bebe el café.

Compresas de col

Compresas de hojas de col

4 hojas de col (repollo, *cabbage*) limpias y frías (ponlas en la nevera, no en el congelador, por una hora al menos)
1 gasa elástica o una tela larga para vendaje

Pon las hojas frías de col alrededor de la zona inflamada y luego la venda o tela alrededor para sostenerla. Deja que actúe al menos 30 minutos. Repite una o dos veces al día hasta bajar la inflamación.

Fresas y bicarbonato

Pasta de fresas y bicarbonato
de sodio

1 fresa madura molida o licuada
½ cucharadita de bicarbonato
de sodio

Mezcla muy bien los ingredientes hasta que quede compacto. Pon la mezcla en un cepillo de dientes de cerdas suaves. Cepilla tus dientes suavemente. Repite este proceso cada tres o cuatro meses. No lo hagas más frecuentemente para no dañar el esmalte dental.

Miel, aceite de oliva y cera de abejas

Labial de miel, aceite de oliva
y cera de abejas

1 cucharadita de miel
1 cucharadita de aceite de oliva
1 cucharadita de cera de abejas
1 recipiente pequeño limpio
(puede ser de una crema de ojos)

En un recipiente pequeño, pon la cera y caliéntala a baño maría o poniendo otro recipiente con agua caliente abajo por un par de minutos, para que se derrita un poco. Cuando esté derretida o más suave, agrégale la miel y el aceite de oliva. Mézclalos y ponlos en el recipiente limpio. Si deseas, ponlo en la nevera para que se condense levemente y úsalo como bálsamo labial. (Mantenlo en la nevera para que sea más fácil de usar.)

Sopa de pollo

Sopa tradicional de pollo

½ pollo o piezas de pollo a tu elección
6 tazas de agua (o caldo de pollo bajo en sodio) o la cantidad suficiente para cubrirlo
1 patata cortada en cuadritos
2 zanahorias peladas y cortadas en rodajas
1 cebolla picada
2 dientes de ajo
½ pimiento rojo, sin semillas
1 taza de calabaza picada en cuadritos
Albahaca fresca picada o deshidratada
Pimienta negra
2 cucharadas de arroz blanco
Sal

Agrega el pollo y el agua o caldo en una olla. Cocínalo a fuego medio alto. Agrega un poco de sal y deja que comience a hervir. Cuando lleve unos 20 minutos hirviendo, agrega la patata, la zanahoria, la cebolla, el pimiento, la calabaza, la pimienta y el ajo. Cubre y cocina hasta que el pollo esté blando, esto es, otros 25 a 30 minutos más, aproximadamente. Cuando falten unos 20 minutos, agrega el arroz. Apaga y agrega la albahaca. Deja reposar por unos 15 minutos. Luego sirve y disfruta.

Té negro

Lavado con té negro

4 sobres de té negro o cuatro
cucharaditas de té negro en hojas
½ galón de agua caliente
Recipiente para poner los pies

Pon a remojar el té en el agua caliente por
al menos 10 minutos. Deja enfriar. Cuela
o quita las bolsitas. Luego, sumerge tus
pies en este líquido. Mantenlos ahí por al
menos 20 minutos. Seca tus pies con una
toalla de papel.

Uvas

Mascarilla de uvas

½ taza de uvas con semillas y piel
(mejor si son oscuras)
1 cucharada de aceite de coco

Muele o procesa las uvas hasta que queden como una crema o pasta y agrégale
el aceite de coco. Mezcla muy bien. Aplícala en el rostro y cuello. Déjala por 15 o
20 minutos. Luego, enjuaga con agua a
temperatura ambiente. Úsala al menos
una o dos veces a la semana.

Vinagre de Marsella

2½ tazas (500 ml) de vinagre
de manzana o vinagre blanco
2 cucharadas de hojas secas
de salvia
2 cucharadas de hojas secas
de tomillo
2 cucharadas de hojas secas
de romero
2 cucharadas de flores secas
de lavanda
2 cucharadas de hojas secas
de menta
2 cucharadas de ajenjo o artemisa
8 dientes de ajo
1 varita de canela
8 clavos de olor
1 hoja de laurel

Pon todas las hierbas y especias en un
frasco de vidrio (de corcho o plástico, nunca de metal). Agrega el vinagre. Revuelve
levemente con una cuchara de madera.
Tapa y deja macerar en un lugar oscuro y
fresco por al menos dos semanas. Cuela
y guarda en el mismo frasco bien tapado,
siempre en un sitio oscuro y fresco.

Diluye una cucharadita de vinagre de
Marsella en un vaso de jugo, té o agua y
bébelo.

Sobre las fuentes

He consultado numerosas fuentes que respaldan científicamente cada uno de los remedios que forman parte de este libro. La mención de los cientos de documentos, estudios y artículos científicos y especializados resulta muy extensa para incluirlos en este volumen. Por lo tanto, invito a los lectores interesados en revisar las fuentes consultadas a descargar la bibliografía completa y ordenada por remedios en el siguiente enlace: www.santoremediobibliografia.com

Agradecimientos

Este libro no hubiese sido posible sin la ayuda de Dániza Tobar, Penguin Random House Grupo Editorial y Univision Enterprises. Tampoco hubiese sido posible sin la comprensión de los miembros de mi familia, quienes me comparten con todos ustedes, pues comprenden también la misión de ayudar a nuestra comunidad.

Doctor
Juan Rivera

Más conocido como Doctor Juan, es médico internista, especialista en cardio-logía, egresado del prestigioso Johns Hopkins University Hospital, en Balti-more, Estados Unidos. Se desempeña como corresponsal médico principal de Univision y es conductor de "Dr. Juan", su propio programa semanal que transmite la misma cadena. El autor, que reside en Miami, ha publicado los exitosos libros *Mejora tu salud de poquito a poco* (Aguilar, 2016) y *Santo remedio* (Aguilar, 2017) con Penguin Random House Grupo Editorial USA.